THREE WISE MONKEYS

THREE WISE MONKEYS

Kikazaru – 'Hear No Evil'

II

Through the Turnstiles of the Mind: White South Africans and the Freedoms of Mozambique, circa 1914–1975

Charles van Onselen

Jonathan Ball Publishers
Johannesburg · Cape Town

All rights reserved. No part of this publication may be reproduced or transmitted, in any form or by any means, without prior permission from the publisher or copyright holder.

© Text: Charles van Onselen (2023)
© Published edition: Jonathan Ball Publishers (2023)

Published in South Africa in 2023 by
JONATHAN BALL PUBLISHERS
A division of Media24 (Pty) Ltd
PO Box 33977
Jeppestown
2043

ISBN 978-1-77619-246-5
ebook ISBN 978-1-77619-247-2

Every effort has been made to trace the copyright holders and to obtain their permission for the use of copyright material. The publishers apologise for any errors or omissions and would be grateful to be notified of any corrections that should be incorporated in future editions of this book.

jonathanball.co.za
twitter.com/JonathanBallPub
facebook.com/JonathanBallPublishers

Cover and slipcase design by MR Design
Design and typesetting by MR Design Proofreading by Paul Wise
Index by George Claassen
Set in Garamond

CONTENTS

The Three Wise Monkeys in Imperial and Colonial Southern Africa .... **VII**

KIKAZARU – 'HEAR NO EVIL'

Introduction **2**

I | Tourist Dreams and Dreams of a Tourism Industry: Johannesburg and Lourenço Marques, circa 1910–1955 .... **13**

II | The Sunday Night Wars: Lourenço Marques Radio and the Triumph of the South African Broadcasting Corporation, circa 1934–1975 .... **77**

Select Bibliography **162**
Acknowledgements **165**
Notes **168**
Index **186**

THE THREE WISE MONKEYS IN IMPERIAL AND COLONIAL SOUTHERN AFRICA

The origins of the three wise monkeys, some speculate, lie in Hinduism, and the maxims surrounding them made their way into the wider world via the Silk Road. Confronted with the choice of going east or west, the monkeys went east, where, they believed, they were more likely to find succour than in the west. Their wisdom was readily adopted, perhaps adapted, by Confucius, making an early appearance in his *Analects* hundreds of years before the Christian era. In the 16th century, Buddhist monks, valuing their lessons, ferried them silently across the South China Sea to take up residence in Japan.

By then seasoned travellers, the monkeys moved easily through the forest of ancient religions abounding on Honshū Island. It was with Koshin, God of the Roads, a friend to Buddhist, Shinto and Taoist wanderers alike, that they felt most at home. Fittingly, they are honoured on a carved wooden panel at the Toshogu Shrine, at Nikkō, in the region where they were widely respected.

How, why or by whom the three were smuggled into the Anglophone world is unclear, but it took some time. Only in the 20th century did they put in an appearance in Western popular culture. An air of mystery clung to them and, perhaps incongruously, they were occasionally reported as having been seen in military arenas where notions of discipline and obedience are always de rigueur. By then, however, their wisdom may already have undergone a rather subtle cultural twist.

In their earliest Eastern setting, the messages of the primates may have come across as a positive proactive injunction to those seeking to live the good life and cultivate a sense of tranquillity. Evil in its many forms existed; it was rooted in place, totem-like. Those in search of wisdom should be pre-emptive and *do something* to avoid it by averting their eyes, not listening to it or speaking of it. Evil was fixed, but intelligent people could navigate their way around it. By acknowledging its existence and acting, the potential for evil could be minimised.

But something had been lost in translation by the time that *Mizaru*, *Kikazaru* and *Iwazaru* got to whisper to English speakers in their customary hushed tones. Wickedness still existed, as it did, always, everywhere, but it was no longer static; it was mobile and on the move towards people. And so, instead of being proactive and doing something, as back in the East, folk needed to sit tight and *do nothing* – see no evil, hear no evil and speak no evil. It was as if people were urged to recognise the presence of evil, and then promptly to deny its existence.

The wisdom of the Three Wise Monkeys came to southern Africa via English, from the West, replete with a cultural coding that encouraged settler ideologies of denial, rootedness and silence when confronted by moral ambiguities. In a setting where colonialism and imperialism posed questions of profound ethical importance about issues of conquest, occupation and gross dispossession, the willingness to see no evil, hear no evil and speak no evil held some appeal. How those ancient directives – in both their old active and new passive form – helped shape the deeply entangled social history of 20th-century South Africa and Mozambique is the subject of these three volumes. Only by seeing, hearing and speaking honestly about the past can we hope to understand a troubled present.

THREE WISE MONKEYS

INTRODUCTION

Calvinism was unloaded in South Africa as an important part of Jan van Riebeeck's conceptual baggage when he and his party disembarked in Table Bay, on Saturday 6 April 1652. Dutch Reformed Protestant churches, without meaningful local rivals among white settlers, remained theologically dominant institutions in a company-constructed commercial dispensation designed to provide passing ships with fresh agricultural products and other necessities. Three decades later, the ranks of the true believers were bolstered by the arrival of the Huguenots, Protestant refugees fleeing persecution in Catholic France.

Commercial farming and Protestantism, the latter in many different variants, became deeply woven into the fabric of rural white South Africa and enjoyed a largely untroubled relationship for more than two centuries as farmers took their religion ever further inland. In 1851, when the Rev N Hofmeyr of the Dutch Reformed Church arrived in the Hantam Karoo, he did not hesitate to name the new parish after perhaps the Reformed Church's greatest earthly hero of all. Calvinia, the only town in the world so named, reminds us of that pre-industrial marriage.

The authority of the Bible in times and places not richly blessed with books or fully literate people, the sovereignty of God in an unpredictable world dominated by nature rather than man, the doctrine of predestination in a continent undergoing European colonisation, along with a strong emphasis on social discipline and scrutiny – all of this settled relatively easily into the countryside, where isolated farmers lived in hope of finding markets for their products. But, as we are often told, beware of what you wish for. Barely two decades after the baptism of Calvinia, diamonds were discovered in the interior of the Cape and, just two decades later, in the 1880s, gold in the trans-Vaal.

These inert, lifeless commodities, destined for purchase and display by the nobility, ruling classes and wealthy around the world – the ultimate outlet for diamonds and gold – could not have been further removed from grapes, maize or wheat than was Christchurch, in New Zealand, from Dutch-speaking Calvinia, in the Cape Colony. The *promise* of the new South African mining towns, from Kimberley to Krugersdorp, was that they provided venerable Calvinists in the countryside with access to the urban markets they craved. The problem was that the same centres became home to tens of thousands of urbanised immigrants, many of them better-educated, English-speaking, literate, secular and resentful of church-driven social discipline that sought to curtail their drinking, modern entertainments, gambling, sport and other forms of recreation.

From the moment that gemstones and nuggets were found in the interior, the question was always going to be how the Calvinist template that had served a dominant, conservative, patriarchal governing rural elite for centuries would hold up when superimposed on an industrial revolution and an urban proletariat. More specifically, how would the entrenched notions of moral propriety and social discipline that emanated from the dominees and the dorps be received by the new mining capitalists and the unruly working class they sought to control? These are questions that economic and social historians have either long avoided or ignored, but that remain deserving of serious answers.

Attempts to curtail the operation of most markets on Sundays, such as the Cape Colony's Ordinance No. 1 of March 1838, predated the mineral discoveries. But the catalysts of urbanisation – diamonds in Kimberley, and gold in Johannesburg – unleashed new commercial pressures and sharpened legislative responses from governments in states that had never advocated established churches. In the Cape, the Lord's Day Observance Act No. 19 of 1895 once again focused on curbing shop and market activity on the Sabbath but also prohibited public performances 'calculated to bring ridicule, contempt or disrespect upon religion or morality'. In Kruger's South African Republic, Act No. 28 of 1896, the so-called Sunday Act, prohibited trading and 'certain games and public entertainments' and provided for 'the seizure and destruction of articles used at such games and entertainment'. Calvinists accustomed to, comfortable with and respectful of the rhythms of church and countryside sought to ensure that the Sabbath was honoured by commercial and social death, by the inactivity of the working classes in the burgeoning towns and cities. Some of that very early litmus legislation remained on the statute books well into the 21st century.

Many urban residents, drawn from different classes, chafed at the restrictive Sunday observance laws, which were among the most consistently debated and sullenly resented in the emerging cities. On the Witwatersrand, the issue was further complicated by the nature of deep-level mining, which demanded continuous maintenance and ongoing operations. It made for a politically sensitive, overlapping three-way contestation between mine owners, white workers and the state.

The Mines and Works Act No. 12 of 1911 legalised essential work on Sundays, but, almost at once, managerial abuses led to the appointment of a wide-ranging Sunday Observance Commission. But so sensitive were the issues, and so complex the possible policy ramifications across town and countryside, that it was not until 1914 that the commission's report was tabled in parliament. White miners had to win the right not to have to work on Sundays, and governments reserved the right to try and determine how their remaining leisure hours were spent on the Sabbath and weekdays.

God-fearing Afrikaners referred to Johannesburg as *Duiwelsdorp* (Satan's City), a name that spoke not only to how Calvinists viewed the place but also to how its cosmopolitan residents, composed largely of young single males, spent most of their leisure hours. Every administration, from the early 1890s until World War I, passed new laws designed to control or eradicate excessive alcohol consumption, gambling and prostitution, which had the effect of driving most such activities underground, where they were controlled by foreign, professional, criminal syndicates.

From the time of Union, in 1910, and for decades prior to that, those leisure-time and recreational activities that failed to qualify as sport and were deemed as being morally abhorrent occupied an ideologically cramped space in the minds of Calvinists and legislators. Crime, place and time clustered together on a conveniently identifiable urban spectrum. God was more at home in the countryside than in the city, but as a predominantly single male workforce gradually gave way to a more settled, family-focused white working class, Protestants had renewed reasons for hope. By the 1920s and 1930s, the state, benefiting from the underlying social changes the Witwatersrand was undergoing, had suppressed many of the most execrable operations associated with morally repugnant criminal activities.

The expanded control of many leisure-time activities by the state and the rigorous social policing of Sunday recreational activities by the churches were, however, never acceded to uncritically by the emerging white middle and working classes in the cities. Indeed, as the economy grew and stabilised during the 1920s, shook off the worst effects of the Great Depression and then positively prospered in the 1930s, the most resented Calvinist laws were often defied, ignored and resisted.

A marginal growth in disposable incomes and increased leisure time won through trade-union struggles encouraged the white middle and working classes not only to partake more freely of the remaining, pared-down recreational activities but to go beyond organised sport and look further afield – including to Mozambique – to escape the clutches of socially oppressive religious dogma. A national movement opposed to almost all forms of gambling other than church raffles, and intrinsic to Calvinist thinking that encouraged thrift, failed to gain traction, and by the late 1930s Protestant leaders across much of the Witwatersrand were feeling somewhat demoralised.

In the cities the Dutch Reformed clergy, along with their English-speaking counterparts, sensed that organised religion was losing some of its traction in white working-class communities. Leading Methodist ministers, raised in the evangelical traditions of Wesley and the industrial revolution, felt that people no longer had a love of the church, and denounced Johannesburg as a 'pagan' city. An interdenominational march called on congregants to return to the fold, and in 1939, the mayor, sensing growing fears about the outbreak of war, led a public 'back-to-church' movement but failed to move the masses.

Some in the slowly expanding middle class, and many in the more populous white working class, had, for decades past, been exploring ways of using such disposable income as they had to escape a tedious working week that culminated in the social death that was Sunday. One of the clues to what they were thinking was to be found in their eagerness to pass through the turnstiles of the Calvinist mind and the South African state and spend their annual vacations in nominally Catholic Lourenço Marques, beyond easy reach of Protestant tethers.

For a time, Lourenço Marques, a sleazy port catering for the leisure and recreational preferences of passing sailors, and Johannesburg, a

'LM' as a white tropical paradise, in the period between the two world wars.

wild frontier settlement catering for miners, shared a not dissimilar social profile in which alcohol, gambling and prostitution featured prominently. But rapidly diverging financial fortunes saw to it that these, initially overlapping, profiles were subjected to change at a different pace. The port retained much of the initial character of its demi-monde even as that of the mining camp-turned-town shrank, with the latter's peripatetic male workers progressively making way for a resident white working class focused on family life.

This, in turn, meant that between 1910 and the mid-1930s, as the South African state clamped down on the classic social 'evils' and 'vices' that slowed Johannesburg's struggle to become a more industrially mature city, Lourenço Marques – hoping to change its own social profile and become a more 'respectable' satellite recreational outlet for better-off Witwatersrand holidaymakers – lagged behind. During those same years, those whites wishing to escape some of the restrictions imposed on them by a Calvinist state continued to frequent neighbouring Catholic Mozambique and partake of its 'social evils'.

Successive South African governments found the annual winter exodus of whites to the fleshpots of the adjoining Mozambican coast distressing. Lourenço Marques was perceived as being at the centre of a morally hazardous zone, posing a particular danger to women testing the outer limits of Calvinism and patriarchal society as they sought to exercise the rights of economic independence and sexual freedom that came with being modern, 'new' women. After World War I, single women were forced to produce a 'letter of permission' signed by a parent or a 'respectable citizen' and presented to a magistrate before they were allowed to proceed to Catholic Mozambique. To the same end – control – the state denied, confiscated or withdrew the 'tourist passports' of women suspected of going to Lourenço Marques to take up positions as barmaids, casino hostesses, dancers or prostitutes. The police circulated the names of women thought to be contemplating marriage to Portuguese nationals. Those who somehow sneaked through the net and ended up working in insalubrious establishments were, under dubious legal provisions, simply deported by the South African consul.

The post-World War I administration in Mozambique, keen to shed Lourenço Marques's dependence on those inland visitors interested largely in exploring morally questionable forms of recreation on low budgets, made a conscious effort to improve the city's infrastructure, hoping that better-appointed hotels might appeal to wealthier South African tourists. But instead of concentrating on the emerging middle class on the Rand, as it did after World War II, it chose to link up with South African mining capitalists and construct a state-of-the art upmarket hotel that, as at Estoril, outside Lisbon, might draw elite visitors from across the Western world.

A serious misreading of the emerging tourist market left the Polana Hotel as the finest of all financial white elephants in southern Africa. While Johannesburg's middle classes helped pump new life into Lourenço Marques during the 1950s and into the 1960s, the Polana Hotel, which changed owners several times, proved to be financially draining for its various proprietors. South Africa's Anglophone upper crust, focused largely on English-speaking Cape Town when they were not in or around Park Lane, felt that Catholic, Portuguese-speaking Lourenço Marques had limited appeal. And, to make matters worse, after World War II, many in the Rand's middle classes abandoned southern Mozambique as a holiday destination, choosing instead to spend their vacations in culturally more comfortable Durban. Lourenço Marques always offered South African tourists what Nadine Gordimer

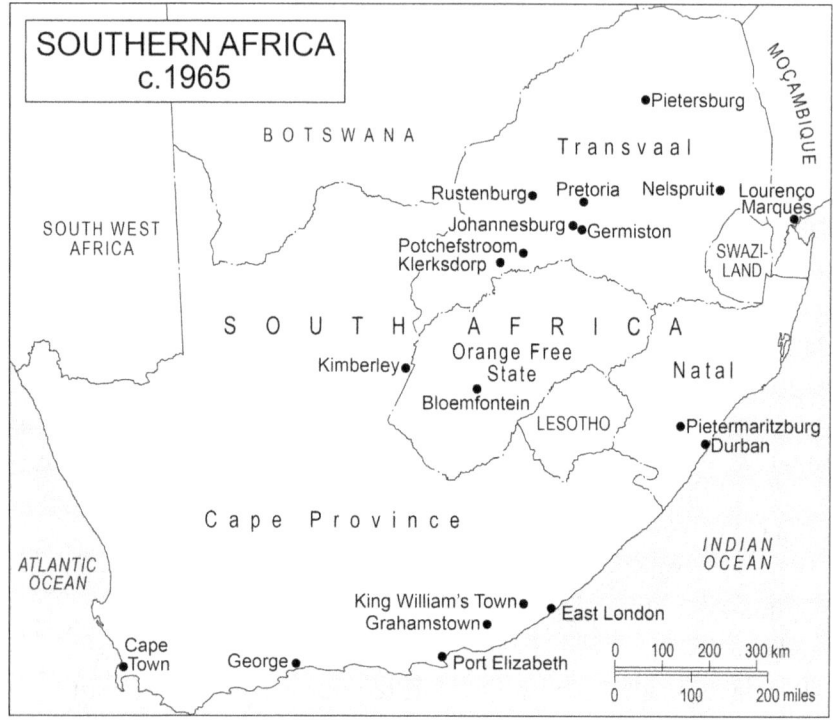

once saw as a 'Little Escape' from the rigours of a church-dominated social dispensation, but it failed to develop a modern tourist infrastructure that could capture – and hold – the white middle classes.

If the Mozambican administration failed in its long-term efforts to hold on to the bodies and holiday spend of South Africa's middle and working classes in the 20th century, then it succeeded spectacularly in securing their minds and money in another venture that exploited interstitial spaces created by Calvinist excess and Sunday social death.

For four decades, from the mid-1930s to the mid-1970s, Lourenço Marques Radio (LMR) was *the* commercial success favoured by those white South African listeners in search of the popular music that helped shaped much of the modern, urban, secular cultures in the United States and United Kingdom. Youthful Afrikaans- and English-speaking audiences in the southern hemisphere may have been locked into a political Calvinist time capsule for the better part of half a century, but they were also increasingly aware that, somewhere out there, in the northern hemisphere, there was a different world, one where greater cultural and social freedoms underwrote a lifestyle they could aspire to. Through their ears, young and young-at-heart South Africans passed through another turnstile of the mind and got a glimpse of modernity.

The irony was that it was Calvinism – narrowly construed – that helped both to create and ultimately, through a devious and dirty war, to destroy LMR. When, in 1934, Prime Minister JBM Hertzog's United Party belatedly stumbled into the need for a state broadcasting system, it chose as its adviser and guide into the modern world the son of a Scottish Presbyterian minister whose private and public morals were not always of a piece. It was Sir John Reith, with his dislike of commerce and jazz, and unwillingness to tolerate anything other than a funereal approach to broadcasting on the Sabbath, who gave Hertzog the BBC-like template that became South Africa's Broadcasting Act 22 of 1936.

The problem was that Reith's legal template was, in some respects, already dated, if not fatally flawed. An islander, Reith thought like an islander. He failed to appreciate fully that radio transmitters were no respecters of national borders. Back in England, the ether was already being exploited by commercial broadcasts emanating from continental Europe. Calvinist South Africa, pushed up against Catholic Mozambique in the northeast, was no less vulnerable to the penetration of its airspace by transmissions originating from beyond the border. Nor did the great man appreciate fully the cost implications for broadcasting in a country that demanded a bilingual service for a white nation in the making. South Africa was divided between rural-based Afrikaans speakers, conservatives spread over an enormous expanse of territory and largely without financial backing, and better-off, low-order English-speaking 'progressives' clustered in cities along the Witwatersrand and with relatively easy access to commercial funding.

The gaps in Reithian thinking may have escaped the notice of Hertzog, who took little interest in the future of broadcasting, but they did not elude GJ McHarry, a young Johannesburg entrepreneur. McHarry hurriedly obtained a concession from the Mozambique administration for a station that would not only carry revenue-generating commercial advertisements but also provide listeners with ready access to popular light music, including on the moribund Sundays patrolled by the Calvinists. Lourenço Marques Radio took to the airwaves in the same year that the South African Broadcasting Corporation (SABC) launched its services.

McHarry did not miss a beat. In the aftermath of World War II, he recruited former British Army officers familiar with monitoring the listening habits of the troops and civilian populations and professionalised the management of LMR. From their Johannesburg offices, the firm of Davenport & Meyer (Pty) Ltd provided the outstanding market research and public relations initiatives that drove LMR's cultural successes. The SABC remained on a tight Calvinist rein and hobbled along beneath the weight of its beloved Sunday shell. By the time the SABC belatedly launched its own revenue-seeking station, Springbok Radio, in May 1950, LMR already dominated the commercial airwaves.

The tide began to turn later that decade, albeit slowly at first. After its electoral triumph in 1948, the National Party's vanguardist think-tank, the Afrikaner Broederbond, took an increasing interest in broadcasting, hoping to consolidate its hold on ethnic loyalists and extend the political and ideological construction of a homogeneous white 'nation'.

In 1959, the inner workings of the SABC were captured when Dr PJ Meyer turned himself into the executive chairman of the board. Under Meyer – apostle of apartheid, Calvinist modernist and ultra-nationalist – the capital-gobbling SABC expanded exponentially and grew increasingly resentful of LMR. Not only did LMR consciously cultivate a secular contempt for weekend social imprisonment, as evidenced by the success of its flagship Sunday-night programme, the 'LM Hit Parade', but it diverted commercial funding into Mozambique.

In Meyer's mind, however, these cultural and financial constraints, in an otherwise economically buoyant decade, were soon eclipsed by new and far more dangerous threats. In the 1960s and early 1970s, African nationalist wars of liberation spread rapidly through much of the wider region, leaving white South Africa increasingly isolated and with the possibility of LMR one day falling into 'enemy' hands. The threat of 'hostile' broadcasts being beamed into the country from Lourenço Marques, by freedom fighters intent on liberating black

South Africans from the heavy burdens of apartheid, was all too real.

For much of the 1960s and early 1970s Meyer attempted, through regular commercial channels, to buy a controlling interest in either the Rádio Clube de Moçambique (RCM), which, in partnership with McHarry, had the licence for LMR, or Davenport & Meyer (Pty) Ltd, the company that shaped the station's ongoing success. More importantly, he also engaged in an overt and covert campaign to gain control of the station.

Always ambitious – to the point where he was viewed with considerable suspicion by leading figures in cabinet – Meyer crafted a Radio Amendment Act, or, as he preferred to refer to it in private, a 'Piracy Act'. The purpose of the draft act was to silence LMR and protect South Africans from 'attacks on the mind'. But his attempt to get new legislation passed that might somehow offend the South African government's military ally in the war against the liberation movements failed, as did his initial endeavour to gain commercial control of LMR.

But the deteriorating security situation in colonial southern Africa played increasingly into Meyer's hands. With the assistance of the Minister of Defence, PW Botha, Meyer cultivated leading figures in the Portuguese Army at home and abroad. By 1970, the Lisbon government, by then the majority shareholder in RCM, was as stretched financially as it was militarily. The SABC signed a contract with RCM in a secret deal, and two years later McHarry disposed of his interests in LMR. The SABC had, after a long struggle, gained covert control of its outstanding regional competitor.

It was, however, a pyrrhic victory since by then, without the drive and thrust of the dynamic, enthused services of Davenport & Meyer, advertising revenue from LMR had fallen drastically. The SABC had won the fight to ensure that the political content of LMR would never pose a threat to the security of the South African state but lost the means with which to finance that control. And, when the Mozambique Liberation Front (Frelimo) assumed control of Lourenço Marques's Radio Palace, the SABC lost virtually all that Meyer and his board had striven to acquire in a decade-long struggle.

At 5 am on the morning of 12 October 1975, after nearly four decades of lively broadcasting to cultural agnostics in South Africa, LMR finally went off the air. Meyer's dirty war for total political control of the national airwaves had received a setback. But such was his Calvinist, ultra-nationalist fixation on the evils of pop music and the need to honour the Sabbath that Meyer had long since put a contingency plan in place. The very next day, 13 October 1975, the SABC's Radio 5 went on air to provide lovers of pop music with a censored, short-back-and-sides version of modern youth culture.

Ever since the formation of the Union, in 1910, Calvinist conservatives tried – with mixed success – to ensure that the South African state controlled those turnstiles of the white mind that led to Catholic Mozambique and unwanted, modern 'liberal' tendencies. Today, it is African nationalists, far more tolerant of cultural differences, who insist on controlling the SABC for party-political reasons. *A luta continua.*

PART I

TOURIST DREAMS AND DREAMS OF A TOURISM INDUSTRY: JOHANNESBURG AND LOURENÇO MARQUES, CIRCA 1910–1955

You must know this, and a number of other things about our life in Johannesburg to understand what Lourenço Marques, a small resort on the coast of Portuguese East Africa, means to us. Indeed, I cannot imagine what we would do without it ... We go to Lourenço Marques, it's our Little Escape.
NADINE GORDIMER, 'SOUTH AFRICAN RIVIERA', 1957

Within months of Nadine Gordimer's murmuring about the importance of having an east coast bolt-hole to elude the rigours of South African life, her *fado*-like refrain was being matched, albeit in prosaic form and at a tangent, by a most unlikely official source – a prominent Afrikaner nationalist. During a brief visit to Lisbon, Dr EG Jansen, the second-to-last Governor General of the Union of South Africa, while bending the diplomatic knee to the cynically propagated myth that Mozambique was a 'province' of Portugal rather than a brutally neglected far-off colony, enthused: 'By a happy accident we are neighbours.'

Jansen's was a cheerfully myopic observation, one that overlooked the fact that he represented a white-minority Calvinist regime deeply committed to an extremist form of racial segregation and social conservatism, while his nominally Catholic hosts prided themselves on a supposedly more open and forgiving form of 'Lusotropicalism', one accommodating of non-racialism. But since diplomacy is the art of sipping arsenic as if it were champagne, he pushed on. 'I believe', he told the press, 'that we should be grateful to history for this accident.'[1]

But mere propinquity is, alas, seldom enough to guarantee a happy outcome when it comes to the historical relationship between countries.

Sharing a border was never in itself enough to draw Mozambique and South Africa into an authentic, closer, organic association. As Edward Said once pointedly reminded us:

> Just as none of us is outside or beyond geography, none of us is completely free from the struggle over geography. That struggle is complex and interesting because it is not only about soldiers and cannons but also about ideas, about forms, about myths and imaginings.[2]

It requires but little reflection to appreciate just how deep such geographically derived complexities can run when reconstructing the intricate historical connections that developed around tourists and tourism between 20th-century South Africa and southern Mozambique and, more especially, between Johannesburg and Lourenço Marques.

A rudimentary settlement on Delagoa Bay since 1544, Lourenço Marques was designated a 'town' in 1876, not long after the discovery of diamonds near Kimberley. In 1887, just twelve months after the opening of the Witwatersrand goldfields and the founding of Johannesburg, a town council cemented its new status. Then, in 1898, unconsciously reflecting the town's rise as a dependency of the mineral revolution on the Highveld, it was made the capital city of Mozambique.

Born a nondescript, malaria-plagued port, albeit one located on a beautifully sheltered Indian Ocean bay, Lourenço Marques struggled to match up to its rapidly changing legal status. Outsiders agreed that it occupied a unique position in the world order of debasement. In 1900, a traveller, apparently blessed with the English gift of understatement, felt that it was the 'vilest, filthiest and most deadly place to white men in all the hospitable world'. Stanley Hollis, the US consul, was even more fulsome when pleading with the State Department to grant him special leave of absence that same year. Lourenço Marques was one of 'the most miserable, unhealthy, desolate and God-forsaken places on the face of the earth'. It was, he said, 'a place destitute of material and social comforts, and filled with the scum of South and East Africa'.[3]

Some of Lourenço Marques's less appealing material conditions could be traced to its unpromising, swampy, riverside location.

Harbours – like mining towns – are sited for the most part where nature dumps her bounty and not where humanity necessarily choses to live and work. Although a cleaner, healthier and infinitely more presentable entrepôt a decade later, Lourenço Marques never fully outgrew its reputation as a grubby port dominated by its cosmopolitan demi-monde. Not everyone found its reputation off-putting, though. Indeed, for many moneyed single male visitors, the demi-monde was the port's principal attraction.

But the port itself shaped only part of the town's complex, evolving, dual social character. Although it remained a preponderantly male-dominated enclave, with an exceedingly modest European population throughout the interwar period, it gradually acquired the infrastructure that allowed it to present the more pleasing 'city' face that it aspired to.

In 1929, on the eve of the Great Depression, a visiting banker noted that the business quarter had not changed noticeably over several years but conceded that municipal affairs were well-managed and public spaces well-maintained. But it was the 'the residential area' that earned his fulsome support. It 'has grown out of all recognition and quite a number of the suburban residences, with their attractive gardens gay with colour, can be classed with the best to be found anywhere in South Africa'. Lourenço Marques was no longer only a sleazy port, to be enjoyed by visiting males with time and money, but a new city on the march, 'and as a seaside resort it is steadily increasing in popularity'.[4]

By the time Nadine Gordimer visited it, in the mid-1950s, Lourenço Marques was a modern colonial city famed for its relaxed 'continental atmosphere'. Many South African visitors nevertheless took some comfort from the fact that, for the most part, it was also racially segregated, and the city's proximity to Johannesburg turned Lourenço Marques into a 'natural playground' for Highveld visitors – much as white Rhodesians turned to Beira, further up the coast, for their vacations.[5] It was, in short, a coastal retreat suitable for a family holiday.

But, for a century prior to that, Lourenço Marques had been little more than a backward bayside settlement replete with many of the social features and structures customarily associated with tawdry ports the world over. After World War I, however, its emerging dual character – as both port and resort, along with the sometimes competing economic imperatives driving each – became more pronounced.

The ensuing tussle, as to which of the city's component parts – port or resort – might emerge dominant, was at its most pronounced during the interwar period. But, by the end of World War II, the outcome was increasingly apparent. As a resort, the city was steadily losing traction in the greater southern African tourist market. A comprehensive, sympathetic survey conducted by a local businessman, in 1950, concluded that, while Lourenço Marques attracted significant numbers of South African tourists each year, the stream was but 'a mere trickle compared to what there should be if only our potentialities were realized and the visitor properly catered for and attracted'.[6] The situation did improve, perhaps even significantly so, over the years that followed and into the early 1960s.[7] But, for many white visitors, the resort remained mired in an indeterminate, surreal blueish haze. Along African coastlines it is often the least threatening mists, those of dreams and potentialities, that conceal the deadliest shoals of all – stark reality.

One such hidden reef lay in the fact that, insofar as the economic fortunes of Lourenço Marques as a tourist hub were tied to another city, the link ran 350 miles west, to Johannesburg and its satellite towns. It was not an affectionate coupling of the type forged in heaven, rather one born of convenience, one compelled by geography. And, just as Lourenço Marques mutated from a port settlement with an adolescent profile, appealing to an adventurous if not always strictly youthful population, into a recognisably more mature resort city with identifiable social parameters, so too did Johannesburg evolve from a rough mining town into an established industrial city.

Like Lourenço Marques in its infancy, early Johannesburg never wanted for critics. God could only do so much. Cast among a few largely treeless quartz outcrops – sentinels guarding the world's deepest and richest gold reefs – the place, despite being blessed with the finest of climates, lacked other redeeming natural features capable of sustaining significant outdoor amusements, entertainment or leisure. Already physically stretched, young miners in search of recreation were, in any case, not much given to hiking, taking in the undulating landscape or contemplating starry skies. Their priorities lay elsewhere. There was no shortage of entrepreneurs, criminal or otherwise, willing to cater for basic and other needs. Man stepped in to plug nature's gaps, giving rise to the mining-camp sociology beloved of filmgoers.

Olive Schreiner was appalled to witness the rape of nature, modest of countenance as it undoubtedly was. 'Here's this great fiendish hell of a city sprung up in ten years in our sweet pure African veldt', she wrote to Edward Carpenter, in 1898. 'A city which for glitter and gold, and wickedness – carriages and palaces and brothels, and gambling halls, beats creation.' Fifteen years later Ambrose Pratt, a visiting Australian journalist, could not even imagine what had gone before and simply recorded what he saw laid out before him. 'Ancient Nineveh and Babylon have been revived', he reported. 'Johannesburg is their twentieth century prototype. It's a city of unbridled squander and unfathomable squalor.'[8]

Up to a point, such descriptions of early Johannesburg and Lourenço Marques seemed interchangeable; the cities could have been twinned. But only up to a point. While both colonial towns shared elements of 'unfathomable squalor', the direction and pace of their trajectories were fated to diverge rather than converge after World War I. White Johannesburg, fed on a diet of gold plucked from sprouting mine shafts, grew plump and wealthy and matured comparatively rapidly in social terms. Lourenço Marques, restricted to feeding off financial scraps discarded along the city's wharves, remained rather thin and lingered in its adolescence.

In truth, what the lean port city wanted most from its fat miningtown twin before World War I was as much of its 'unbridled squander' as it could effectively lay its hands on by way of tourism. What the Rand miners wanted from their port counterpart was a bit of its 'unfathomable squalor'. A successful socio-economic exchange along those lines worked reasonably well into the early 1920s, while both cities remained overwhelmingly shallow, male-dominated centres in which drinking, gambling and whoring formed an important part of a pared-down social life.

Economic and political realities in southern Africa checked the pace at which Johannesburg and the surrounding mining towns came of age in purely social terms. The persistently high cost of living on the Highveld, along with the attendant ease of international migrancy in the late 19th and early 20th centuries, made it difficult for British and other Anglophone migrant miners to contemplate settled life on the Rand. True, the political uncertainties of life in Kruger's South African Republic were partly resolved by the outcome of the Anglo-Boer War (1899–1902). But the war, in turn, gave way to the upheavals occasioned by the new political configuration that came with Union, in 1910. Union was followed, almost immediately, by World War I, which was tailed by a 50 per cent increase in the cost of living between 1917 and 1920.[9]

In 1897, barely 12 per cent of the Witwatersrand's European mine employees were married and had their families living with them in the republic. It was a moment when Johannesburg's Big Three social pathologies – illicit alcohol consumption, covert gaming and organised prostitution, all deemed illegal yet partially tolerated – were at their very height.[10] It was not a time when Lourenço Marques had much to offer the Rand.

Immediately after the war, in 1902, that figure crept up to 20 per cent as the Milner reconstruction administration, riding in on the coat-tails of British military power, clamped down on gangster-driven illegalities as it sought to bring greater regularity and normality to questionable recreational excesses. By the same token, it was a time when some of the more adventurous and cash-flush white miners had to look further afield for the Big Three.

A decade later, in 1912, when organised crime's hold on the Big Three was largely broken, the figure had doubled to 42 per cent; after that, it is almost impossible to find reliable figures.[11] The arrival of Afrikaners on the mines in significant numbers, during World War I, may have seen a spike in the number of married miners living in family homes, but it seems that it was only in the early 1920s that something approaching a social norm for white working-class life was achieved along the Witwatersrand. Ironically, however, and as the 1922 white mineworkers' strike confirmed, the post-war period was also one of growing financial and job insecurity. For most white mineworkers, the delights of Lourenço Marques were increasingly out of financial and social reach – except for the purchase of lottery tickets. For many, the hope of securing a fortune in a frontier town had given way to grinding out a more tenuous living.

Taking in the picture as a whole, then, what male tourists and others spontaneously set out to find in Lourenço Marques during the

An appeal, in both official languages, to white South African tourists, c. 1950. DETA was a charter airline set up by Mozambique's colonial administration in 1936.

early 20th century, and the nature of the families and visitors that the port was forced to try and attract from Johannesburg after 1920, have to be aligned with the changing socio-economic profiles of both cities. The success or failure of the port-turned-city's fortunes as a tourist hub for visitors from a mining-town-turned-city thus hinged partly on the former's ability to read the changing patterns of disposable income, by class, and to adapt its supply of leisure and recreational amenities accordingly. It also depended on ease of access to the seaside resort.

During the opening decades of the 20th century, a narrow-gauge rail journey of around 17 hours separated Johannesburg from Lourenço Marques. It required negotiating a formidable mountainous section en route, followed by a tedious border stop at Komatipoort. Steam and time were pitted in an unequal contest that time almost always won. By the late 1920s and early 1930s, however, the same expedition could be tackled by car, the average journey taking between 10 and 12 hours. By 1947, for the well-off, just an hour's flight separated a dusty plateau from a muggy coast. Dream time and real time, separated by class, colour, culture and technology, were constantly changing.

Tourist Dreams, Coastal Escapes and the White Working Class, circa 1906—1922

It may be true that there are certain elements that cut across ideas of class when we try to understand how people from different walks of life pursue leisure during short breaks or extended stays away from home. As the adage has it, a good number are, no doubt, looking for a 'complete change', for something fundamentally different. But closer examination suggests that they may be a minority, and that by probing their underlying motivations we may arrive at a more nuanced interpretation. It may just be safer to assume that, while most holidaymakers want to revel in new experiences and altered rhythms to offset the dulling effect of the routines of domestic life, there are limits to their capacity for tolerating changes and disruption. Most vacationers want contrast and novelty, but they seek to do so within identifiable parameters that do not imperil comfort or security.

The contrast in environments between Johannesburg and Lourenço Marques was as obvious as it was stark. Most white miners, breathing the thin air of a dry grassy inland plateau 6 000 feet above sea level when they were not underground, were drawn from a damp, wooded, island kingdom where no point was further than 70 miles from the sea. The desire, if not the need, to swap the omnipresent dust and noise of mining towns for fresh coastal breezes and the relative tranquillity of the humid seaside required little prompting by way of advertising. Indeed, it was only after the advent of Union that one or two of the more reputable hotels in Lourenço Marques thought it profitable enough to advertise their 'holiday rates' in Johannesburg's English newspapers.[12]

As marked as the inland–coastal dichotomy was, so was the difference in climate. Despite sharing an almost identical location latitudinally, around 25 degrees south, the contrast between winter and

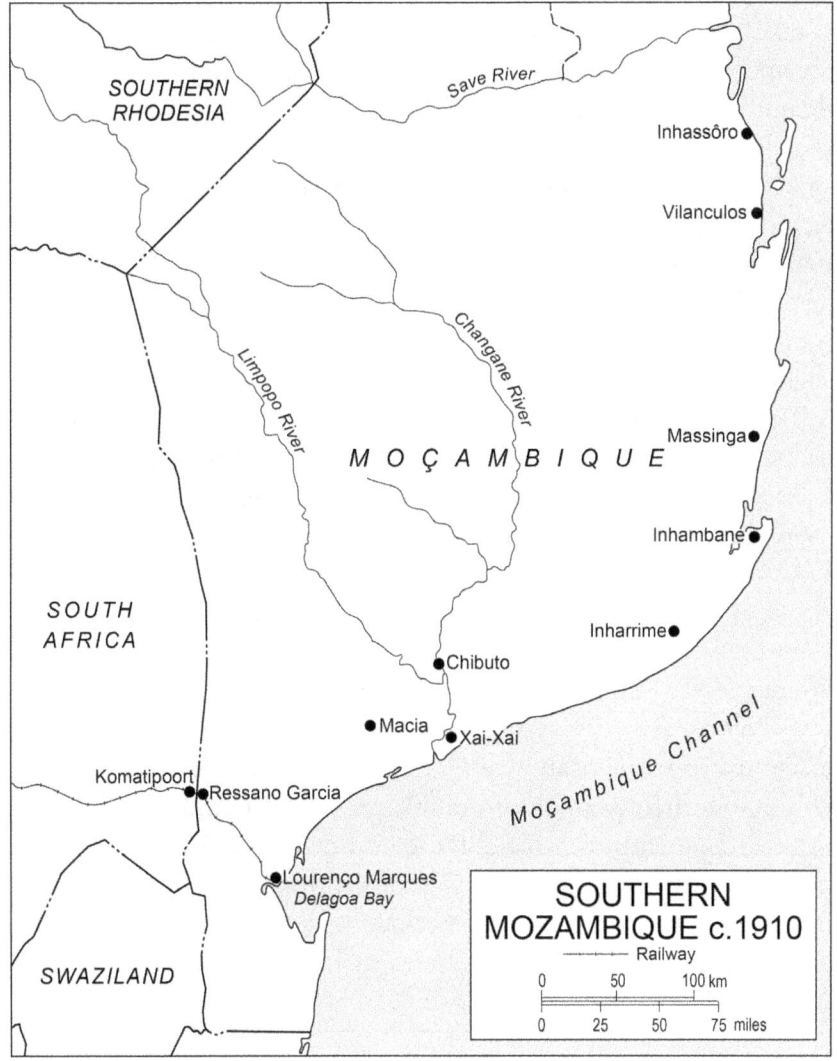

summer in the two cities was especially marked. Highveld winters – in which South African stoicism made few concessions to reality – could be bitterly cold, with night-time temperatures sometimes falling below freezing. At precisely the same time of year, southern Mozambique bathed in balmy subtropical weather. The basic appeal was obvious.

Many northern-hemisphere immigrants, like their white South African counterparts raised in the Christian tradition, were inclined to take their annual family holidays over Christmas. But, because December and January were unbearably hot and humid in Lourenço Marques, they were encouraged to take a winter rather than a summer break from work. Thus, while those white families on the Highveld who could afford it went off to much cooler South African coastal resorts over the Christmas period, European migrant miners with more discretionary income – bachelors, or nominally 'single' men away from their northern wives and families, operating by a different calendar – chose to make their way to Mozambique between May and September, the height of the longer of the two tourist seasons in Lourenço Marques.

These immutable coastal–inland, cold–warm, dry–humid, up–down distinctions temporarily disrupted the everyday, as well as the seasonal, realities and rhythms experienced by many working men and women. It inverted the physical and temporal demands placed on them by industrial capitalism on the Highveld. In much the same way, the change in climate and weather assisted in disrupting the diurnal rhythms of those who – unlike shift-working miners – were accustomed to the patterned difference between days and nights in Johannesburg.

FJ Nance, a travel writer on a commission in 1920, and Gordimer, nosing into an American magazine noted for accommodating those with serious literary ambitions in the mid-1950s, both revelled in the way that Lourentinos avoided the enervating heat by turning night into day. At the docks, African waterfront workers who started their morning shift not long after daybreak under Portuguese, Mauritian or *mestiço* supervision, were rested between 11 am and 2 pm. And as the blacks along the wharf stopped working, whites started appearing in nearby cafés and hotels for either a late breakfast or an early lunch.[13]

Lazy afternoon hours flowed into early evenings, and around 9 pm a frisson of sexual tension could be detected in the air as bars, cafés, hotels, restaurants and waterfront dance halls – 'that would provide material for a Toulouse-Lautrec' – began to come alive. 'When night comes, Lourenço Marques is one of the pleasantest places imaginable', Gordimer observed from her comfortable mid-20th-century perch. 'Nobody goes to bed until near morning', she continued, and 'the pleasures of the town', which she elsewhere describes as 'mildly wicked', 'are not confined, after eleven o'clock as in Johannesburg.'[14] Clock and calendar were upside down.

But it was not only the daily disruption that appealed; a pleasant change in the all-too-familiar cadence of weekly working life was also on display. Nance, closer by several decades to the 'single' miners' long weekends or annual excursions than was Gordimer, was struck by how free the town was of the shackles of the Highveld's steely grip when it came to Sunday observance. 'It is true,' he noted, apologetically, that 'alcoholic drink can be obtained freely at almost any hour', including Sundays. The Pope, it seemed, was more than a match for Calvin. But that was an old struggle, and Nance, a modern man, counselled tolerance: they should give 'their Latin neighbours the benefit of the doubt'.[15]

Such exceptions had an appeal of their own for vacationers. But for many male visitors to Lourenço Marques before World War I, they were complemented by other personal indulgences that were becoming increasingly difficult to satisfy back on the Witwatersrand. Middle-class Protestant Johannesburg, keen to get the city to shed its old Mr Hyde outfit for one of Dr Jekyll's suits, was set on controlling what it saw as the crude excesses of white working-class social behaviour.

The interwar period, from 1902 to 1914, and a few years thereafter, were marked by the way that the state at every level – city, provincial and national – sought to cast aside the last of the 'naughty nineties', of the mining-camp-turned-town, and draw an ever-tighter net around white working-class gambling and recreational activities in an aspiring city. The ever-stricter insistence on Sunday observance cast a shadow as large and intense as that experienced over the entire Witwatersrand during a total eclipse of the sun. It helped set the tone for governing the days and hours at which all citizens – Christian and non-Christian alike – might attend cinemas, concerts, dance halls or sports events, or have a drink in a hotel or pub. The Calvinist disapproval of wealth gained without work informed legislation aimed at controlling and regulating gambling on the outcomes on anything from professional athletic competitions to dog and horse racing and, the ultimate horror, lotteries and sweepstakes. Tolerance for human frailties and weaknesses pointed to Catholicism, and the train pointed to Delagoa Bay.

In Lourenço Marques, the Estação Central was first mooted in 1906, but the grand station building, originally designed to partly

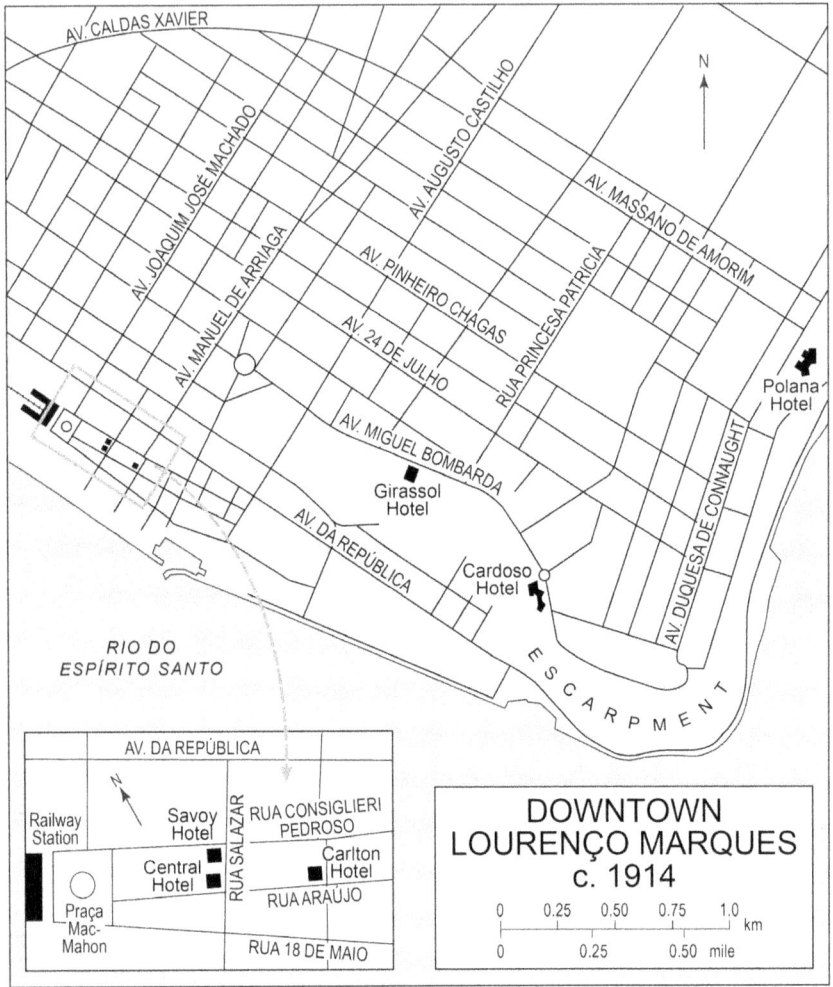

match the façade of its counterpart in Johannesburg, Park Station, was only completed in the Beaux-Arts style four years later. Once Johannesburg was directly linked to the eastern main line, shortening the journey time by two hours – by avoiding an unnecessary diversion via the capital, Pretoria – travel by rail became less arduous and offered tourists a genteel reception.

Disembarking passengers crossed the Praça MacMahon, a square leading directly into the main street of a downtown area characterised by its cosmopolitanism. Rua Araújo, also known as 'Whisky Street' – and other names that did not bear repeating in polite company

– boasted the offices of some leading port businesses and commercial agencies, as well as many more hotels, bars, boarding houses and cafés and kiosks. The adjacent backstreets housed cheaper accommodation and places of amusement.

The only decent hotel in town in the late 1890s, it was said, was the Cardoso. It was some way off, far away from the docks, and situated on the cliffs overlooking the bay. The hotel was named after its proprietor, the naval officer and noted explorer Augusto Cardoso, who had found himself in charge of an expedition to the shores of Lake Nyasa (Lake Malawi) when Alexandre de Serpa Pinto fell ill, in 1885. Cardoso went on to become the Port Captain, a significant post in an often venal civil service and one not entirely divorced from financial opportunities. His hotel, successfully managed by an Italian, was reconfigured several times and dominated the upper end of the local market until 1924.[16]

In truth, it was not all that difficult to be the best. During the Anglo-Boer War, Hollis, as insightful as he could be irascible, noted that 'there are no low-priced decent boarding houses or hotels in town'. 'The cheap hotels', he complained, 'are nothing better than brothels.' It was not surprising, since, as Bertha Goudvis, the South African novelist and playwright who, with her husband, owned the Royal Hotel, off Rua Araújo, noted, 'it was a known fact that *anyone* could acquire a hotel licence'. But even at the decidedly middle-class Royal, which charged ten shillings a day, and which Hollis deemed 'reasonable for Lourenço Marques', the perky, always adventurous Mrs Goudvis 'would never go near the bar as no respectable woman was ever seen near one'.[17]

During the Anglo-Boer War, an influx of Highveld refugees enabled most hotels to concentrate on their core function by providing guests, including somewhat more women than usual, with accommodation and meals at smartly elevated rates.[18] The same held true for the two world wars. Wartime was harvest time along the Bay. Peace was bad for business; it dried up the supply of better-off guests, trimmed margins and eroded profits, forcing many proprietors to try and attract new clients by reverting to the age-old dockside formula noted by Hollis.

Lourenço Marques had delivered clients to prostitutes of all classes and colours ever since the first ship berthed in the modern port, but after 1895, once the railway line inland was completed, it became a favoured point of entry and transmission for the international white slave traffic. Pimps and procuresses operating out of continental Europe used the southbound ships of the German East Africa Line, passing through Suez, to transport their prey into border-porous Lourenço Marques, from where they were forwarded by train to gangster-controlled Johannesburg.[19]

But during, and more especially after, the Anglo-Boer War, scores of these women, including numbers of Jewish prostitutes, had either been abandoned by the former New York City gangsters who controlled most of the trade or fled Johannesburg. Many found themselves stranded in Lourenço Marques, where, passing as spinsters or widows, they ran boarding houses at the lower end of the market offering a range of home comforts of the sort that Hollis, and Rabbi Joseph Hertz – passing through the city in 1899 – disapproved of. Many remained in the port and their graves lie in the Jewish cemetery.[20]

Prostitutes approaching the end of their working career, middle-aged at best, tended to seek a measure of concealment and protection from the passing trade by taking up positions in boarding houses or cheap hotels. New entrants to the profession, younger women wishing to parade their attractiveness and in search of above-average earnings, knew that the passing traffic needed to be courted, not shunned. Bertha Goudvis pointed out that the 'few professional barmaids in town' – those working in bars or hotels – 'were classed as courtesans'.[21] As with brothels that were legal, at various times in the 20th century the state appreciated what the earning capacity of a 'courtesan' might be. Between the world wars the cost of a bar licence reached £60 sterling per annum, while each barmaid had to be licensed at a further cost of £40.[22]

Arguably better and more numerous opportunities for identifying potential clients were to be found by working as waitresses in the 'kiosks' – 'like continental cafés' – spread around the main plaza, where the military band entertained the public in the evenings, or near a few smaller parks.[23] After World War I, the old kiosks were supplemented by a half-dozen new and larger cafés that offered meals by day, only to be transformed into clubs at night staffed by youngish 'dance hostesses'.

To be sure, however, even before the Great War the town offered a few other – less ambiguous – allures that might appeal to middle-class, if not middle-aged, males or even the odd married couple with children. The smooth Polana Beach could be reached by bus or tramway along an asphalt road, and on most days was as pleasant as it was safe. By night, more confident swimmers could use a lit diving tower to enjoy the sea. Sailing or tennis presented other diversions for a minority.

After 1908, bullfights, cultivated amid an Iberian blur, drew their share of spectators looking for the precise point where athleticism intersected with blood. Those with less robust constitutions could, by 1910, retreat to the 'opera house', the Teatro Varietá, or to two smaller theatres. By 1920, the town was also served by two cinemas, with one offering films for mainly Portuguese audiences, the other for English speakers. Nance argued that Lourenço Marques could offer a 'quiet holiday'.[24]

But tranquillity was not what those headed for a place where men vastly outnumbered women for decades were looking for. 'The strolling crowd is', EC Scully noted, around 1910, 'almost wholly composed of men. By day or by night, it is but rarely that one sees women abroad.' A decade later, Nance, an apostle of resort over port, was still battling a 'fantastic misconception'. 'Lourenço Marques', he assured his nervous South African readers, 'is not a continental fastness where self-respecting mothers cannot take their babies without returning monsters of depravity.'[25] Not everybody was easily reassured. As late as 1970, a guidebook warned naive female tourists that Portuguese men 'liked to admire the passing parade of girls', but then hurriedly proceeded to reassure them that 'unlike the Italians they are not bottom pinchers'.[26] Some earlier white working-class tourists could not have cared less.

In the wake of the 1906–1908 depression the last of the 19th century's 'sporting men' – those who prided themselves on fighting, drinking and womanising – along with miners with or without their wives in tow, descended on the port in growing numbers.[27] A few headed straight for the Savoy Hotel, notorious for its rowdy drinking parties, the singing of obscene songs and generally disturbing the peace. By 1912, there were so many canteens – more than 950 in the Lourenço Marques district – that the police could no longer maintain public order and the Governor General, for a time, banned the issuing of any further liquor licences.[28]

Lourenço Marques street scene, c. 1920, white and male.

Lesser mortals pushed on to the Central Hotel, owned by Johannesburg Consolidated Investments (JCI), a Rand mining house. It was, the manager boasted on an impressive promotional photograph, 'the most best family hotel', situated on the Rua Araújo, matching a similar nearby establishment, the Carlton Hotel. But *família* and Araújo went together about as well as did heaven and hell. When a fire started in the tellingly named Klondike Bar at the Central, around midnight one evening in May 1910, the hotel was gutted and the corporation owners rushed to rebuild it. The building changed but the clientele did not. Three years later so much noise was coming from the bar, around closing time, that no one was able to sleep, and the authorities had to place the owners on terms.[29]

Just as the social lives of mining towns all along the Reef were being sedated and trussed up by the church and suburbs for a slow death by respectability and Sunday observance laws, the port's demi-monde was becoming ever livelier and kicking. Johannesburg could not get enough of it. In March 1912, the *Rand Daily Mail* warned readers that Lourenço Marques had become so popular as a holiday destination that all hotels were fully booked for the upcoming winter season, and that there was probably insufficient accommodation to satisfy all visitors.[30]

The seasonal influx of upcountry visitors appears to have tailed off briefly during the closing years of the war, but by 1919 a lack of sufficient accommodation for tourists, let alone of the required quality, was again manifest.[31] The long-standing problem went beyond the physical provision of beds, rooms and meals. It stretched the port's always generous supply of indigenous African women at the lower end of the market and contributed to a marked shortage of English-speaking, more culturally attuned barmaids, café attendants and waitresses, as well as prostitutes based either in licensed brothels or in rooms in the downtown area. Demand trumped supply.

Throughout most of its history, Lourenço Marques never wanted for some 'coloured' (mixed race) or white women who had been coerced or forced into a life of prostitution. Many more might have consciously chosen it as a profession to support a preferred lifestyle. What is striking, however, is how, before the mid-1920s, many were lured into service in the port, and how many more arrived seemingly cheerfully and voluntarily after the Depression. Either way, their arrival reflected two things: the ongoing proletarianisation of 'poor whites' on the Highveld as the South African industrial revolution progressed, and the increased repression of white working-class social life in urban areas.

Starting in 1910, with the formation of Union, the authorities in Pretoria – overwhelmingly male and white – viewed Lourenço Marques as an especially morally hazardous enclave, a zone that exposed white South African women to unspeakable dangers at a time when the 'country' was creating a bureaucracy to serve the new state and busily forging a largely mythical 'national' identity that excluded black people. Thus, while white men were free to indulge in away games at a time when organised crime was on the retreat along the Witwatersrand, white women travelling to Mozambique were viewed with great suspicion.

Seen through the official eye, unattached young white women making their way to Delagoa Bay were either embarrassingly deficient in morals when it came to lives of prostitution freely entered into, or they were the hapless victims of a new traffic in white slaves. Both extremes were, of course, in evidence but such mutually exclusive interpretations allowed for neither agency nor choice. They left little room for other women, those in search of adventure, those wanting to exercise their sexuality more freely or those who, for a time only, wished to become financially independent by occasionally prostituting themselves.[32]

Bar owners, forced to look beyond the port and to Johannesburg for a new intake of assistants from among the daring, desperate or naive, used employment agencies or newspaper advertisements to entice young white women to the Bay at salaries purported to be between £10 and £15 per month.[33] Many barmaids, however, not only served customers from behind the counter but worked on a commission basis. They took seats at small tables and engaged clients in pleasant conversation or danced with them, and by so doing prolonged their stay and ensured they drank more than they might otherwise have done. What the happy couple did after the establishment closed was for their own account.[34]

But what the printed word could not do a few Johannesburg-based procurers, procuresses and pimps, and one or two sent up from the Bay, sometimes could. They focused on the poorest white working-class suburbs, centres for cheap labour such as Fordsburg and Vrededorp, where a generation of South African-born prostitutes was beginning to fill a gap in the market occasioned by the large-scale departure of international gangsters and 'continental women' from 1908 to 1910.[35]

It was part of a new response, one evolving across southern Africa, that the British consul in Lourenço Marques considered to be akin to the older white slave traffic of the 1890s. But instead of the Witwatersrand being only an importer of prostitutes from the northern hemisphere, as was the case before the South African War, it now exported a small number of home-grown white prostitutes to the coast. And, despite efforts by detectives attached to the South African Police (SAP), who – with or without the approval of Mozambican authorities – slipped in and out of Lourenço Marques as it suited them, the trade in women gained in momentum and public prominence between 1910 and 1916.[36]

The Union government, struggling to establish a full-fledged state with muscle, and egged on by the British consul in Delagoa Bay, Errol

MacDonnell, aspired to control the movement of *all* women entering or leaving southern Mozambique. By 1913, the local Portuguese authorities, already deeply alarmed by the number of licensed liquor outlets, attempted to clamp down on what they saw as the most flagrantly immoral and rowdy bars operating in the downtown area.[37]

MacDonnell, seizing the moment, issued a notice informing bar owners that he would refuse to countersign the paperwork from barmaids unless he was furnished with 'documentary proof as to the identity, age, nationality and civil state (i.e. spinster, widow, divorced)' of the applicant.[38] Not content with that, he drafted a series of by-laws for the consideration of the Portuguese administration that would prevent the employment of any 'girl' under the age of 21, deny her the right to change employers without the prior approval of the relevant consul, and force her to re-register should she ever be absent from the city 'for more than 48 hours'.[39] In Johannesburg, the Inspector in Charge of the Criminal Investigation Department (CID) aspired to making it compulsory for all employment agencies to provide him with the names of any white South African woman proceeding to Lourenço Marques and to have the right to interview them, in person, prior to their departure.[40]

Neither the proposed by-laws nor the mandatory interviewing of European women making their way to the east coast came to fruition. The British and South African authorities had overreached themselves in their attempt to control what they saw only as weak and vulnerable women entering a zone filled with potentially lethal moral danger. Lourenço Marques's popularity grew and the news about its various attractions began to spread slowly beyond its old working-class core.

Portugal's belated and reluctant entry into World War I – at Albion's behest – further boosted the momentum of a tourist trade that had been growing rapidly for half a decade. At 8.45 pm, three nights a week, the mail train roared out of Park Station only to arrive, all puffed out, at the Estação Central 17 hours later. But at the height of the season the thrice-weekly wartime service proved inadequate. Seeking to bolster its seasonal carrying capacity on an increasingly attractive route, South African Railways (SAR) took its cue from a once-off special rail-and-steamer excursion that, in 1914, offered a Johannesburg–Lourenço Marques–Durban–Johannesburg round trip. To the delight of Delagoa Bay hoteliers, SAR ran special winter excursions in both

1915 and 1916, only to be eventually overtaken by wartime realities.[41]

A steady growth in tourist numbers and the potential for attracting more South Africans – perhaps of a different class with greater spending power – did not go unnoticed by a local administration that had struggled for some time to maintain control around the docks. What the authorities and a few wealthier entrepreneurs wanted most for the city was to cultivate more refined visitors drawn from the white middle class by providing them with the better-quality accommodation, recreation and leisure activities that would set them apart from the base of mass tourism centred on Rua Araújo. Decree No. 1029 of 7 August 1914 provided them with the instrument that would help turn the port into a resort.

The Conselho de Turismo (CDT), like the town council, was essentially a supervisory panel consisting of local notables who were nominated by, and reported to, the Governor. Set up within days of the outbreak of war, at a time when Portugal was still neutral and at the end of an era during which the escudo had held up reasonably well against the pound sterling, the CDT had several functions.

First, it would assist in identifying and championing the development of new tourist attractions that might help the city compete more effectively with other southern African holiday resorts, and more especially its noted rival, Durban. Second, through an agent and office in Pretoria, it would act as a publicity association, drawing visitors' attention to existing attractions though brochures and pamphlets and facilitating travel arrangements and bookings by cooperating with the expanding SAR. Third, it would help oversee the spending of a modest state grant.[42]

By 1916, after a sluggish start, the CDT, chaired by Augusto Cardoso – he of hotel fame – including nine other prominent men, was functioning reasonably well. A modest budget, based on the reasonably buoyant escudo, allowed it to subsidise various upmarket attractions, including a new golf course and the existing yacht club, as well as the ever-popular military band on the plaza. As importantly, however, Cardoso's committee had the ear of the city authorities when it came to suggesting policies and practices needed to appeal to the middle-class white South African tourists they hoped to entice eastward. [43]

But it was precisely in its endeavours to draw in these elusive, relatively more affluent new tourists that the CDT ran into competing political and ideological demands and tensions that proved extremely difficult to reconcile in practice without succumbing to crass pragmatism and gross opportunism. How was an allegedly open and tolerant non-racial port city, one supposedly infused with the spirit of Lusotropicalism, to retain its core values while attempting – simultaneously – to accommodate a class of tourists increasingly defined by an evolving identity constructed around notions of class, colour and nationality?

The Union, not yet a decade old, was, like the former Boer republics that it had effectively incorporated, built around the idea that there would be no equality between black and white in matters relating to church, state or society. Indeed, from the outset its governments had set out to systematically widen rather than narrow the already formidable gap between the races by colour and by class. Moreover, the outbreak of war, the introduction of passports and – paradoxically – the very act of travelling by train across borders by privileged and poorer whites alike were all feeding into the emerging South African 'national' identity.[44] In fair measure, then, middle-class white South Africans were busy defining themselves ever more narrowly, and whatever they *were*, they most certainly were not like Mozambicans, black or white.

The question then became how to square the circle when dealing with the visitors. As in many places the world over, filters of differing gauges could be employed to encourage, or enforce, the separation of races. The first, the crudest mesh of all, and the one most loved by white South Africans, was to declare selected public spaces to be off limits to people of colour. But, precisely because it was a practice as crude as it was illegal in a nominally non-racial dispensation, it was not readily achievable. 'The difficulty', as Cardoso reluctantly admitted when dealing with a South African objection, in 1916, was 'insurmountable'. Three white women, visitors, had written a letter of complaint to the local *Guardian* newspaper, objecting to the presence of black men in the swimming pool at the Polana Beach. 'The provision of a place specially reserved for coloured people', said Cardoso, who wanted to stimulate the tourist trade, would be 'illegal'.[45]

The beach presented itself as a site for a potentially serious explosion of racial tension triggered by the underlying insecurities and sexual tensions that formed part of the visitors' psyche.[46] Young white women, pared down to their swimsuits, in full view of black men, and accompanied by white males, made for a volatile mixture. Indeed, most of the tourists were drawn from a city that had been, and still was, in the throes of a protracted moral panic, one occasioned by precisely the same ingredients – class, race and sex. The 1906–1908 recession on the Witwatersrand had set off hundreds of so-called Black Peril cases in which dozens of white women were subjected to real, but many more to imagined, violent sexual assaults by their African servants or others. It all came to a head in the 1913 Commission on Assaults on Women.[47]

Not all white South Africans hoping to take in the sun on the Polana Beach before World War I were in a settled frame of mind. But neither were their hosts. City authorities, aware that the beach area might be morally hazardous, a place that lent itself to cultural and sexual indiscretions, had to find other, less direct ways of encouraging racial segregation.[48]

The fact was, most Portuguese residents, including a good number on the state payroll, longed for more stringent, legally enforceable separation of the races. In the local hospital there was a 'separate ward and rooms for white patients'. Local administrators were impressed by South Africa's oppressive mine compound system, which incarcerated black workers – including thousands of Mozambican migrant labourers – and openly expressed their admiration of the 1923 Natives (Urban Areas) Act, which formalised and refined the grid for segregation in the Union's cities. Few Portuguese would make South African tourists feel unwelcome on the grounds of their political views; there were underlying affinities.[49]

A second segregation filter – colour prejudice hidden beneath what, on the face of it, presented itself only as class privilege – was more subtle, less easily exposed. Whereas the exclusion of blacks on the grounds of colour alone was more likely to be expressed in public places or in the lower reaches of the civil society, class-colour separation was more characteristic of the middle reaches of colonial society. In Mozambique, class-colour exclusion was the preferred method of achieving what amounted to a great deal of de facto racial segregation within a larger *de jure* dispensation that eschewed racism.

One South African who epitomised an appreciation of class privilege over colour and who was apparently taken in by, and content with, the manner in which the class-colour filter operated in colonial Mozambique, was the founding father of the African National Congress (ANC), Pixley ka Isaka Seme. Seme advocated the assimilation of Africans into Anglophone South African society and dismissed those whites who thought that they might be overrun by the indigenous peoples in search of 'social equality' as just 'silly'. 'We Africans', he wrote, 'don't waste time thinking about that. Just look at Lourenço Marques where there is not even a bit of restrictions [by colour], there is no invasion of European hotels and places by the Blacks.'[50] It was a lesson that smart Portuguese and South Africans had long since learnt.

A third segregation filter, strictly by class – as underwritten by displays of European education, privilege and wealth so complex and profound that it was unthinkable that the code might be cracked by any black intruder – operated in the most exclusive and private locales of all. The beach might well have to be patrolled but there was no need to police those trusted redoubts of class snobbery, the golf, tennis or yacht clubs. Their whites-only membership was secure even though they were served by a phalanx of black cleaners, guards, cooks and waiters.[51]

The existence of these everyday filters sustained a parallel universe in what otherwise supposedly was a Lusotropical, non-racial paradise. They also encouraged the CDT to push on in its efforts to attract more upmarket white tourists to the city. But then, in February 1917, just as the council was settling into its new role, Portugal entered the war on the side of its hectoring old ally, Britain. The war, part of it fought against the Germans in east Africa, caused some disruptions. But it was the economic consequences of the conflict that did more to place the tourist industry on the back foot. War and post-war inflation, along with a crippling lack of foreign exchange, put a brake on most new developments. Instead of heading upmarket in a search for hard currency derived solely from tourism, the administration was forced to look for another source of more broadly based South African revenue.

The Lourenço Marques Lottery was never focused primarily on tourists, nor did it depend directly on visitors for its mainstream of revenue, even though, as a tourist attraction, it soon occupied an important role in the city and colony's economy.[52] It also, unintentionally, became a geopolitical template for how to locate, and manage, a gambling enterprise that was in, yet out of, the country for those South African hotel magnates later praised for their 'pioneering' insights.

The original concession to run a lottery in Delagoa Bay dated back to the financial crisis in Portugal in the early 1890s, but, having been acquired solely for speculative purposes, it remained moribund for two decades. Shortly after the outbreak of World War I, the concession was purchased by an enterprising if rather shady duo: Rupert 'Rufe' Naylor and José Vicente.

Vicente, a lapsed Catholic missionary who had effectively been defrocked by the Vatican for financial impropriety and preferred to cast himself as 'Padre José Vicente do Sacramento', provided the political contacts for the pair to win the bid but died a poor man. Naylor, a charismatic Australian entrepreneur based in Johannesburg – where the lottery was illegal – defied easy description. Big-time bookmaker and impresario and small-time gangster and politician, Rufe Naylor brought the start-up capital and low-level underworld contacts on the Witwatersrand for the Delagoa Bay 'Naylor' Lottery.[53]

The tickets, for prizes ranging from £1 000 to £3 000 during the post-war period, when the value of wages was being seriously eroded by inflation, sold to white and black miners in and around Johannesburg, and to others further afield, as readily as did baked beans at breakfast time. Neither undercover SAP detectives dispatched to Lourenço Marques to monitor the draw nor frequent police raids on the Johannesburg premises of the business could shake Naylor's rapidly growing reputation as an honest operator of a legitimate offshore lottery famous for its prompt payment of winnings. Seeking to capitalise on, and further burnish, the positive publicity surrounding the lottery, Naylor, always inspired in his thinking, came up with an arresting innovation.[54]

He hired a train to provide his clients – almost without exception male and mostly single – with a direct, exciting and speedy link to the after-dark delights of Lourenço Marques, one that also afforded them the opportunity of personally witnessing the daytime draw of the lottery. Once a month, early on a Friday, from around 1919 until at least 1926, the 'Rufe Naylor Express' sprinted out of Park Station, stopping only at the border, and headed for Delagoa Bay.

There, men with money indulged their leisure-time preference on the Rua Araújo. On Saturdays, heads permitting, they awoke to displays of lottery tickets in most shop windows and took in the gaily clad, uniformed and licensed black vendors peddling yet more working-class dreams. Once the draw was done, a few had both the reason and the resources to indulge in more weekend carousing, while many had the opportunity to reflect on the arbitrariness of life and luck. The Sunday-night train back up was less noisy than the journey down.[55]

The monthly influx of merrymakers delighted bar owners, barmaids and hoteliers alike, providing them with a ready source of hard cash in hard times. It may, however, also have further encouraged a belief among some of the less perspicacious members of the CDT that South Africa and the Witwatersrand were the financial source of a future almost without bounds. Unchecked by reality, dreams of a tourism trade could be just as dangerous as the dreams of tourists.

The Riviera Reveries, circa 1918–1929

The balloons of capitalist development – the dreams of entrepreneurs – remain tethered to the weight of financial reality until they have secured sufficient helium-capital to ensure a successful lift-off and flight. But problems can emerge if, during the interval between the inflating of the envelope and casting off, an unexpected downpour makes the trailing tethers heavy and soggy, imperilling launch and flight alike. For the first two decades of the 20th century, the hotel and tourist industry in Delagoa Bay promised much by way of expansion and profitability, but from the end of World War I, and until 1925, Lourenço Marques was drenched in a deluge of economic uncertainty. Projects conceived of in sunshine had to be nursed through chilly, damper financial times.[56]

Back in 1895, at the height of Britain's imperialist ambitions in southern Africa, the great 'Kaffir Boom' and the opening of the Kruger republic's rail link to the east coast, Barney Barnato's JCI spun off a subsidiary company, the Delagoa Bay Lands Syndicate (DBLS). Shortly thereafter, the DBLS acquired a disputed concession, which had once changed hands for £80, for £30 000. The eight-acre clifftop property overlooking the Bay formed part of the most desirable Polana estate.[57]

Family tradition had it that it was Barnato's nephew, Solly Joel, the mining millionaire, gambler and thoroughbred horse-racing enthusiast who, in the late 1890s, first took a 'group of mine magnates' to the coast to view the new site. During a picnic on the property an 'affluent' member of the party – unnamed, but who may well have been Gustav Imroth, a first cousin to Ernest Oppenheimer and another of JCI's 'sporting men' – lamented that 'there were no [legal] facilities for gaming' in Johannesburg. That complaint, supposedly, gave Joel the idea that 'this would make an ideal spot for a resort hotel and casino'. If that indeed was the birth of the idea, then it was doomed to lie idle for at least two decades before being reactivated via a different route.[58]

Backed by capital of £1.6 million and supported by various loans from JCI and the Lewis & Marks company, yet more extensive adjoining property was acquired before and after the South African War. The DBLS eventually owned most of a sprawling 40-acre lot that fell partly in, and partly beyond, the Lourenço Marques municipal boundary. Encouraged by the influx of South African tourists after 1910, the success of the JCI-owned Carlton Hotel, and an underlying belief – which persisted into the 1920s – that one day the Sul do Save might well be folded into the Union, the DBLS began to develop the estate slightly more actively. By 1913, most of the property had been surveyed and divided into parcels, a few of which were disposed of very profitably.[59]

Under the beady eye of its local agent, Leāl (Leon) Cohen – politically well-connected on the Rand and in Lourenço Marques but hopelessly inept and a shady businessman – DBLS properties continued to be managed as a largely speculative concern.[60] Company and city alike remained pregnant with 'potential'. But the persistent shortage of suitable hotel accommodation, other than the mid-market Cardoso, and the absence of a genuinely first-class establishment capable of attracting upmarket tourists and visitors, was becoming increasingly apparent amid the otherwise workmanlike efforts of the CDT.[61]

In 1917, the Governor General appointed Colonel Alexandre Lopes Galvão, the recently returned military engineer responsible for public works in the city, to the CDT.[62] A graduate of the University of Coimbra, the Colonel was, by temperament and training, as energetic as he was outcomes-driven. Galvão bewailed the absence of an impressive landmark hotel in the city commensurate with Portugal's status and stature as an imperial power. His wartime lament came in an era when dozens of ports around the Indian Ocean boasted grand hotels – among others Raffles in Singapore, the Strand in Rangoon, the Grand Oriental in Colombo and the Taj Mahal in Bombay – that served colonial elites and visitors with distinction. Lourenço Marques, though it faced inland – like Macau – was also part of what was a far larger 'eastern' world.[63]

Moreover, Galvão was well acquainted with recent developments in the tourist trade in Portugal itself. His friend, Leonida Costa, editor of the influential railway travel magazine *Gazeta dos Caminhos de Ferro*, had been instrumental in organising an international congress of tourism in Lisbon, in 1911. There had been extensive discussions about the importance of luxury hotels, and by 1916 the President of Portugal, Bernardino Machado, had laid the foundation stone of what was destined to be one of the greatest casinos in Europe, at Estoril.[64]

The Colonel brought some of the very latest thinking about luxury accommodation and a practical bent to Cardoso's sluggish council. In 1917, when Galvão shared with his friend Adriano Maia his disappointment about a lack of creative thinking at the CDT around a grand project, Maia told him that he had excellent connections in Johannesburg who had once expressed an interest in building a hotel on Delagoa Bay and who had access to vast amounts of capital. And, indeed, he did.[65]

Maia had, until 1910, been Portuguese Curator of Natives in Johannesburg, an office notorious for the amounts of money that its incumbents siphoned off from the remittances of black miners indentured to the Witwatersrand Native Labour Association.[66] He was well acquainted with senior figures in the mining houses. By the time Maia retired to Lourenço Marques, in 1913, he had sufficient funds to purchase several properties and was known to Cohen and the DBLS. Maia was well-placed to act as the middleman for any new initiative.[67]

Galvão was unlike Augusto Cardoso, a man whose sympathies lay with local political activists who resented foreign capitalists threatening to 'denationalise' the economy. Galvão was a military modernist, one accustomed to operating with private investors.[68] Like many engineers, he had spent much of his career working on infrastructure projects in the capital-starved Portuguese colonies, and, like most in his profession, he focused on developmental outcomes. It was, then, perhaps predictable that Cardoso would be poorly disposed to Maia's going to Johannesburg to seek out a company closely tied to Witwatersrand mining capital. Galvão, sensing a problem in the making, thus chose *not* to take to the CDT his idea of using Maia to get the DBLS to underwrite the cost of erecting a new luxury hotel on the Polana Beach.

Cardoso had other reasons for objecting to the erection of an upmarket hotel. As the owner of the only half-decent hotel in the city he, together with Luigi Boschian, the manager of his establishment, stood to lose a large part of a legitimate income stream, as well as a front for a profitable sideline that they appear to have developed during the latter part of the war.

With the help of Italian connections, Boschian imported large quantities of Chianti, sherry, spirits and pasta products from Europe.[69] The goods were then stored in the port's bonded warehouse before being exported to leading firms in Johannesburg, including Castle Wine & Spirits and Luigi Fatti's famous Italian food store. It was all legitimate and above board – up to the point where Boschian claimed the imports but then failed to pay duty on the products before going on to export them. It was a practice that could not have occurred without the Port Captain and Chief of Customs – one man, Augusto Cardoso – turning a blind eye to an allegedly fraudulent practice. It would have provided Boschian and/or Cardoso with very competitively priced goods and enhanced their profit margins. Almost certainly, it would also have helped Boschian – an employee rather than a business partner – with the capital necessary to buy the hotel from Cardoso in 1920.[70]

Since there were apparently insurmountable differences separating Galvão and Cardoso – age, ethics, temperament, army vs navy, colonel vs captain, committee member vs CDT president and unencumbered state official vs vested interests – Galvão resolved to bypass the tourism council and pursue the idea of a luxury hotel through a different channel. In April 1918, with the colony's finances still in reasonable shape, he set out his stall before the new Governor General of Mozambique, PF Massano de Amorim. De Amorim – who was in office for only a year – was anxious to make his mark in the new position. He told Galvão that Maia was free to embark on negotiations with the DBLS and to explore any interesting possibilities that might arise.

With Leon Cohen acting as his intermediary with the DBLS, Maia acted immediately. When Cardoso got wind of what was happening, he called a meeting of the CDT and asked the members if they had any knowledge of an approach to the DBLS. Galvão said that he did, but that since the matter was in the hands of the Governor General, he was not at liberty to discuss it. Cardoso then approached de Amorim and, with the rumour confirmed, wrote the Colonel a letter breaking off all relations – personal and professional – with him. Galvão then used a mutual friend to try and bring about a reconciliation, but it failed.[71]

Much to the distress of Cardoso and Boschian – the one by now bent on selling, and the other buying, the Hotel Cardoso – Galvão's project took wing. Maia and Cohen had little difficulty in reaching an agreement, in principle, with the financiers on the Witwatersrand. Within weeks, DBLS representatives appeared in Lourenço Marques to sign a contract drawn up by a senior officer of the administration.[72]

Everything proceeded at pace and went well. The sun rose in the east and set in the west, and the escudo and *libra esterlina* – 'Portuguese sterling', backed with gold from the issuing bank, the Banco Nacional Ultramarino (BNU) – held firm. But the Mozambicans were supplicants in the courts of mining capital and perhaps, in retrospect, the administration may have come to regret a few of the provisions in the contract, even if at the time of signing they appeared to be in line with market realities.

The fully furnished 150-room Polana Hotel, with a dining room and ballroom, would be built at an estimated cost of £200 000 (around £11.5 million in inflation-adjusted terms today) within 19 months, and was completed by January 1920. A large generator provided it with its own source of electricity to power the lighting, cooling and refrigeration facilities and every other conceivable modern convenience, from separate elevators for guests and staff to a state-of-the-art kitchen, an in-house laundry and a soda-manufacturing unit.[73]

It was indeed to be – as was proclaimed at the time, and long thereafter – the finest hotel in southern Africa, but the devil lurked in the details of the contract. The most startling of these was that, for an initial period of ten years, the Mozambican administration guaranteed the DBLS an annual return of six per cent on any capital invested in the project, in addition to various other handsome concessions in terms of taxes. In effect, the South African mining-house financiers, who already dominated the city's waterfront businesses, were to be guaranteed a profit regardless of how well or poorly the business functioned. It was a precedent-setting clause that was to be repeated in various forms for decades thereafter.[74]

An elitist project inscribed in a contract that privileged a foreign company in questionable fashion, and that excluded local investors, raised the ire of several of the city's more successful businessmen and citizens. Sensing their frustration, Cardoso and Boschian authored an emotive, 'patriotic' petition objecting to the terms of the contract.[75] But the die had long since been cast by the Governor General, as advised by his Inspector of Public Works, Galvão, and the petition fell on deaf ears. Adding insult to injury, the contract and plans for the hotel were then publicly displayed in the offices of the neutered CDT.

It got worse. In addition to ensuring a six per cent return on capital, the DBLS made certain that the most important parts of the project – notably the design and construction of the hotel – remained firmly in the control of the mine owners and their networks. With profits guaranteed by the Portuguese administration, this meant that any delays and cost overruns were unlikely to be contested by the architects or the builders.

Seven architectural firms, six from Johannesburg and one from Lourenço Marques – the sole Portuguese bidder – competed for the tender. The contract went to an established, reputable family firm, AH & W Reid, which underwent a couple of changes after 1920, bringing in new partners. There were, perhaps still are, some in what once was Lourenço Marques who lived in a fog of European romanticism. Like the dome on the Estação Central, incorrectly attributed to Gustave Eiffel (of Tower fame), it was put about, and still is, that the hotel was designed by South Africa's most famous architect, Sir Herbert Baker. It was not. But it is easy to see how the glossed story gained such lasting traction.[76]

The architect was Walter Reid's partner, William Delbridge, assisted by Reid's son, Cyril. Delbridge, a leading Cape Town architect with a reputation for bringing out the best in new entrants to the profession, was closely associated with Baker, who, as the resident architect, had overseen the completion, in 1899, of that famous Cape landmark, the Mount Nelson Hotel. Indeed, if the Polana Hotel, which, like the majestic Mount Nelson, came to stare out across a bay from a hillside, owed anything in its elevation of comfort and modernity, its scale or its large, imposing profile to another hotel, it was probably the 'Nellie'.[77]

The contract for the building of the Polana went to a Lourenço Marques resident, but, in truth, it was just another part of the mining industry's extensive Sul do Save network. Hugh le May, the 1906 Mozambican Open Boxing Champion, an engineer by profession, had made his fortune on the Witwatersrand before retreating to the coast, where he ran the Delagoa Bay Engineering Works. It is highly unlikely that Le May was not well acquainted with Gustav Imroth, a keen amateur boxer who, in 1908, had also been a referee at the London Olympics.

Le May was acutely aware of, and sensitive to, the patriotic misgivings that Cardoso and Boschian had expressed in their petition to the Governor and decided to box clever. He created a new special-purpose vehicle for the hotel project, Consolidated East Coast Engineers, which had the ring of a consortium to it and provided a few of the locals with some crumbs from the main table. But Consolidated was clearly in no hurry to expedite the hillside building operations.[78]

The Governor General was out of town, in Inhambane, when the contractors prepared to move onto the site, in late 1918. But, even before the first sod could be turned, de Amorim received a telegram from a frustrated Cardoso and a clearly unsettled Boschian objecting to the construction of the new hotel. De Amorim did not bother to reply. He told Galvão to simply inform the unhappy partners in the port, and in criminal business, that the Polana project would proceed as planned.[79]

Le May's team set about building operations, but progress was slow and the escudo and *libra estralina* began to lose value at an alarming rate. This raised a question: if the Portuguese administration were called upon to make good on the six per cent guarantee, where would it find the currency needed to meet its commitment? The year 1919 came and went, as did the original completion date of January 1920, and the hotel was nowhere near completion. So, too, did January 1921. Unlike with the Mount Nelson, where Baker was the resident architect, neither Delbridge nor Cyril Reid were on site when alterations were made to the original plans.

The DBLS did not appear to be unduly perturbed, but the principal

The Polana Hotel, Lourenço Marques, c. 1925, financed by South African mine owners and with the return on investment guaranteed by the Mozambican administration.

shareholder, JCI, was becoming less sanguine about the project. In mid-1921, Solly Joel was dispatched to Lourenço Marques to 'do what was possible to facilitate progress'.[80] It was a rare visit from a senior partner in the business, and there was a good reason for it. Building costs, like the clouds above Delagoa Bay on a summer's day, were simply floating out of sight. What had started out as a £200 000 project had rapidly escalated to £250 000, and in the end would cost £300 000 sterling. Put in today's terms, the cost of the hotel had risen by a third, from an estimated £11.5 million, in 1918, to £17 million, in just 36 months.[81]

Amid growing impatience on the part of the Portuguese administration, and with building operations 'by no means yet completed', the Polana Hotel took in its first winter-season guests in June 1922. A few weeks later, on 3 July, the hotel was officially opened amid much speechifying in the presence of newly appointed High Commissioner Brito Camacho, and what probably was the most distinguished set of guests, numbering 130, ever assembled for a luncheon up or down the east coast. In difficult times, one of Portugal's least promising colonies had suddenly acquired an asset that could easily hold its own among the best the continent had to offer, including South Africa, and throughout an Indian Ocean region dominated by imperial powers. And the Rand mine owners knew how to play up to that sense of pride.[82]

The occasion marked a rare, spectacular showpiece for a financially stretched Mozambican administration that was chewing up, and spitting out, governors general at a pace that would have embarrassed a hardened tobacco addict. Military modernisers, Portuguese and nationalist to the core, had achieved what the colonial businessmen had not been able to do on their own, and each successive senior officer bearer had little choice but to take up the torch as it was passed to him.

The hotel showed a profit for July 1922, but within four weeks, so much uncertainty was prompted by the rapidly deteriorating financial situation in the colony and confusion surrounding vexed currency issues that 'business is adversely affected, and visitors are not attracted to the town'.[83] The fragility of the colony's economy and the hopelessly precarious position of the BNU, which was without access to credible reserves, was indeed deeply alarming. But the Portuguese administration did not see in this any reason to retreat from the direction that it had set out on from midway through World War I.

On the contrary, the Mozambican administration was of the view that what was needed was for it to redouble its efforts to draw in badly needed foreign exchange through tourism that might rescue the BNU and colony from imminent bankruptcy.[84] The success of the lottery concession (1917) supported such reasoning, as did the opening of the Polana Hotel, which had kicked off in reasonably promising fashion, though it lacked the elusive magical ingredient that gave Estoril its sparkle.

The big lunch at the Polana was still settling when the administration, nudged along by Colonel Galvão, called for tenders for a casino that would form part of the beach complex. Just as the faintest trace of blood in the water attracts distant predators, so the whiff of a possibility of a lucrative deal on the east coast was detected almost instantly – first in Lourenço Marques, and then on the Witwatersrand.

Perhaps closest to the bait in the Bay, and hoping to use the strong undercurrent of anti-foreigner sentiment unleashed by the hotel scandal, was Paulino dos Santos, arguably Lourenço Marques's most successful businessman. Yet, maybe closer still was Leon Cohen, pilot fish for the DBLS, which wanted to guide the Polana into more lucrative waters still. The biggest fish of all, however, may have been the ironically nicknamed 'Little Man', the American-born Rand financier, property developer and insurance mogul IW Schlesinger (1871–1949). Schlesinger could well have been alerted to the attraction of doing business on the east coast by the lottery concessionaire, Rufe Naylor; the two men's paths had converged around the Rand horse-racing business.[85]

By the first week of November 1922, the *Rand Daily Mail* already knew who the principal bidders were, although it politely declined to name them.[86] The DBLS, but more especially the omnivorous, well-travelled Schlesinger, who instantly developed an appetite for east coast prospects which never quite left him, put in grand – no, grandiose – proposals for a casino complex.[87] The bidders consciously pushed comparisons not with Estoril – perhaps more appealing to Portuguese nationalists – but with the French Riviera, where rich English speakers from around the world went to play. There was apparently little that the developers could not achieve. The beach-casino complex would be rendered modern beyond recognition and served by chalets, a cinema, theatre and restaurant, and sports facilities.

Information that readily found its way into the Mozambican and South African press inflated the propaganda balloon, which soon cleared its moorings, floating gently away from reality. As the bidders intended, the DBLS, JCI, Naylor, Schlesinger, the lottery and the Polana Hotel made for an intoxicating mix, and there was loose talk of Delagoa Bay as a new Côte d'Azur and of Lourenço Marques becoming a touch like Monte Carlo or Nice.[88] Late 1922 saw the ideological high point in the struggle to turn the port into a resort. It promised much and, on the grapevine if not on the Rialto, the news long remained positive. 'The Polana is the best hotel I have so far been in in South Africa', wrote WM Leggate, the Southern Rhodesian Colonial Secretary, in 1925. 'It is ahead of the Carlton at Johannesburg and the Mount Nelson at Cape Town.'[89] But of the grand casino itself there was no sight, only the dying embers of yet another seaside vision.

The casino project had come to nothing. The would-be operators, eyes literally and metaphorically fixed on the precedent-setting

Polana Beach Pavilion, c. 1930.

Polana deal, made such onerous demands, by way of guarantees, leases and a monopoly, that the administration was forced to back off from the project. Lourenço Marques never got the great casino that modernisers dreamt of and, from then until into the 1950s, had to content itself with one or two licensed, but modest, casinos along with a few illegal operations. The retreat towards a resort more in keeping with white South African preferences continued, and by 1970 all casinos were deemed to be illegal.[90]

The hasty retreat from the casino project was probably wise; the news from the Polana Hotel was not good. It was running at a loss and the DBLS invoked the six per cent guarantee. In 1924, the loss was a bit more than £3 000; in 1925, it was £8 000; and in 1926 the Portuguese administration had to pay the syndicate more than £12 000 (close on three-quarters of a million pounds today).[91] And, since about 30 per cent of the Mozambique administration's revenue derived from taxes levied on African migrants, it meant that white guests in a luxury hotel were having their stay partly subsidised by indentured black mineworkers locked into southern Africa's cheap-wage regime. The mine owners, however, did not have it all their own way, since the administration chose to make good on the guarantee not in British sterling but in their own bloodless, devalued currency, the *libra* – so-called Portuguese sterling. This gave rise to a dispute that lasted until at least 1928, when the DBLS finally received its guaranteed payment in hard currency.[92]

Truth was that, from the outset – even before the Portuguese currency collapsed – the hotel was always more of a metropolitan than a Mozambican project, both in conception and in execution. Military modernisers, out of imperial and nationalist pride that went on to acquire its own hubristic financial logic, had indulged themselves in a vanity project that bore little or no relation to the real needs of the colony's tourist industry. An elitist, top-down enterprise born of Lisbon-think could not readily be grafted on to the port of Lourenço Marques.

The Portuguese administration had misread the culture, class structure and politics of white South Africa. It believed that the large-scale influx of immigrant working-class and lower-middle-class tourists might prove to be the vanguard of an admittedly smaller, but far wealthier, set of visitors from the Highveld. But it was not. The higher up one went into the white 'South African' class structure, where many were still uncertain as to what precisely their two-decade-old 'national identity' really was, the greater their prejudice about things considered foreign.

In a country that acquired a national flag for the first time in 1928, many better-off English-speaking South Africans were Anglophiles with barely hidden contempt for the Catholic Portuguese.[93] Lourenço Marques was no Riviera, and many English-speaking South Africans – who constituted the majority of the country's affluent – went either to Europe or to Anglophone South African resorts for their vacations.

If the Portuguese administration wanted its tourism sector to move beyond an established white working-class base, it had to cultivate another way of looking to South Africa's emerging middle classes for its salvation. The Polana was antiseptically international and luxurious in the experience that it offered opulent guests. But, unlike the Mount Nelson, it was insufficiently 'English' in character to capture most of South Africa's wealthy, and unable to offer the upcoming middle classes an exotic vacation that was authentically 'Portuguese'. Lourenço Marques, a port hoping to become a resort, remained trapped between the incoming and outgoing tides of its largely white tourists.

Nadine Gordimer visited the city in the mid-1950s and wrote about the city without so much as a hint at the hidden umbilical cord of cheap black labour that tied it to Johannesburg. She nevertheless captured the ambivalent feelings that beset her and other well-heeled white visitors when having to choose an appropriate hotel for their winter vacation:

> Once in Lourenço Marques, we Johannesburgers divide ourselves into those who stay at the Polana Hotel, and those who don't. This division, which began as simple snobbery, has developed the subtlety of snobbery in reverse. It is now also the thing *not* to stay at the Polana, because you want to live 'Portuguese' rather than in an anonymous convention of luxury.[94]

Somewhere between tourist dreams and dreams of tourism, somewhere between port and resort, lay a ragged-edged, white middle-class world.

Matching Imperfections: Aligning White South African Perceptions with a 'Continental Atmosphere', circa 1922–1955

The economic fortunes of Mozambique were never determined by the success or failure of its efforts to encourage tourism in the Sul do Save, although the sector did assume greater financial significance by the 1950s and beyond.[95] Generally, the fate of the sector slotted into the broader rhythms governing the economy, responding reasonably well during periods of stability but lagging during the Great Depression and World War II.[96] In searching for patterns, however, it is probably wiser to focus on some underlying continuities rather than the few disruptions.

In the early 1920s, taking their cue from the immediate post-World War I success of the Naylor Express, South African Railways and the

Caminhos de Ferro de Lourenço Marques (CFLM) joined forces to offer special winter excursions to the east coast. The frequency and popularity of these round trips, which peaked around 1928, were squeezed into the few years between the end of the currency crisis, in 1924–1925, and the first bite of the Depression, in 1929–1930. Unlike the Naylor Express, which aimed at the dwindling number of unattached males on the goldfields, the SAR-CFLM offer had one lazy eye focused on the white working-class family, which, with the help of the Labour Party, was being transformed into something approaching a 'labour aristocracy' under South Africa's 'Pact' government (1924–1933). In an appealing tourist brochure outlining the many attractions of Lourenço Marques and the surrounding areas, in 1928, it was suggested, 'The people living along the Reef are, perhaps, of all the several South African communities, in greatest need of an annual respite from their labours.'[97]

The SAR-CFLM's stronger eye, however, was already focused on a new target. In line with the thinking of the Portuguese administration and the CDT, which sensed that the Polana Hotel was never going to trigger a significant influx of wealthy visitors, the railways sought to cater for that part of the Anglophile white South African middle class that could not quite muster the funds necessary for the mandatory trip 'home', to the United Kingdom, or on to Europe, in one of the Union-Castle liners that dominated intercontinental travel between the two world wars.

Every ship that left Cape Town, the brochure noted, had its quota of tourists headed out of Africa, but 'for every one that goes to Europe, many thousands have, perforce, to remain behind, feeling, no doubt, disappointed'. But there was no need for despondency, since close at hand 'stands the city of Lourenço Marques, a little continent on its own'. And whites flexing their new national-racial identities had nothing at all to fear: 'Despite its African setting, European ideas and fashions predominate.'[98]

But it was never an easy sell. Constant effort was required to shake off the port's pre-war reputation as a hellhole and to foreground its emerging middle-class credentials as a resort. 'It is extraordinary how legends persist', the *Rand Daily Mail* complained in 1927. 'There are some who still regard Lourenço Marques as an Alsatia. In reality it is as harmless and orderly as is Yeoville or Westcliff.' Except, of

The 'Rufe Naylor Express' ran between Johannesburg and Lourenço Marques from 1922 to 1928, providing monthly weekend excursions for lottery aficionados.

course, it was not. Just 18 months later the same paper had to reassure readers that new 'stringent' controls were being contemplated to control bars, boarding houses and hotels, which would be subject to new classifications: bars would have to close at 9 pm unless they had a special licence; establishments would be restricted to two barmaids each, who could not be away from the premises for more than eight days without police permission; no other women were to be allowed into bars; and dancing and singing would be prohibited. The port was being pushed to get into line with the resort, but many still preferred the docklands to decency.[99]

Rail excursions to the east coast, including the popular 'Round-in-Nine', which took in parts of the eastern Transvaal and Lourenço Marques in the same number of days, became a feature of the 1920s. Before the mass-produced motor car began to eat into rail travel a decade later, these excursions briefly extended their reach into the upper echelons of the white middle class. After that they died

Assembling for a bullfight in Lourenço Marques between the wars.

a lingering death; the last such 'mystery tour' promoted by SAR-CFLM was around 1935.[100] A few years later, and for some time into the 1940s, the SAR's luxury Blue Train also ran to the east coast, providing a link to the Polana and beyond at a time when cruise liners were calling at the port more regularly.[101]

Brochures promoting rail excursions to Lourenço Marques in the interwar period were at pains to highlight every 'respectable' diversion that might appeal to white visitors from upcountry. The usual suspects lurked everywhere – the beach, shopping, cinema, theatre, golf, tennis and yachting, along with out-of-town land or sea excursions. It was quintessential middle-class tourist fodder. The administration and the CDT augmented the list with new cash-raising concessions, including late-summer bullfights that proved popular enough to last several decades.[102] A second concession, to a Johannesburg-led syndicate to run the Delagoa Bay Turf Club, proved less successful. It went the way of the Polana Hotel and probably for the same reason – too few wealthy patrons. The push was upmarket, to sell the city as a resort, and of bars, brothels and illegal casinos there was just no mention.[103]

The discreet interwar silence in the SAR-CFLM brochures about the other part of the city, the port's vibrant demi-monde, which continued to attract its fair share of visitors, pandered to some white females' and most families' middle-class notions of 'respectability'. But the same silence, the dog that did not bark, hinted at another ominous development. The Portuguese administration and the CDT were having to take more notice of the emerging 'South African' national identity. Not only were most South African tourists white, middle class and racist but – in the eyes of their government, if not themselves – they were also Protestants playing in what was seen as a dangerous libertarian space.

Thus, while Highveld tourists were free to take part in the lottery or visit the Delagoa Bay Turf Club, which 'ran sweepstakes on important South African racing events', colourful SAR-CFLM brochures contained a discordant warning: 'It is, however, illegal for persons in the Union to take part in these ventures.'[104] Successive South African governments, believing that wealth could only be legitimately acquired through work, had long been policing men, but especially women, moving between a zone of Calvinist zeal and one of Catholic influence.

Casinos, cultivated by the Portuguese administration in the hope that one day they might match the Polana in terms of class, elegance and prestige, posed a double threat to nervous South African authorities watching from afar. Casinos not only encouraged the gambling horror but, in 'continental' fashion, employed dozens of South African women as 'hostesses' who drank, danced and, after hours, did what they pleased with their guests for as many days as they chose. For much of the interwar period and beyond, the port-resort was served by two licensed, class-crossover casinos – Bello's and Costa's – along with one or two illegal downmarket establishments. As ever, the hope was to drive the casinos upmarket, and so, in 1936, visitors were assured that two outlets had been reconstructed and 'refurnished on lavish lines'.[105]

Throughout the interwar years, the fate of the Lourenço Marques tourist industry remained in the balance. It was difficult to tell where things would settle – with the earthy attractions of the port, clinging to declining numbers of working-class tourists, or with the emerging resort, slowly coaxing in an increasing number of 'respectable' upmarket

Bello's Casino, set in 'South Africa' for those white tourists with an imperialist mindset.

middle-class visitors. The same unhurried see-saw motion could be detected when one examined the provision of appropriate hotel accommodation for the shifting class base of the incoming tourists.[106]

By 1928, the SAR-CFLM publicists were confident enough to list, and sometimes provide photographs of, a score of hotels in the city that might appeal to either the single male visitor or the white working-class family. Prices, per room, per day, ranged from 8/6 (eight shillings and sixpence) at the Majestic to 17/6 at the Cardoso, and a hefty 40/- at the Polana.[107] At first glance, the choice of accommodation seemed sufficient and the prices reasonable, but not everyone was convinced. Certainly not the Minister of Colonies, DFV Machado, who, in 1939, bemoaned the lack of a 'decent' casino and the shortage of hotels.[108]

Beneath all the incremental bricks-and-mortar, train-and-track adjustments revolving around the city's tourist hub, however, there were other socio-economic changes and struggles taking place. It is true that some of the least visible tussles harked back to the formation of the Union of South Africa, in 1910, and up to 1929. But many more dated from the post-World War II period and the closing years of the 1940s and 1950s as Afrikaner nationalist governments and the South African state stepped up their surveillance of the neighbouring Catholic colony, slowly extending their bureaucratic reach. The elusive new 'white South African' identity, already some three decades in the making, had to have its Protestant underpinnings reinforced both at home and abroad. Those developments, in turn, had socio-economic repercussions in various parts of the city, which the Portuguese administration tried to adjust to.[109]

As the socio-economic base of South African visitors to the city after World War I slowly became more middle class in its composition, so its reputedly less race-conscious hosts – Portuguese proprietors of boarding house and hotels – were called upon to accept and adjust to the tourists' preference to be seen and identified as respectable whites.

To be 'respectable' was to be white, and to be 'white' was to be respectable, but class retained a logic of its own. In the barely racially integrated bars, brothels, cafés and casinos of the city, partly or wholly hidden from the public view and close by the port, this white identity, at play, relaxing and paying, merged – and was encouraged to merge – with the famed 'continental atmosphere' cultivated and marketed for its consumption. But beyond the twilight and after-dark venues, out in the glare of the sun and in full public gaze, notions of respectability and whiteness had to be catered for, and the hosts obliged.

Among the earliest public conveyances from hotels to business and tourist venues, in a city where, until after World War I, equine sicknesses largely precluded the use of horse-drawn cabs, were African-operated rickshaws. Born of necessity, the rickshaw service matched similar offerings at many of the grand colonial hotels spread around the Indian Ocean. Rickshaws hinted at a romantic 'eastern' identity for a port city already catered for in other ways by a Chinese minority. But the combination of a lack of capital and the arrival of motorised transport heralded the end of the black rickshaw-pullers' business. By the mid-1920s, the city and its hotel ranks were dominated by white Portuguese cabdriver-owners. The remarkable ethnic homogeneity at the taxi rank was not a product of economics only; it reflected customer preferences.[110]

After the Great Depression there was more, anecdotal, evidence of South Africans asserting their racial prejudices in hotels, and some Portuguese may have followed their lead. In the two decades following on the financial downturn, suggests one authority, there was evidence of 'mounting colour consciousness' among the Mozambican Portuguese. If so, they were marching in time with many, if not most, of their cross-border visitors. By the mid-1950s, racial friction, including incidents in hotels, were being attributed to the 'greater number of tourists from the Union and the Rhodesias' and were 'no longer isolated cases'. First segregation and then, after 1948, apartheid cast lengthening shadows over the supposedly non-racial experiences of tourists in the emerging resort.[111]

In Mozambique, the seeds of these crass expressions of white South Africans' class and colour consciousness and 'national' identity were sown largely during the interwar period. But they became ever more pronounced after World War II, and then blossomed in the decade after the election of the first fully fledged Afrikaner-Calvinist nationalist government, in 1948. The new nationalists inherited what seemed like an intractable problem. How were they to remain on good terms with a neighbouring regime which provided them with most of the cheap black labour for the mining industry, but was also a Catholic enclave presiding over a moral sinkhole that attracted around 15 000 South Africans each winter? And, more painfully still for a 'nation' priding itself on its Christian morality, as well as its supposed cultural and genetic superiority, among the thousands caught in the warm embrace of Lourenço Marques's demi-monde were scores of Afrikaner women.

From 1910, when formal surveillance of South Africans crossing the border into Mozambique picked up – and probably for years before that – Delagoa Bay beckoned to certain young and middle-aged white women from the dominee-dominated platteland and new mining towns. Initially, these women undertook the move voluntarily, but some of them were primed by procurers. What began as a trickle increased markedly after World War I as 'poor whites' became a more notable feature in South Africa, and flowed steadily throughout the 1930s and 1940s and on into the 1950s.

Lourenço Marques presented different faces to Afrikaans- and English-speaking South African women on the move, those without steady partners. The city enticed adventurous, young 'new women' keen to throw off the parental yoke, earn their own living and explore their sexuality in a socially remote yet geographically proximate setting where they could adopt new names and identities without interference from the family or drawing moral censure. For others – middle-aged divorcees, spinsters and widows – Lourenço Marques was a line of retreat, a nearby yet hidden venue in which to assert a new side of their personalities while making a living in the entertainment, leisure or recreation sector. For yet others, the city was a fortress, a refuge where, under a new identity, they were safe from abusive partners, bad marriages, unwanted pregnancies or other painful personal traumas.[112]

These women were either running *towards* what they saw as greater individual freedom in Delagoa Bay, or *away* from constraints and other personal demons. In both instances, they abandoned the Highveld and headed towards, or were directed to, the city's bars, brothels, cafés, casinos and nightclubs. Working on commission, earned via the number of drinks they could unload on clients between 9 pm and 3 am, and aided by a chit system, most were licensed as 'barmaids' or 'dance hostesses'. Others, in yet another bow towards a broader port culture around the Indian Ocean, like their counterparts in Singapore and elsewhere, were termed 'taxi-girls'.[113] At the lower end, some were registered as prostitutes in a few state-sanctioned brothels.

Clearly not Portuguese-speaking or Portuguese, most Highveld women could only partially conceal their South African origins, and once they became the subjects of official interest in Pretoria, their true identities were soon revealed. Here, in no particular order, are the names of a few who came to the authorities' attention between 1913 and 1955: Groenewald, Joubert, Fagg, Nel, Beukes, Hatting, Bosch, Meiring, Horak and van Niekerk. These individuals hailed from, again in no special order, Pretoria, Johannesburg, Germiston, Bloemhof, Bloemfontein and Barberton.[114]

There were any number of other African, Asian or 'mulatto' prostitutes working in the poorer parts of Lourenço Marques. But in those outlets frequented mostly by upcountry white male tourists, South African women were in a clear majority and the Pretoria government always found their prominence embarrassing.[115]

As noted earlier, the first attempts to control the efflux of South African women dated back to 1913 and, in large measure, were intended to help curb the recruitment of the naive or vulnerable as barmaid-prostitutes. Even then, however, it was mooted that women – *all* women – might be required to produce a 'certificate of good character' before they would be granted residency in the city. It was, however, World War I and the introduction of passports – a widespread occurrence – that did most to extend Calvinist scrutiny and patriarchal control over single and married women seeking to travel to the east coast for whatever reason.

What started out as a wartime stopgap measure soon took root. When FJ Nance visited Lourenço Marques in 1920, he complained that 'the passport nuisance has to be endured' but that once the 'orgy of hate' unleashed by the war abated, 'there should be no more restriction on going to Delagoa Bay than to Cape Town'.[116] It was wishful thinking. The South African government, out to extend control and cultivate a sense of nationhood, insisted on the presentation of passports, and, as Nance implied, it checked the free flow of tourists into the city, much to the distress of the Conselho de Turismo.

Not long thereafter, at the request of the Portuguese, travel restrictions were eased through the introduction, in both countries, of cheaper 'permits' and 'tourist passports'. The new documents encouraged the flow of visitors from Johannesburg to Lourenço Marques but, for reasons that seem obvious, did little to promote a flow of tourists in the opposite direction. The process of acquiring one of the new 'permits' or 'tourist certificates' – valid for three months – was far from being gender-neutral.

To acquire a permit, a woman had to provide evidence of her age and identity, and to state her reason for wanting to travel. This had to be supported by either a 'letter of permission' signed by a parent or one attested to before a commissioner of oaths by any 'respectable citizen', and had to be presented to a magistrate before a permit would be granted. The system was, nevertheless, not entirely foolproof, and fraudsters, or very determined women, could, and did, circumvent it.[117]

Since applying for a 'tourist passport' – also valid for three months – presented fewer obstacles, most women destined for the coastal demi-monde opted out of the permit system. The passport did not entitle the women to take up employment in the city, and at the end of the three-month period, they were supposed to present themselves before the commissioner of police in order to be allowed to extend their stay.

But, in a setting where the white stick of bribery was never far from a blind official, women often remained at work for as long as it suited them. The timing may simply have been serendipitous and attributable to Portugal's own centralising propensities, but once the Afrikaner nationalists settled into government, the possibility of bribing officials to obtain residency rights in Lourenço Marques declined. In 1949, the South African consul in the city reassured the Secretary for External Affairs that resident permits for women were no longer locally obtainable and had to be authorised by the 'government in Lisbon'.[118]

Ignoring the paperwork and overstaying their welcome during the interwar years left women on tourist passports vulnerable to deportation not only by Portuguese officials whose authority might not have been bought and then flouted, but by the South African consul, who, with the support of Pretoria, willingly extended the reach of a strengthening state. While no male appears ever to have been sent back across the border for violating the conditions attached to their entry into Mozambique, scores of women who had failed to comply with the unwritten terms of what was a form of Calvinist and patriarchal control were sought out and then summarily sent back to South Africa.

It is difficult to determine when the deportations started, but the system was already functioning smoothly by the end of the Great Depression and may have been in place several years before that. In 1934, the consul, General Pienaar, furnished the Governor General with the names of five women – three married, two unmarried – informing him that 'it is the desire of the Union authorities that they should return to the Union at an early date' and that the 'necessary railway tickets will be furnished by this office'. One of the group, Miss Ruby van Zyl (aka Ruby 'Steen'), was a dancer at the Cosmo Club and had been traced by her family, who insisted on her return. In another case, Mrs EJ Saunders and her sister, Mrs Maritz, had both abandoned their husbands and children and were living in the house of Captain Carlos Lorentz in the city. They, too, were put on the train to the Union without a hearing.[119]

After World War II, South African women continued to use 'tourist passports', which allowed them to make their own choice of career or lifestyle, often centred on that part of the port most dependent on the tourist trade. And, the more they did so, the more interest the

South African state took in them and their documentation. Some of the caution was born of genuine concern about occasional instances of trafficking in women, but these had to be offset against the growing desire to police the behaviour and morals of independent-minded women crossing borders as it suited them. Some were denied passports; others had them confiscated or withdrawn. The SAP circulated the names of a few 'contemplating marriage to Portuguese nationals'.[120]

South African notables made it clear that white women in the Lourenço Marques demi-monde drawn from upcountry were compromising a 'national' identity in the making. In 1928, Leslie Blackwell, Unionist Member of Parliament and later Supreme Court Judge, said that 'he had been to Lourenço Marques and the most sickening sight to any South African was to see the South African women standing in the bars'.[121] The passage of time, and the persistence of a dominant South African female presence in the clubs and dives around the port, only deepened the moral outrage of law-makers and law-enforcers. After World War II, such disapproval was increasingly expressed in reputational terms by both the consul in Lourenço Marques and the police in Pretoria.

In 1953, Consul General WC Naude, supported by the Lourenço Marques police, took up the case of 42-year-old Gertruida Meiring, who, after working in the city for a decade, had applied for a new passport. 'Nothing detrimental can be found regarding her in our files', wrote Naude, 'but she is well known as a "dance hostess" at the Penguin Café, a place of ill repute.' If her passport were to be renewed in customary fashion, he suggested, she would remain in Mozambique, where she could 'bring no credit to either the Union or to herself'. Under the circumstances, it would be advisable to renew her passport for only six months, which 'would give her ample time to settle her affairs here and to find some means of livelihood in the Union'.[122]

Naude's hypervigilance around the Penguin had a history. In 1946, Charlotte Beukes, 19, formerly of Piet Retief, had collapsed and died in a stationary train at Komatipoort from causes that were never determined definitively. She had abandoned her position as a clerk in Pretoria and made her way to Lourenço Marques, where she became a dance hostess at a café. The death and the circumstances surrounding the case, involving a clutch of Afrikaner women leading what were perceived as disreputable lives, alarmed many in official and senior police circles and embarrassed the Portuguese authorities.[123]

The Beukes case triggered an aggressive response in South Africa on the eve of what was going to prove to be a decisive phase in the quest for power by Afrikaner nationalists. Within weeks the Secretary for the Interior informed magistrates that 'all applications by young women to proceed to Lourenço Marques [should] be referred to the local police before passport facilities are granted'. In a 'secret' communication, the South African ambassador in Lisbon was instructed to approach the Portuguese government to raise the problem of those 'of the female sex' who were 'a discredit to the Union' and request its cooperation in adopting measures necessary to control women in the tourist sector.[124]

No South African woman was to be employed in 'cafes, night clubs, casinos or similar places of entertainment' without the 'written concurrence' of the country's resident moral authority, the consul. Moreover, any woman who 'generally acts in such a manner as to arouse reasonable suspicion' that she was surreptitiously receiving commission or compensation from the proprietor of any such establishment was to 'be deported'. For the South African authorities, it was no longer enough for Calvin to police the behaviour of the public at home and at work; it was necessary to police females employed in a neighbouring colony and, indirectly, any male tourists on vacation.[125]

As a comparatively weak European imperial power, the Portuguese were accustomed to riding the waves of diplomacy. They had no intention of entertaining strictures that might undermine their sovereignty and responded in ad hoc fashion, as and when it suited them. In 1949, responding to the political change across the border, a new commissioner of police in Lourenço Marques claimed that dance hostesses in casinos and nightclubs were going to be 'forced to leave the Colony immediately'. But it never happened, compelling the South African authorities to fall back on old, passport-manipulating, methods. But it was never easy. Members of the CID policed trains arriving from, or departing to, Lourenço Marques but then complained that they had no way of easily telling 'prostitutes' from 'respectable' women.[126]

After the Beukes case, in 1946, and more especially after the Afrikaner nationalists came to power, the SAP effectively exercised a veto when it came to the issuing of passports to women they disapproved of wishing to travel to Mozambique. After half a decade there were signs that they were succeeding in starving Lourenço Marques of the supply of South African women intent on entering the demi-monde and hoping to escape the suffocating embrace of life under Protestantism on the Highveld. In yet another 'secret' communication, in 1951, the SAP Commissioner was informed that the police and immigration authorities were working closely together to ensure that only respectable women obtained passports. Then unable, or unwilling, to see the link, he went on to suggest, hopefully, that there may have been a change of heart among women – 'local young women are no longer attracted by the casinos in Portuguese East Africa'.[127]

By then, however, there were larger although less visible forces reinforcing the wishes of the South Africans. By the mid-1950s the authoritarian, if not fascist, tendencies in Lisbon and Pretoria were coming into closer alignment on social policy. In April 1954, a decree was issued in Portugal 'prohibiting the exercise of prostitution in all the overseas provinces'.[128] It was more wishful thinking, but the covert social policies of authoritarian regimes often precede, rather than follow, the overt restrictions that come with the centralisation of political power.

In the same slightly haphazard, pragmatic fashion, the Lourenço Marques and Pretoria administrations cooperated to formally shape the social profile of the tourist sector in the port's demi-monde. This was mirrored, in part, in the informal manner in which Portuguese proprietors accommodated the ever more manifest racial prejudices and segregationist wishes of white South Africans in the post-World War II period.

In the 1950s and 1960s, as apartheid legislation designed to increase the social distance between the races became ever more draconian, Lourenço Marques became a favoured port of call for white South African males willing to pay African or *mestiço* ('coloured') women for sexual encounters.[129] As elsewhere in the world, women of colour on the east coast – and more especially those of mixed race – were thought of as possessing a certain sexual mystique. In Portuguese literature they were often portrayed as being part of a 'lushly exotic – and erotic' tropical universe.[130] These notions of sexuality were never incompatible with structured racism; indeed, they may have fostered it.

There was never a moment when coloured women, including a fair number of South African origin, were *not* represented in those bars, brothels, cafés, casinos and nightclubs of Lourenço Marques frequented mostly by upcountry tourists during the winter season. A few were recruited in South Africa by procuresses at £10 per head, but most found their way to Delagoa Bay, often via Durban, under their own steam. But whether it was the carrot of dreams or the stick of nightmares that drove them to the supposedly colour-blind east coast, it failed to free them from many of the shared and structured racisms of southern Africa. Coloured hostesses had to be content with £6 a month as a retainer, while their white counterparts earned between £10 and £15 per month. This could lead to friction, and a coloured 'rival' was – wrongly – suspected of having poisoned Charlotte Beukes.[131]

As already noted, by the mid-1940s white South Africans were becoming more self-confident about asserting their 'national' identities and racial privileges in hotels and other public spaces while on holiday. Their colour prejudices were successfully transmitted to and acted upon in Mozambique and neighbouring areas. In 1946, Costa's Casino – with a staff of 50 females – the Imperium Café and several other nightclubs underwent 're-organisation', which included replacing 'Coloured girls by white women'.[132] Could it be that some white South African men, sensing that cross-racial liaisons were increasingly frowned up by their Calvinist overlords and peers, were adjusting their vacation sexual preferences, even before the notorious Immorality Act 21 of 1950?

Ensuring that South African coloureds or Mozambican *mestiços* assumed their proper places as second-class citizens in the racial pecking order was never confined to females working in the demi-monde; it applied equally to coloured clients and tourists. Some idea of the social pressures exercised on people of colour who dared to frequent public spaces is, again, most manifest in the post-World War II period.

In November 1946, a certain Romeu de Sousa organised a Christmas excursion to the coast for members of Johannesburg's coloured community. It was sufficient to send the resident pack of class-colour-morals-visa watchdogs in Lourenço Marques into a fit of snarling. First to raise the alarm was the Lourenço Marques *Guardian*, the long-standing English-medium east coast mouthpiece for South African business interests and the gold-mining industry. It is worth quoting at length:

> It is to be hoped that if such a party should visit Lourenço Marques they will behave themselves. Although there is no colour bar in Lourenço Marques the non-European section of the population never abuse their privileges. If they visit a casino or night club, they select a secluded table and keep to themselves causing no disturbances. Lourenço Marques is a city where hooliganism and drunkenness is unknown. If non-Europeans from the Union wish to visit us, they are welcome, but they must not come here with the intention of becoming a public nuisance.[133]

Not content with snarling, Consul General EF Horn then barked loudly enough to wake the living dead. He sent the visa-authorising officer-in-chief, the grand protector of the Union's reputation, the Secretary for External Affairs in Pretoria, an extract from the article in the *Guardian*.

But Lourenço Marques's reputation as a tropical paradise permitting sexual adventure, experimentation and indulgence was never confined by class or by colour. There is anecdotal evidence suggesting that, as white South Africans became more affluent, in the politically tense 1960s, the city, easily accessible by air, grew in popularity among white businessmen as a venue for extramarital affairs. In the late 1960s, a South African opened an upmarket private detective agency in the city, seeking custom from 'anxious spouses wanting to keep tabs on errant partners on so-called business trips'. But the agency never got off the ground because, as the Portuguese security police quickly explained, private detective agencies were prohibited by law in Mozambique.[134]

Lourenço Marques, Segregationist Thinking and 'Tourist Zones': The Conceptual Roots of Leisure under Grand Apartheid, circa 1922–1979

If the 1940s saw the last of the dreams of South Africans visiting or working in the Lourenço Marques demi-monde recede in the face of growing state control and surveillance, then so too did the city's dream of commanding a growing tourist industry capable of competing with the increasing popularity of Durban for the white working class or

Cape Town for South Africa's wealthiest visitors. And, as before, it was that sentinel by the sea, the Polana Hotel, that lay at the core of the Portuguese administration's dilemma as to whether it wished to hold on to what it had – 'the port' – or to develop as a resort. It was a problem that dated back decades, one with cosmopolitan roots. How do you build a holiday resort in an ostensibly non-racial colony to cater for a clientele drawn from a neighbouring segregationist state?

IW Schlesinger was a product of New York City's Bowery. As a boy, he sold newspapers in the city and may have known about the specially commissioned, elegantly designed and lavishly furnished, yet outwardly discreet, 'House with the Bronze Door' (1891–c. 1916), around the corner from the Waldorf-Astoria Hotel. The House, the grandest of casinos imaginable, opened in 1891, three years before IWS left for Johannesburg, where he made a fortune after starting out as an insurance salesman to become – arguably – one of South Africa's most ambitious, business-versatile and successful entrepreneurs ever.

Although by his own telling never a man for games of chance, Schlesinger had a long-standing interest in hotel-casino complexes catering for the wealthiest of the wealthy. Unlike the conservative mining capitalists of the DBLS who built the Polana Hotel, IWS felt that the long-term success of the upmarket hotel could only be ensured by coupling its fortunes *directly* to an exclusive gaming house, bypassing the seedy legal and illegal casinos to be found around the lower port area. As already noted, in 1922 he made an unsuccessful bid to run a casino serving the Polana.

The early setback did not deter him. In 1934, with the Depression behind him, Schlesinger again floated the idea of a hotel-casino complex to another of Mozambique's constantly coming-or-going governors general. But for reasons that are not clear, the Lourenço Marques administration – which may have had growing reservations about the Polana's chronic subsidy-consuming propensities – failed to rise to the millionaire's bait. So IWS acted. In 1936, using the good offices of the DBLS's local director and a friend of the Schlesinger family, J Dias Monteiro, he bought the loss-leading Polana for £400 000. By this point, JCI had little, if anything, to show for a decade and a half's investment in what was largely a vanity project.[135]

Monteiro was installed as manager of the hotel, which abutted on surrounding property owned by the DBLS, but he failed to check the Polana's near-insatiable appetite for funding.[136] Unlike the gold-cushioned mining capitalists, Schlesinger had little interest in guarantees, or in long-term speculative profits – he wanted large returns, immediately. So, in 1939, he returned to a concept that harked back to his proposal in the 1920s, and again pushed the idea of developing a larger and far more substantial 'tourist zone' that would be anchored by an extended Polana Hotel and, of course, a new profit-generating casino.

The idea of an exclusive 'tourist zone', separated from the city and port by a bus or tram ride, was not without precedent either in Portugal or elsewhere in Europe. But a 'zone' – an area that, by definition, included the few while excluding the many – located in the heart of a nominally non-racial society in Africa, owned and controlled by a South African notable, for the benefit of South African tourists, most of whom insisted on parading their national and racial identities as 'whites', raised the spectre of the age. In an era already scarred by the growing economic, geographical, political and social distance between the races throughout much of southern Africa, a 'tourist zone' came with undertones of racial segregation.[137] The filter might be of the 'class rather than colour' variety favoured by Pixley Seme of the ANC, but the net effect would be the same – to marginalise all those of more modest means, not just the white working class but, more importantly, those Africans and coloureds who might not, in the words of the *Guardian*, willingly 'seclude' themselves in public.

Schlesinger acknowledged that the casino would be *the* centrepiece of the complex, but it would also boast 'championship swimming baths, bowling greens, and other outdoor amenities, as well as a cabaret hall and a restaurant' with extensions to the Polana 'to accommodate the expected influx of visitors'.[138] But Governor General JN de Oliviera, like Brito Camacho before him, in the 1920s, was not biting. The Portuguese, for whatever reason or set of reasons, were not convinced.

When war broke out in 1939, Portugal remained neutral and the slightly run-down Polana became a centre for espionage, the contact point of preference for Allied, German and South African spies. The idea of creating a 'tourist zone' was in danger of being lost amid wartime concerns. But IWS made certain that Monteiro kept their casino project

A Lourenço Marques tramcar in the 1920s, at the high point of the Riviera-like reveries.

plans in clear view of the administration. Indeed, Schlesinger got him to submit a radically new proposal for an 'ultra-modern casino' in 1942.

The following year, Schlesinger toured the western Atlantic. In South America, he visited casinos in Buenos Aires and Rio de Janeiro, which, along with a trip to the United States, served only to remind him that the Polana would remain a pig in a poke until a casino unlocked its full potential. It may, or may not, have been entirely fortuitous that it was only 24 months before Schlesinger called in at New York City, in 1941, that Bugsy Siegel and Meyer Lansky began investing in Las Vegas as a casino-in-the-desert project. Upon IWS's return to South Africa, he and Monteiro began tossing telegrams and memos at Governor General Tristão de Bettencourt as if they were conceptual hand grenades, but these failed to penetrate his defences.

Bettencourt *was* interested in developing a resort 'tourist zone' that might help check a growing threat from Durban as a vacation destination that he was increasingly aware of. But he was powerless. Lisbon balked at the idea of a 'tourist zone' being financed by a foreign-owned casino offering uncertain returns. Indeed, the Governor General had forewarned IWS of this via a telegram in which he pointed out that no less than the Minister of Colonies himself had ordered that the question of 'gambling should be set aside'.[139] An irresistible American entrepreneur was up against immovable Lusitanian objector.

By the time that Schlesinger got back to his desk in Johannesburg, in November 1944, his frustration was at detonation point. He wrote Monteiro a long letter that, he knew, would be passed to Bettencourt.

'I am back' and 'no time has been lost in getting to grips with the various aspects of this project', Schlesinger wrote. He was, he claimed, willing to invest £500 000 sterling in the scheme – a sum that exceeded that which had been paid for the Polana. It was, he implied, the last chance for Lourenço Marques to offer that additional magic something that Durban, locked into a Protestant hinterland, never could – an internationally sought-after casino and resort drawing on an Indian Ocean constituency. It was to be a seaside Sun City decades before Sun City – the geographically isolated bushveld resort developed by another Johannesburg-based Jewish entrepreneur, Sol Kerzner, in 1979. Only, the Lourenço Marques tourist mecca was to be on a hemispheric, not a national, scale. But it *had* to have a casino:

> [W]ithout the lure of gambling the place would not be patronized by the wealthy people of the Union, large numbers of whom are noted for their sporting instincts, or from other parts of Africa, neither from India, nor from the luxury liners that doubtless will visit your ports again in the years after the war. In short, unless the casino I have visualized for Lourenço Marques is to be modelled on those of the Riviera, South America and other parts of the world where a tourist industry has been permanently established, it would be doomed to failure.[140]

And then came the warning: 'the prospect of failure is not one that I could face.'

Schlesinger, American outsider and capitalist visionary, had set himself an extraordinary objective. He wanted to blend international business best practice, colonial realities and white southern Africans' dreams of wealth, along with their racial nightmares, into a class-segregated recreational zone that could contribute to the long-term development of a viable local tourist industry. But, as a conceptual juggling act, it failed to convince the Portuguese imperial overlords, who saw too many plates and too few hands. A consolidated investment of £1 million in a hotel-casino complex, for the wealthy, may have nudged Lourenço Marques a bit further along the road in its quest to develop as a middle-class holiday resort, one that eclipsed the baser attractions that the port held for working-class visitors, but the outcome was not certain. As it turned out, the city had to continue its efforts to develop a middle-class base for the industry without the benefit of one outstanding attraction.

Tourists from elsewhere in continental Africa never arrived in Lourenço Marques in noteworthy numbers. The Indian Ocean gamblers never appeared. The luxury liners, too, failed to disgorge passengers in the numbers hoped for.[141] After World War II, white South Africans, comfortable in their own skins at home but increasingly uncomfortable abroad, were constantly on the retreat from political realities. They dug themselves into ethnic or racial trenches and became ever more selective in their choice of vacation destinations that did not threaten their fragile and troubled 'national' identity.[142] Border formalities, passports, permits and visas, the use of Portuguese rather than English at a time when their country was developing a world-class road infrastructure serving psychologically secure domestic holiday destinations – all helped undermine the appeal of an east coast vacation.

It was not as if Lourenço Marques and the rest of the Portuguese colony did not try to attract their share of the South African market for tourism. By the late 1960s, as the world was growing ever smaller for white South Africans, the colony was said to be attracting over half a million tourists each year. Hotels, including the upgraded Cardoso and the new Girassol, all pulled in the direction of a modern resort, but they were never enough to put the issue beyond doubt. Lourenço Marques, languishing halfway between port and resort, never became the habitual, preferred holiday destination for most white South Africans of either its growing middle class or shrinking working class. IW Schlesinger, who died in 1949, might have been forgiven a wry smile.

More than 150 years ago, first diamonds and later gold triggered an industrial revolution in colonial southern Africa. It was consciously managed by successive white elites to exclude and marginalise Africans, Asians and people of mixed race, preventing the benefits from being distributed fairly, let alone equally. In so doing, it also drove a wedge between class and colour and militated against the emergence of a more cohesive economic, political and social dispensation. Driving those corrosive processes through most of the 20th century were political parties dependent, to differing degrees, on the voting power of a white working class fearful of being replaced by cheaper black labour, and a deeply politically insecure middle class.

These basic truths, along with the tragic consequences that they gave rise to in a country always set on ethnic-driven self-destruction, have – rightly – done much to set the intellectual agendas of many historians. But here we are, a century later, and the social history of southern Africa is still largely in its infancy. While we have learnt much about the economic and political struggles of a white working class that arrived to great fanfare and then disappeared, unloved and almost unnoticed, we still know little about the psychological universe that it occupied while at play and beyond the world of formal employment.[143]

The culture of South Africa's white working classes, and the middle class it gradually gave way to, is never going to be understood in the round until we transcend the important, but limiting, structural dimensions of their history and begin interrogating their lived experiences with more comprehensive, subtle, supplementary questions. Writing such a social history is neither an exclusionary exercise nor part of a stand-alone project, but rather is complementary in nature and builds on the solid platforms provided by existing economic and political histories. It is within this rather broader context that a focus on working-class tourists, the places that they chose to spend their vacations in and a nascent tourism industry might be of assistance.

The choice of venue for a short-stay excursion, or for a lengthier annual vacation, never was – or is – an elementary exercise. Answers could vary, among many other things, by age, culture, class, gender, language and marital status. The choice of a holiday destination involved complex trade-offs between a host of variables that went well beyond the obvious considerations of cost and time available. Core considerations included having to reconcile inherent tensions between a desire for change and continuity that might help regenerate the spirits, on the one hand, and measures of comfort and familiarity that ensured a pleasing, secure environment, on the other. The flip side to musing about the demand generated by prospective visitors was the supply thinking coming from a developing tourism industry across the region.

For those single males in Johannesburg with an eye on Lourenço Marques as a holiday possibility in the early 20th century, the continuities, as well as the contrasts, between the two cities lent themselves to a potentially rewarding vacation experience. Altitude, climate and position made for stark physical contrasts, while exposure to a different cultural universe made for a tolerable if not altogether welcome change. But it was the last echoes of a frontier town that lived on in Lourenço Marques, providing the familiar social institutions of beer, barmaids and brothels, that offered the cultural continuities sought by many a youthful immigrant miner.

Many colonial port cities – dominated by sailors with pent-up consumer power destined to be spent on alcohol and women – shared certain features that bore a passing resemblance to inland mining towns on Friday nights. Lourenço Marques did not have to invent, or reinvent, itself to become the sociological twin of early Johannesburg. Indeed, before World War I and into the early 1920s, all it had to do was to attempt to control and expand its existing tourist infrastructure in ways that coped best with an annual influx of winter visitors. The principal instrument for that came with the establishment of the Conselho de Turismo in 1914, which, and probably not by chance, was the same year that its rival, Durban, set up a 'Beach and Entertainments Committee'. The opening of the prestigious Polana Hotel in 1922 was followed, in 1923, by the launching of the 'Durban Publicity Association', which coordinated attractions for upcountry visitors. From World War I on, Lourenço Marques and Durban were locked in a covert struggle for the custom of holidaymakers from the Witwatersrand.[144]

Primed by the early success of Lourenço Marques's demi-monde in attracting working-class visitors, the Portuguese administration set its sights on expanding its share of the market in the interwar years by catering for the Witwatersrand's emerging white middle class by providing more and better hotel accommodation. In theory, the port's earthy attractions would gradually make way for the more respectable holiday attractions of a typical English colonial resort city. But military modernisers in the CDT attempted to add yeast to that slow-rising dough by persuading Rand capitalists to enter a joint venture, in the shape of the Polana Hotel, which, at best, proved to be a limited success.

Between the wars, all attempts at aligning the vacation dreams of white middle-class upcountry visitors with an east coast tourism industry played out against another underlying logic. South African visitors were, for the most part, drawn from an Anglophone, Calvinist, industrial and urban dispensation and committed to a state intent on pursuing explicitly racist policies. Not only were the configurations of South Africa's class structure and consumption patterns changing rapidly, but they were increasingly informed by mindsets in which a 'national identity', crystallised around interchangeable notions of respectability and whiteness, were linked directly with class and colour.

By contrast, Mozambique was Catholic, Lusophone, commercial and, nominally at least, committed to a greater imperial, and smaller colonial, state supposedly characterised by a spirit of tolerance that refused to fetishise racial differences. Moreover, Lourenço Marques itself had a flatter and looser settler class structure, with a significant *mestiço* population that had ambivalent feelings about nationality and differed greatly from Johannesburg's in scale when it came to social interaction.

Privately, many Portuguese and most white South Africans shared a general contempt for black Africans and hankered after increased racial and spatial segregation, prompting a convergence of views. But, at a formal public level, Mozambican and South African policies diverged, tending to increase the political and social differences between the neighbouring states. In the long run, reconciling this tension between the public and the private perceptions of racial difference may have contributed, albeit only in small measure, to Lourenço Marques's inability to compete successfully with segregated Durban for tourists in the 1950s – a trend that, for other reasons, including bureaucratic and economic, was briefly reversed in the more racially fraught 1960s.

But, between the wars, the widening gap in policies between

Protestant Pretoria and Catholic Lourenço Marques, particularly regarding games of chance that might be linked to a nascent tourist industry, was bridged by a cross-border pipeline that a few entrepreneurs were quick to exploit. The bookmaker Rufe Naylor and his partner, José Vicente (Padre José Vicente do Sacramento), paved the way after World War I by demonstrating that white miners were willing to spend a weekend in Delagoa Bay in order to witness the drawing of lottery tickets sold along the Witwatersrand.

The monthly arrival of a trainload of moneyed gamblers on the east coast was not lost on IW Schlesinger. Throughout the 1920s and 1930s, Schlesinger sought to exploit the counterflow between neighbouring Catholic and Calvinist regimes by trying to persuade the Portuguese administration to create an identifiably distinctive, Riviera-like 'tourist zone' in Lourenço Marques.

Schlesinger saw the zone as catering for exceedingly wealthy and ordinary gamblers not only from socially repressed South Africa but from all round the Indian Ocean, including India and the Far East. But the faltering success of the Polana Hotel, and the reluctance of the Portuguese administration to guarantee the profitability of the scheme through the granting of a casino licence, scuppered the scheme. After that, the future of the Lourenço Marques tourism industry lay somewhere between those middle- and working-class white South Africans searching for an affordable 'exotic' vacation on their doorstep.

But hidden within that potential market lay another growing problem. The 'national' identity of some increasingly assertive Protestant white 'South Africans', drawn from an economically successful neighbouring state, saw them demand more considered segregationist measures from their poorer Catholic Mozambican hosts. The terms of social trade between tourists in Lourenço Marques and their hotel-sector hosts, as well as the terms of political trade between the two states, were being eroded steadily as the class base of the industry shifted from working- to middle-class whites.

As with the hill stations frequented by the British in India, Delagoa Bay had, since the 1890s and well into the 1950s, been a 'site of refuge as well as of surveillance' for the white men and women of the southern African Highveld.[145] Broadly speaking, it was never a site of refuge for white men but more of a proximate retreat offering some respite from the remorseless industrial routine, physical demands and social patterning that came with working in the mining and allied industries.

But for poorly educated, economically vulnerable white and coloured women placed in social jeopardy by having been forced off the land, or for those locked into mining towns during an unforgiving industrial revolution, the demi-monde of the tourist sector in the Lourenço Marques economy was a site of comparative safety. Marginalised, naive or vulnerable women, of all ages and marital and social standing – out of strength or out of weakness, having been coerced or having gone voluntarily – went to the port city in their several hundreds if not low thousands. There they independently found, or were set to, work as barmaids and dance hostesses in bars and brothels or cafés and casinos.

From the birth of the Union, Lourenço Marques – at least insofar as white South African women were concerned – was both a place of refuge *and* a site of state surveillance. The South African government saw Mozambique as a Catholic enclave, as part of a zone of sexual danger for adventurous or depraved women, that either lured them into the attractions of the tourist demi-monde or offered unwanted sanctuary to irresponsible women fleeing the supposedly legitimate, ultimately patriarchal control of their families or some unwanted spouse. This invasive policing of South African women abroad, during the construction of a 'national identity' for whites, was often reluctantly facilitated by a cowed and silently resentful Portuguese administration.

From the Great Depression and perhaps for a decade before that, the South African consul in Lourenço Marques and Mozambique's Governor General agreed, seemingly without legal sanction, to have coloured or white women whom they considered, or sometimes merely suspected, of being in dereliction of their moral obligation, to be deported at the expense of the South African state.

And, where deportation was not feasible, women suspected of having 'loose morals' had their passports confiscated, curtailed or withheld unless they had obtained approval from the police prior to leaving South Africa. After the unexplained death of a 'dance hostess' in 1946, but more especially after the coming to power of the explicitly Calvinist Afrikaner nationalist government, in 1948, these measures were tightened further. The consul kept a file on South African women working in the demi-monde and tourist sector and appears

By the mid-1920s, the Polana Hotel rivalled the Carlton and Mount Nelson hotels in Johannesburg and Cape Town.

to have become more inclined still to arrange for the deportation of coloured or white women suspected of earning a living from overt or clandestine prostitution. Yet again, the Portuguese administration cooperated with its counterpart.

The social pathologies accompanying the South African industrial revolution – excessive alcohol consumption, legal and illegal gambling, prostitution and the white slave traffic – all manifested themselves fully within the national boundaries between the mineral discoveries and the outbreak of World War I, after which they tapered off quite significantly. But the changes wrought by capitalist expansion and the social disruptions that it occasioned were never confined within the national boundaries or for the duration of wars. They spilt over into adjacent states, and nowhere more so than in the southern part of Mozambique.

Both white South Africans and Mozambicans indulged the idea that Delagoa Bay – part port, part resort – could cosset white visitors in an all-enveloping social mist, in a 'continental atmosphere'. The city, it was believed, was a place capable of conjuring up exotic and erotic adventures that somehow eclipsed the more familiar, mundane, vacation experiences to be found along the rest of the often very dreary southern African coastline. And, in some important respects, there was a measure of truth to it all, and, typically, the romanticised version of that myth gained expression in at least one Mills & Boon novel.[146]

But, for those daring to peer through the mist and wanting to see a little further, there were other, more menacing social realities to be detected. These derived from an unequal, uncomfortable relationship between two neighbouring states locked in the embrace of a sprawling industrial revolution engineered along unforgiving racial lines. Maybe Nadine Gordimer got it right after all when she noted of the city: 'no, this isn't Europe', 'no, this is not Africa' – 'this is simply Lourenço Marques'.[147] Lourenço Marques was part of a liminal space, a place always in the throes of becoming, never quite arriving, covered in the dust of leaving.

PART II

THE SUNDAY NIGHT WARS: LOURENÇO MARQUES RADIO AND THE TRIUMPH OF THE SOUTH AFRICAN BROADCASTING CORPORATION, CIRCA 1934–1975

If we are victorious in one more battle with the Romans we shall be utterly ruined.
PLUTARCH, *LIFE OF PYRRHUS*

It is true, as African nationalists like to emphasise, that the dominance and oppression of blacks by European settlers across much of southern Africa stretches back more than 300 years. It is also true that, in good measure, such sustained pre-eminence was partly underwritten by the relative ease of access of whites to education and technology and that the dominant historical narrative in a sad country known only by a geographic signature – 'South Africa' – is one of race-based conflict.

But, hidden within that narrative that cannot, and must not, be forgotten lie many other political struggles to achieve ethnic and political dominance within the ranks of the whites that should not be lost sight of. Pale in complexion when compared with the epic, bloody conflicts waged over the *longue durée*, such encounters nevertheless offer important insights into the emergence, nature and trajectory of white supremacy as it entrenched itself over the miserable 20th century.

Taking a similar longer view, but seen only in constitutional terms, the European 'South' – as opposed to the broader, more inclusive 'southern' – African experience was as fraught as it was short-lived. It lasted a little over eight decades, from 1910 to 1994, when hard-pressed whites eventually chose to vote themselves out of power. In those 80 years the same narrow, racially defined but largely economically successful 'Union' experienced a rural rebellion and a full-scale urban revolt, and entered two world wars with its two language groupings, English and Afrikaans speakers, divided largely along political lines.

Viewed through those same 80-year binoculars, deep-seated political fractiousness, born of restrictive colonial experiences and imposed imperial domination, comes as no surprise. Torn between the numbers of relatively recently arrived Anglophile English speakers, urban immigrants who were ideologically locked into the British Empire and Commonwealth, and a larger number of native-born 'Boers', Afrikaner farmers firmly grounded in the countryside, with sentiments almost instinctively republican, such political contestations proved to be reasonably protracted. The echoes of the last ideological shots fired during the Anglo-Boer War (1899–1902) could still be heard in the early 1950s and 1960s, as the 'Union' finally made way for the realities of a republic.

Very little, if any, of this manifest trauma was the product of spontaneous political combustion. Underlying it all, provoking, stoking the flames of contestation and conflict among the whites, was an industrial revolution driven by the mining of precious minerals that pre- and post-dated the formation of the Union of South Africa, in 1910. While the outcome of the South African War was a watershed moment in the history of the region, opening the way for accelerated capitalist development underpinned by the systematic creation and exploitation of pools of cheap black labour, there was significant collateral economic damage in the vulnerable parts of white society.

The need to feed growing numbers of industrial workers housed in the towns, cities and mine compounds triggered an expansion in commercial mechanised agriculture. That, in turn, gave rise to larger farms raising specialist crops or dairy products, and to increasing landlessness that left pockets of 'poor whites' stranded in rural and urban areas. Competition among the whites for semi- and unskilled positions in mines, factories and railways, fought against the perceived threat of being replaced by even cheaper black labour, further heightened political differences within the European population.

All of that, along with the normal vicissitudes associated with periods of marked expansion or sharp contraction in a developing, market-driven economy, played out within the same small 80-year window of white dominance. From the 1950s on, however, these 'white' problems increasingly gave way to the Afrikaner nationalist government's preoccupation with allocating, controlling and regimenting cheap African labour condemned to a politically rightless existence on the rural and urban margins of an industrialising society. Predictably, that fed into racist white regimes that were increasingly authoritarian.

After the 1960 Sharpeville massacre, the government, up to then more concerned about forging and strengthening political solidarity among whites, was forced to pay increasing attention to the challenge that African nationalists posed to state security. The presence of a growing number of black militants outside its back door – itself encouraging of greater cohesion among the whites – did not, however, allow the government the luxury of neglecting an electorate camped outside its front door. Indeed, the magnitude of the challenge at the back door made it that much more important to ensure that the front was secure.

The political oppression of the African majority over several centuries through the exercise of brute force did not call for the reinvention of the wheel on the part of the government. But it did call forth adaptive and more subtle strategies to divide and rule through the manipulation of ethnicities, by encouraging class, cultural and geographical separation among blacks. Likewise, the three decades of Afrikaner authoritarianism after the achievement of a republic called for new forms of discipline and unity within a white electorate often still divided along class and cultural lines, though amid growing political solidarity.

Looking back, then, over eight decades of turbulence, white South Africa was cradled in an unstable union struggling to give birth to a republic. Within that context it becomes easier to understand how forging a broader 'national' white identity from competing strands was never going to be a straightforward exercise. Like modern African nationalists, forever chanting 'nation-building' while engaged in smuggling racist contraband across the borders of common sense, Afrikaners, too, chanted *'ons bou 'n nasie'* (we are building a nation) when peddling items of self-interest. Even then, it was a long and difficult road. It took fully 15 years – out of the 80 – for Afrikaans to be recognised as an official language and another two before the white nationalists more or less agreed to adopt a 'national' flag that ignored the majority of citizens.

The struggle to build a more inclusive white 'South African' national identity may have been most evident at the hustings, at the polls or in the columns of Hansard. But the deeper, sometimes more meaningful, contestations took place around everyday cultural interactions relating to unarticulated or unsolved issues of ethnic or linguistic inclusion or exclusion. The drive towards white unity, during the interwar years, made for slightly more pragmatic accommodation and a limited tolerance within the country's formal political structures as evidenced by the relatively long-lived 'Pact' and 'Fusion' governments. Between them, the two accounted for 15 of the 84 years of white rule, even if it did pale beside 35 years of authoritarian rule from 1960 to 1994.

Once the African nationalists appeared outside parliament's back door, members of the House of Assembly became increasingly dictatorial and insecure, and the government devoted more effort to excluding political dissidents within the ranks of the whites at the front door than it did to fostering a much broader South African 'national' identity. What Afrikaner nationalist governments, intent on entrenching white political dominance at the expense of a disenfranchised African majority, yearned for most during the closing decades of white supremacist rule was a fully compliant electorate. The electorate, the government hoped, would behave like the three wise monkeys of Japanese folklore. It would see no evil, hear no evil and speak no evil.

Governments ensured that no political 'evil' was to be seen by banning 'undesirable' literature of all sorts and by delaying the introduction of television until 1976. White ultra-nationalists guaranteed that no 'evil' would be heard by maintaining close control of the airwaves through the South African Broadcasting Corporation (SABC), which enjoyed a near monopoly of the airwaves that lasted until a democratic dispensation was eventually agreed upon in the mid-1990s. The ultras also used the security police – the Special Branch – to discourage the speaking of any 'evil' by equipping them with a barrage of restrictive and oppressive legislation that made for arbitrary detention, banning and house arrest.

And, truth be told, for the most part, the three white monkeys were usually content to play their part in underwriting a monstrous regime.

Staking Out the Battleground, circa 1920–1939

Neither politics nor its cousin, culture, can operate entirely free of other considerations, and more especially so in the case of scientific advances whose societal impact is not always easily foreseen or readily discounted. Nowhere is the importance of this third force – the impact of science on politics and culture – more evident than in the fields of radio and public broadcasting. For white South African nationalists, it was a problem that went all the way back to the 1920s.

The Pact government (1924–1933) was the product of an uneasy and pragmatic alliance between the secular, all-white Labour Party and the National Party, committed to an Afrikaner Calvinist tradition. Beyond an interest in fostering state-owned enterprises that would enhance primary industrialisation, it was not a government especially concerned about, nor well equipped to deal with, rapid developments in commercial radio – beyond the obvious temptation to collect revenue from licences. The rapid advances in radio technology that came in the wake of World War I slithered into southern Africa largely unnoticed by either the outgoing South African Party administration or the new government, largely preoccupied with aligning race and class in an industrial revolution deliberately skewed so as to give priority to white interests.

However, in the economic heartland of the country, on the Witwatersrand, members of the Associated Scientific and Technical Societies (AS&TS) were fully alert not only to new technical developments in radio transmission but also to the long-term commercial potential of radio. In 1924, the promise evident in early experimentation assumed a corporate dimension with the registration of the AS&T Broadcasting Company Ltd. Granted an operating licence by the state, AS&TS launched Johannesburg's 'JB' radio station, just 24 months after the BBC took to the air in the United Kingdom. A painful lesson followed. With the wind of science fully in its sails, JB scudded along well enough, but, lacking economic ballast, it was simply a matter of time before it toppled over. White South Africans, never shy of preaching to others about the link between ethics and economics, were simply not willing to come forth in sufficient numbers to pay for radio licences and ensure JB's financial viability.[1]

In 1927, the Pact government was still searching for a clear-cut policy as to the long-term future of public broadcasting. The American-born millionaire IW Schlesinger, who had a growing interest in cinema and a liking for capital-intensive enterprises driven along monopolistic lines, was then persuaded to take over AS&TS's licence to keep JB on air. But not even Schlesinger's new African Broadcasting Corporation (ABC) could afford to keep a station going with a licence that restricted advertising to a mere ten per cent of its airtime. ABC depended, quite substantially, on income derived from whites who lived within a 100-mile radius of the wealthiest city in the country, but were unwilling to pay for a service that entered their living rooms freely and invisibly.

ABC never got a meaningful return on the £50 000 invested in what ostensibly was 'commercial' radio. By the end of the Great Depression, Schlesinger was looking for a way out of the business just as a new government, fully ten years after the starter's gun had sounded, was waking up to the possibilities of radio as a tool for prompting cultural cohesion among linguistically divided whites. Elected in 1933, the new 'Fusion' government comprised the old South African Party and the National Party, leaving the Labour Party denuded of support and largely powerless. With the dominant new United Party, under the leadership of General JBM Hertzog, effectively in control, conservative nationalists, overwhelmingly Christian, were well-placed to use radio for cultivating a more inclusive 'two-stream' centre for white culture.

In July 1934, Prime Minister Hertzog issued an invitation to the then Sir John Reith (later Lord Reith) of the BBC to take stock of the South African situation and come up with a broadcasting policy acceptable to the government that could be tailored to the country's needs. Hertzog's choice of investigator was a canny one, albeit partly obvious, blending an element of English imperial deference with a larger devotion to conservative Afrikaner values. Reith was well-placed to pinpoint the political crossroads where the interests of town and countryside met.[2]

The son of a Presbyterian minister, Reith was steeped in the same Calvinist values that came to many Afrikaners as so much mother's milk. Puritan in taste, to a fault, and set against the commercialisation of radio, Reith posed little threat to the underlying beliefs of the nationalists. Moreover, his technical expertise as an engineer and manager of the BBC resonated positively with businesslike Anglophiles. He was also considerate and generous in his interactions with Schlesinger, opening the way for a financial settlement between the ABC and the state, though one that, in the end, had to be decided through costly arbitration.

Sir John Reith, of the BBC, who helped shape South Africa's conservative Broadcasting Act 22 of 1936.

Reith's report emphasised the need for public control of policy, the importance of appropriate expertise and that there should be no outside political interference in the management of the service. The primary task of a public broadcaster, Reith maintained, was to inform, educate and entertain. With programming designed to be more uplifting than popular in nature, it would, of necessity, also be radio that drew more heavily on the strands of haute culture than on what was merely fashionable. Accommodating of white cultural diversity and conservative almost to the core, Reith's report chimed almost perfectly with the times and was tailor-made for a Fusion government driven by the United Party. It formed the basis for what, with broad-based agreement, on 1 August 1936 became the Broadcasting Act 22 of 1936. The South African Broadcasting Corporation was born that same day.

But, as lawyers remind one, it is not always what is in the document that counts; sometimes what is *not* on paper counts for more. Reith failed entirely to see the possibility of a challenge by commercial radio to a South African state monopoly of broadcasting other than that provided within the national borders by Schlesinger's ABC, which was about to be bought out. Raised as an islander, Reith thought as an islander. In England, he effectively ignored the country's geographical setting amid a European context, and in Africa he likewise confined his thinking to the emerging white nation-state and failed to locate South Africa in its wider, regional setting. It proved to be a costly oversight and one that he might have been expected to be more aware of. At the time of writing his report for Hertzog, the BBC's own monopoly of the airwaves was already being challenged by offshore commercial broadcasting. In the United Kingdom, as with the ABC in South Africa, these strains were not new and dated back at least a decade. It was not a question that Reith could claim to be wholly unfamiliar with.

Problems for the BBC first surfaced in the early 1920s when broadcasts by a French amateur radio enthusiast, based at Fécamp on the Normandy coast, crossed the English Channel and penetrated southern England. The problem was self-limiting while the operator of the French station lacked the capital necessary to invest in a stronger transmitter and confined itself to broadcasting in French. But the problem became more pronounced once an English businessman, Captain Leonard F Plugge, and a few associates sensed the possibilities for offshore commercial advertising. By the late 1920s, Plugge's International Broadcasting Company (IBC) had bought time on several continental stations, including Radio Luxembourg, had renamed the French station 'Radio Normandie' and was beaming advertising into the English heartland.[3]

In March 1931, IBC increased its holding in Radio Normandie fourfold and proceeded to boost its powers of cross-Channel transmission. By 1933, the company had a fee-paying 'club' for listeners, with a reported membership of 90 000, and had at least one programme on Radio Normandie sponsored by the American radio manufacturer Philco. IBC was quick to appreciate that the BBC's strict policy regarding religious observance made for either dull listening, or complete silence, over the latter part of the weekend – the notorious 'Reith Sundays'. Radio Normandie seized the opportunity to plug the gap for English listeners. As we will have reason to note in due course, this pioneering experience of advertising by personnel at Radio Normandie later exercised considerable influence on the management and marketing strategies adopted by Lourenço Marques Radio (LMR). In one sense, then, the idea of LMR was born on the shores of northern France.

Officials at the BBC were equally quick to note these developments and, during the Great Depression, at a time when advertising had assumed heightened importance, attempted to come to terms with the challenge as best they could. But, given Reith's unwavering insistence on strict Sunday observance, they were denied a direct competitive response to Radio Normandie. Instead, from 1931 to 1933 the corporation made repeated – but largely unsuccessful – attempts to limit or undermine the legitimacy of cross-Channel commercial broadcasts by going through the Foreign Office, or by lobbying the UK's powerful National Publishers Association, 'which was unhappy about the possible diversion of advertising money from the press to radio'.

Reith became personally involved in several of these covert indirect oppositional moves. When, in April 1933, a former BBC employee complained to the International Broadcasting Union that such stations could 'become a source of international friction', Reith wrote back telling him that he had been 'quite right' to do so. In the year leading up to his South African visit, Reith was regularly engaged in the challenge that commercial radio might directly pose to a state monopoly.[4]

In South Africa, too, there were signs of an early interest in the potential that offshore commercial broadcasting might hold. In 1932, two years before Reith even set foot in the country, the owner of a small printing works in Johannesburg, GJ McHarry, an avid jazz and radio enthusiast, produced the first issue of *The African Radio Announcer*.[5] The very name of the journal pointed to a proprietor capable of thinking beyond national boundaries. *The African Radio Announcer* provided readers with bread-and-butter details about programmes and different wavelengths, but McHarry's curiosity about broadcasting went further.[6] He knew of the South African ruling elite's hesitancy about advertising on radio, and was intrigued by the emergence of offshore radio in France challenging the BBC's monopoly in the UK.

Just months later, in 1933, McHarry's thinking about the potential of offshore commercial broadcasting took on an exciting new dimension. He happened to catch a late-night transmission by a group of amateur enthusiasts in Lourenço Marques, men with scientific interests, calling themselves the Rádio Clube de Moçambique (RCM).[7]

But, like AS&T Broadcasting and Schlesinger's short-lived ABC, RCM was gasping for financial air.

With its back to the Indian Ocean, RCM was broadcasting to a catchment area of 180 degrees rather than 360 degrees. A small number of poor settlers and a large pool of even more deeply impoverished Africans spread out along an extensive coastline meant that RCM was effectively transmitting into an economic void at the tail end of the Depression. In 1934, RCM went off the air for financial reasons, and McHarry, sensing that the optimal moment to strike a deal had arrived, hurriedly made his way to Delagoa Bay.

He was not the first to realise that, as a site for a potential offshore business, Lourenço Marques presented itself as the obvious venue for anyone interested in circumventing the deep conservatism born of white South Africa's Calvinist tradition. That honour fell to Rufe Naylor and Padre José Vicente do Sacramento, who, some years earlier, had secured a concession for a lottery from the Mozambican administration that operated successfully, albeit supposedly illegally, in South Africa.

As McHarry already knew, the South African government was finding it extremely difficult, if not downright impossible, to prevent Naylor and a few brothers from selling lottery tickets, undercover, to miners all along the Witwatersrand. Trying to prevent radio broadcasts from the Portuguese colony reaching the commercial and industrial heartland of the country would be even less feasible – like attempting to bottle the breeze. Moreover, the South Africans were unwilling to jeopardise an already testy relationship with the Mozambicans, who supplied the gold mines with cheap, unskilled black workers drawn from the Sul do Save.

With McHarry's financial support, RCM resumed broadcasting in 1935, buying him a certain amount of goodwill locally and gaining him some political traction. He then pitched the idea of an English commercial radio station based in Lourenço Marques but directed at a South African audience and underwritten by advertising revenue derived from the same industrial heartland. Always stretched financially, the Mozambican administration granted McHarry a five-year concession as the sole proprietor of Lourenço Marques Radio in 1936. It was subsequently renewed, on the same terms, for five more years, until 1946, when RCM became a partner in the business. LMR started broadcasting in 1936, the very same year as the SABC.[8]

Looking back, the economics of the Depression and the politics of recovery on either side of the border, in 1934–1936, were decisive in shaping the origins and nature of the great war of the airwaves that followed until 1976. John Reith came to South Africa in 1934 to determine the future of public broadcasting within the country, just as McHarry went to Mozambique to establish private broadcasting beamed into the country from just across the border.

What had happened, in effect, was that McHarry had created a corridor for radio transmissions that, by 1936, linked commercial Lourenço Marques to industrial Johannesburg and the Witwatersrand heartland. Rigorously policed but not yet fully controlled, repressed urban Calvinist South Africa was suddenly placed within earshot of more socially liberal, and nominally Catholic, Mozambique. The corridor carried more than shortwave radio signals. From the outset, LMR sent out not only the overt content of its broadcasts but covert subliminal messages that were wholly at odds with official broadcasting policy in South Africa. Freed from the onerous Sunday observance legislation that governed South Africa, LMR was free to transmit as and when it pleased to a country that, over most weekends, was socially comatose.

As importantly, unlike the SABC, which was overseen by a state-designed and -operated bureaucratic structure that became increasingly cumbersome over the years, LMR's management structure was as flexible as it was lean. So, while on Sunday evenings the SABC dragged around the ball and chain of highbrow culture and classical music destined for older listeners, nimble-footed LMR was free to play popular music and jazz. Lighter content on LMR made for a larger audience of younger listeners with growing spending power who were also more receptive to commercial advertising, which, unlike on the SABC, was presented without set limits. Sponsors knew this and responded accordingly, which meant that, as ultra-nationalists often complained, there was a growing stream of advertising revenue flowing out of South Africa.

In short, from the outset the McHarry corridor operated smoothly and profitably as far as LMR and the Mozambican administration were concerned, and largely without the need for public financing. The SABC, by contrast, plodded along a Reithian path, weighed down by its Calvinist outlook, seeking financial relief along the way via outstretched palms begging for licence fees from a reluctant electorate. But the 50-year war between the SABC and LMR was never confined to commercial rivalry, important as that was. The conflict assumed different complexions at various historical moments. If we are to understand the conflict and conquest that followed, it is necessary to chart the evolution of the war by breaking it down into discrete phases.

Mobilising Ultra-Nationalists for the Coming Culture Wars, circa 1918–1939

Gabriel Johannes McHarry was of Irish stock, possibly from County Down, and probably Gaelic 'Meharry' rather than McHarry. A husband and wife of the latter name emigrated to the Cape Colony in 1845, and soon had two sons. But tragedy struck almost immediately. Within three years both parents were dead from a disease that no one bothered to record. The two infants were adopted by a large Afrikaner farming family and provided with new first names to help anchor them in their new surrounds. Michiel Johannes McHarry, father of 'our' GJ McHarry, became a *bywoner* (sharecropper) on a farm in the Venterstad district of the northeastern Cape. But after he was declared bankrupt, in 1885, he made his way north to the newly discovered Witwatersrand goldfields. His son, GJ McHarry, was born in Fordsburg, already a cosmopolitan, racially diverse working-class suburb of Johannesburg, in 1892.[9]

Caught amid yet another economic downturn, the hapless father simply disappeared from the family home, leaving GJ, or 'Gabby', to be raised in a poverty-stricken female-headed household. There were, the boy later recalled, always 'more breakfast times than breakfasts'. Low on cereal, high on cortex, the curious youngster took to schooling and, very soon literate, was apprenticed to a printer at the age of 12. Mastering his craft, he stayed with his employer for the better part of a decade.[10]

World War I seemed to prompt opportunity, and in 1915 McHarry opened his own, modestly successful, printing works. But 36 months later he too was bankrupted by a client who, having ordered thousands of waxed-paper butter wrappings, could not pay for them. Undaunted, McHarry took the wrappings and set out for the Cape, intent on selling to farmers and hoping ultimately to get to another famed land of opportunity – Argentina. But he got only as far as Kimberley. There he met and married Irene Rainsford, in 1919, and together they returned to Fordsburg where he set himself up as a printer for a second time.

McHarry's interest in radio was piqued when the Philips Company gave him a contract to print their in-house magazine and which he then turned into *The African Radio Announcer*, in 1932. By the time he got the concession for LMR four years later, he was thoroughly acquainted with recent developments in radio transmission and alert to the commercial opportunities it presented. When LMR took to the air in 1936, he and Irene went to the coast over weekends and used his interest in and enthusiasm for jazz to present programmes in person.

Although baptised in the Nederduitse Gereformeerde Kerk (NGK) and a firm believer, McHarry wore his childhood Calvinist Christianity lightly; it seldom impinged directly on his business decisions. Catholicism in Mozambique and Portugal, too, was never an issue. He greatly enjoyed the hospitality of both Lusophone countries and named his own beach cottage, at Uvongo on the Natal South Coast, 'Coimbra'.

An adolescence spent in multicultural, partly multiracial, Fordsburg lifted McHarry above the anti-Indian and antisemitic prejudices that pervaded Johannesburg at the time, as did his love of gambling. He mixed as easily with the Mauritian-born, Edinburgh-trained Indian Dr William Godfrey, an early associate of MK Gandhi's, and Godfrey's Scottish wife, Catherine Swan, as he did with the Jewish gambler Max Friedman.[11] Smart, and able to slide easily across ethnic, personal and national lines, McHarry, elusive and shy, was well-suited to running, from behind the scenes, an enterprise that often required lateral thinking when responding to new developments.

With McHarry's nose for business, LMR made steady progress during the buoyant mid- to late 1930s.[12] While RCM members in Lourenço Marques concentrated their marketing efforts on the lively commercial and tourist area around the Rua Araújo, in Portuguese, McHarry used RCM to encourage South African advertisers and listeners to follow the English-language transmissions of LMR. Such advertising as he did attract, for LMR and RCM, he personally sold to Witwatersrand-based companies, steadfastly refusing to entertain the idea of working through the emerging advertising agencies, which in his view only hiked prices unnecessarily as middlemen.[13] By 1941 McHarry had succeeded in persuading several leading companies, including General Electric, Geen & Richards, Castrol Oil, Ford, Palmolive and the Carlton Hotel in Johannesburg to advertise via LMR and RCM.[14] In chronically cash-strapped Mozambique a stream of hard-currency revenue proved most welcome and paved the way, in 1941, for the renewal of McHarry's concession for five more years.

While the McHarry corridor – advertising-transmitting and revenue-receiving – was growing steadily in significance in Lourenço Marques, it was the source of increasing economic disruption in Johannesburg. Reliant on the state and licence fees for its income, the SABC was bleeding commercial income because taxpayers were listening freely – quite literally – to LMR. But the corporation's financial predicament went deeper than that. Unlike Reith's BBC, it was under pressure to air programmes in both English and Afrikaans, doubling its expenses.[15]

The challenges that came with treating two official languages equally became more acute over the following decades as the relative tolerance of the 'two-stream' Fusion government gave way to more militant ethnic administrations. After 1948, Afrikaner nationalist governments were intent on capturing the state in all its dimensions – culturally, economically, socially and politically. McHarry's long-term problem lay not so much with the relatively free-and-easy listening habits of white South Africans but with those emerging Afrikaner ultra-nationalist organisations bent on gaining total control of the country.

The interwar period saw the transformation of Afrikaners from a reasonably diversified but overwhelmingly rural community of interests into an increasingly urban population. That transition was partly managed and shaped by several functionally specific, but frequently overlapping, organisations overseen by a tightly interconnected, ultra-nationalist racist elite. The ultras, unlike those more pragmatic Afrikaners previously drawn into the hybrid Pact or Fusion administrations, shared a few determinative characteristics.

The pre-eminent importance of their identity as Afrikaners left the ultras with little, if any, interest in forging a broader white 'South

African' unity. For them, to be an Afrikaner was to be a South African, and to be an authentic South African was to be an Afrikaner. For the ultras, parity between the languages was not an end but merely another step on the long road to achieving cultural dominance in the land of their birth. Republican to the core, they rejected any constitutional arrangements that folded the country into the British Empire or Commonwealth. Unlike most other conventional advocacy or pressure groups, ultra organisations catered for an extraordinarily wide spectrum of interests, covering most walks of life, and concentrated on strategically determined, practically applied interventions often underwritten by the most modern social-scientific research techniques. Moreover, as either parliamentary or extra-parliamentary groupings, the ultras were for the most part – a small paramilitary grouping aside – content to remain minorities until such time as political power was within reach and they could establish a hegemonic Afrikaner order.[16]

Almost without exception, the ultras tended to cast themselves merely as nationalists of firm conviction rather than as extremists. An ethnic enclave within a larger and more diverse population, they, along with their organisations of choice, had their heads in politics and their feet in the bedrock of Calvinist beliefs as espoused by the three Dutch Reformed churches in the country. In the mid-1930s, even though there were tens of thousands of ultras locked into scores of different organisations, almost none had a developed interest in broadcasting, or in the commercial or political potential of radio, or could see any further than the need to pursue the goal of language parity for whites.

Indeed, few politicians of any stripe had spotted the potential that radio held for promoting social cohesion. JH Hofmeyr, then the Administrator of the Transvaal, which had undergone a revolutionary spasm at the hands of white miners in 1922, appears to have been an exception. Opening the AS&TS's JB station, in 1924, he observed:

> I am glad that this station has been established in Johannesburg. Not least regrettable has been the lack of contact and of sympathy prevailing in the past between the Rand and the rest of South Africa. By many of those who live in other parts of the Union,

> the Rand has been regarded as something un-South African, alien, incapable of assimilation, a disconcerting excrescence which appeared on the smooth surface of South Africanism. Many on the Rand, to those living outside, must seem peculiar people, strange in their ideals, their customs, and ways of thought. Yet the last few years have seen a breaking down of many barriers of misunderstanding. Links have been formed between the Rand and the Platteland. Each has begun to realise its dependence on the other, its inability to live unto itself alone. This station will surely help to break down what remains of the barrier.[17]

Early lessons on linking a modern means of mass communication and political mobilisation may have been lost on most people but clearly not on all, not in Europe, and certainly not in Germany.

In 1933, Oswald Pirow, Minister of Defence in Hertzog's Fusion government, met and was impressed by Adolf Hitler. He later went on to meet the other big three dictators – Franco, Mussolini and Salazar – all of whom he admired. When Reith interviewed Pirow, a ranking politician, the following year, the latter's ideas about how best to link broadcasting and politics were already clear. Pirow 'told Reith bluntly that he "would like to see something approaching Nazi rule" [and,] Reith confided to his diary, "hope to use broadcasting as an adjunct thereto"'.[18]

Pirow may have been ahead of his peers, but his pattern of thinking was not lost, and in the 1960s it was dusted off and used by another neo-fascist. In 1934, when Reith briefed Hertzog before returning to England, he got the impression that the 'Prime Minister had obviously given little thought to broadcasting', and he noted that many influential citizens in the country felt that it was 'in effect ruled by rural "poor whites"' and, that if South Africa was to make real progress, the 'franchise would have to be reduced'. Hertzog failed to appear in the House for the second reading of the Broadcasting Bill. He, orthodox nationalists and ultras alike had other priorities, and a relatively tame debate centred on the equal treatment of the two official languages.[19]

The issues of substance that surfaced thereafter, in the years leading up to World War II, were the relatively high price of radio listeners' licences and the complaints, often by intolerant middle-class English speakers, objecting to the SABC's 'enforced bilingualism' on air. The questions around the disliked 'bilingualism' were addressed in 1937, when parallel services in English and Afrikaans were introduced. The former, sporting a Reithian pedigree, was deemed to be the 'A' programme and the latter the sad, revealingly named 'B' programme.[20]

Despite their initial lack of interest in broadcasting, two ultra organisations that, along with the churches, eventually came to exercise a profound influence over the fate of the SABC and LMR were already shuffling into position in the wings of the 'nation's' exclusivist white history. First and always foremost among ultra organisations was the elitist Brotherhood of Afrikaners, the Afrikaner Broederbond (AB).

The AB was founded, in 1919, by an eclectic grouping of middle-class, semi-professional Afrikaners hoping to find a toehold in the urban dispensation on the Witwatersrand. Intent on furthering ethnic unity, religious adherence to Calvinism and – rather modestly – 'every concern of the Afrikaner nation', the AB almost immediately buckled beneath the weight of some factional differences. The response of the organisation, in 1921, which soon became one of its defining features, was to go underground and thereafter enforce Masonic-like secrecy. This was followed by a successful stiffening of its professional, intellectual backbone and character by appealing strongly to a base of high-school teachers.[21] Over the following five decades the Bond became *the* intellectual powerhouse of Afrikaner nationalism, defining and researching cultural and other issues, and debating them rigorously before moving to have them translated into party policies.

A secretive, vanguardist Rand-based political organisation such as the Bond, by definition, lacked broad access to the public it sought to direct through the raising of Afrikaner consciousness via everyday popular cultural activities in the pre-radio era. In short, it needed a credible, cross-country front organisation, one considerably lighter in touch than the AB and capable of informing the day-to-day activities of those Afrikaners whose first ports of call were not necessarily the church or the nationalist parties. Unintentionally, such a broad cultural front would subsequently also be well-placed to serve as a pressure group when it came to developing broadcasting policies.

Established in 1929, when the idea of an ears-only audience was still largely in the domain of a few progressive-minded scientists, the

Federation of Afrikaner Cultural Organisations (FAK) was a carefully engineered offshoot of the Broederbond. Cast on the same sturdy foundation of teachers, the FAK did all the active proselytising that its older sibling could not. It helped straddle the cultural gap between city and platteland in an era marked by the migration of poorly educated whites to the new industrial centres. The AB and the FAK marched in lockstep. And 'in the process, the general meaning of the word "culture" shifted from emphasis on the creative arts to a more technical and ethnic sense that limited "culture" to the civil-religious conception of traditional forms of Afrikaner life'. Significantly, the FAK was the '"first [organisation] to concern itself with the right of Afrikaans to equality on the radio"'.[22]

The ultras, like ethnic nationalists everywhere, hoped to impose an exclusivist, politically hegemonic order on the land of their fathers as exercised through man, mind and muscle. The Bond provided the mind, the FAK the muscle and thousands of Calvinist patriarchal males the political coordination. It would, of course, be doing violence to the historical record to suggest that the two organisations were ever dominated by just one man. But if one *were* forced to choose a person who might have gone on to qualify as the Commissar of Radio Culture in the latter part of the 20th century, it would have to be Brother No. 787 – Dr PJ Meyer, as he was better known to the public.

His pedigree as an Afrikaner ultra was beyond dispute. Son of a South African War veteran and former inmate of a British prisoner-of-war camp in Ceylon, 787 was born in the Ladybrand district in 1909. As a young man, he attended the University College of the Orange Free State where, on the eve of the Depression, he obtained a first degree, majoring in ethics. He rejected the chance for further study, in English, at Oxford University when he won a Rhodes scholarship, and later chose to go to the culturally acceptable Calvinist Vrije Universiteit, in Amsterdam.[23]

The 1930s were exciting times for a young firebrand to be in Europe and he undertook 'several study tours to Germany', where he became reasonably well acquainted with a few members of the Nazi hierarchy: 'He wrote afterwards about his excitement that Rudolf Hess, Reich Chancellor and Hitler's chief of staff at the time, taught him to ski, and that he had seen Hitler close up.'[24] It was also the era of Joseph Goebbels, the Nazi propaganda chief.

A love of learning and a thirst for formal qualifications that testified publicly to his achievements never left him. In the 1930s he obtained a string of degrees, including a doctorate that focused on psychology but also explored other, more philosophical issues. As a dedicated Afrikaner intellectual and a staunch Calvinist, he considered himself to be a philosopher of sufficient standing to exchange views across a desk with Martin Heidegger. He developed a special interest in what, for him, were the inseparable issues of *haute culture*, politics and religion.

In Harrismith, in 1931, during a short interlude between formal studies and teaching, 787 was recruited into the AB, which, three decades later, he became chairman of (1960 to 1972). The groundwork preparing him to become Leader of the Unseen Elect had been decades in the making. As a student leader, he had been present at the founding congress of the FAK in 1929. By 1936, No. 787 was, simultaneously, the assistant secretary to both the AB and the FAK, and in the years leading up to and into the war he was active in many initiatives ranging from organising miners to the financial upliftment and economic salvation of vulnerable Afrikaners. His loyalty to the nationalist cause was never in doubt. But, by the end of the war, his role in the AB and FAK and growing stature began to trouble other ambitious politicians in the National Party, which was becoming an electoral force of note.[25]

It was the man who later became the architect of grand apartheid, Dr HF Verwoerd, who did most to check what he saw as the gathering momentum of 787's political career. As editor of the party's northern mouthpiece, *Die Transvaler*, as well as its powerful chief organisational mechanic, Verwoerd was well-placed to assess 787's growing influence in the wider nationalist movement. In 1943, Verwoerd pressured 787 into choosing between being in the cockpit of ideological power, in the AB, or serving a choice of cultural meals to FAK passengers in the rear of the craft. Number 787 resented having to make the choice and chose to stay with the Bond, abandoning his role in the FAK. The two men were cut from the same authoritarian cloth, and 787 never forgave Verwoerd. Years later, he forced Verwoerd to supplicate when the latter, by then Prime Minister, wanted 787 to assume control of the SABC.[26]

Wings clipped, 787 looked around for opportunities in business to broaden his experience and better manage his involvement in the core ultra organisations. Never much interested in the pursuit of personal wealth, an unsuccessful venture in publishing was followed by a spell as political correspondent for the newly launched Afrikaans Sunday newspaper, *Dagbreek*. The real breakthrough, however, came in 1951. He was made head of public relations at Anton Rupert's Rembrandt, a tobacco company closely linked to the Broederbond and central to activities ranging from charity to employment creation for women. Working for Rembrandt not only increased 787's business experience but gave him time and space to re-engage more vigorously with his political work, and more especially that of his beloved Broederbond.[27]

By 1953, when DF Malan's National Party was in full control of the House of Assembly, 787 was both qualified and well-placed to take up almost any senior position within the gift of the party. That call duly came, in 1959, when another of the Unseen Elect, Dr Albert Hertzog, the Minister of Posts and Telegraphs, asked Meyer to take control of the board of the SABC. It was not the best of times at the corporation. Having long prided itself on standing above the commercial fray, but keen to advance a 'separate development' agenda that would eventually extend to separate, ethnically aligned broadcasting channels for Africans, the SABC was feeling the pinch that came from neglecting the market. Meyer accepted the position only after Verwoerd wrote requesting him to take it up, and after agreeing to their setting aside political differences.[28]

Looking back, then, it is hardly surprising that the professional careers and life trajectories of Piet Meyer and Gabby McHarry failed to intersect for the first 50 years of their lives. The two men simply occupied very different universes. But history had long since demarcated the battlefield on which they would encounter one another, and by the 1950s the stage was set for the coming conflict about broadcasting and popular culture.

The reclusive McHarry was an ambitious capitalist, autodidact and entrepreneur. He was adaptive and pragmatic, a low-key Christian, free-spirited and capable of thinking and acting transnationally. Meyer, driven by a rigid Calvinism and relentless pursuit of exclusivist Afrikaner nationalism locked into its historically proclaimed boundaries, sought – and was rewarded with – public acclaim for his academic and other achievements, and relied on collective or state finances to further a political agenda that transcended the accumulation of personal wealth.

But, for all that, McHarry and Meyer shared important traits, including the love of a formidable challenge and a determination to win. Given their personality differences, however, their competitive spirits operated optimally only on vastly different terrains of conflict. When it came to commerce, out in the open market, McHarry displayed the adaptability and fleetness of foot that gave him the short-term advantages of a sprinter. But when it came to staying power, being backed by the public and covert resources of the state, Meyer, a marathon man, was probably always going to outlast his nimbler opponent. McHarry might triumph in strictly commercial contests but Meyer, operating above and beyond the marketplace, was better suited to harnessing state apparatuses for a public, or a dirty secret war.

The War in the Marketplace and LMR's Pre-Emptive Strike, circa 1941–1959

In 1939, South Africa's decision to go to war, on the side of Britain, imposed renewed strains in the ranks of Afrikaner nationalists, forcing important organisational breaks and realignments.[29] Re-establishing political unity became a priority, leaving broadcasting policy and listening habits flapping in the cultural breeze for most of the 1940s. The pursuit of unity became a preoccupation that left the AB and FAK without policies to hand when the National Party won the 1948 election, and their cultural watchdogs were playing catch-up politics well into the 1950s. However, money and the markets were not diverted, and not everyone had fallen asleep while guns were booming over much of the world.

The war, for reasons that are partly obvious, heralded a spurt in the numbers of those tuning in to the radio in South Africa.[30] In 1939, it was claimed, there were 200 000 listeners, most of them reluctantly coughing up an annual licence fee of 35 shillings that critics coupled to the price settled on by arbitration for the Schlesinger deal in 1936.[31]

In Johannesburg, the financial benefits of McHarry's initial investment in RCM and LMR in 1934–1935 were becoming tangible. Even

The 'Radio Palace', home to Lourenço Marques Radio (LM Radio), which came to dominate commercial broadcasting in southern Africa from 1936 to 1970.

before the war he had commissioned the building of a spanking new home in the upmarket suburb of Saxonwold.[32] In Mozambique, too, the flow of new funding lubricated the renewal of his LMR concession and partnership with RCM for a further five years. The partnership soon took on tangible form, and by 1948, a little over a decade after initially going bankrupt, RCM moved into the stylish new four-storey 'Radio Palace' in Lourenço Marques.

These highly visible developments, along with admiring whispers in the market, laid bare McHarry's alchemy – the trick of turning airwaves into offshore banknotes. Old wizards and young, would-be sorcerer's apprentices were drawn to Mozambique and began supplicating for additional commercial radio licences. First to stir was Schlesinger, the veteran broadcaster, who, in 1941, approached the

Lourenço Marques administration with a request to sanction a new commercial station.

McHarry family oral history has it that, in an unsuccessful bid to sway influential members of RCM, Schlesinger, a capitalist warhorse whose interests had long since embraced advertising, embellished his lobbying efforts by leaving six new American sedans, complete with ignition keys, outside the Clube's premises.[33] But the Lisbon government was keen to assert Portugal's neutrality in the war, and the Lourenço Marques administration, true to a successful partnership with McHarry, turned Schlesinger down, citing – privately – an apparently bogus concern about being sensitive to 'American' influences.[34]

By the mid-1940s, the potential that commercial radio held for bailing out the faltering finances of the SABC's two sluggish relatively highbrow channels had become so obvious that even the South African government could sense it. In September 1946, Prime Minister Smuts, a lawyer by profession, appointed Dr AA Schoch KC – a former career legal adviser to the government with a pair of hands so safe that they barely moved – to head a 'Commission of Enquiry into the Operations of the SABC' with a view to exploring new possibilities.[35]

But commissioners, usually let loose only on questions to which the answers are largely self-evident, sometimes feel duty-bound to be even more ponderous than politicians when providing answers. By the time Schoch KC presented his wavering – 'on the one hand, and on the other' – findings, in 1948, the pragmatic nationalist Gideon Roos was the recently appointed Director-General of the SABC, and the newly elected, apartheid-obsessed National Party the incoming government.

At that time, neither the vanguard Broederbond nor the trailing nationalist administration had any clear-cut, let alone strongly held, views when it came to the future of broadcasting. The government was content to graft what it had been presented with onto the stem of the SABC. On the one hand, Schoch endorsed competition and the free market, and, on the other, reiterated a few classic Reithian objections to the commercialisation of radio. The answer lay in squaring the circle.

The Schoch commission freed up the space for the coming of South African-based commercial radio, in the shape of Springbok Radio, which went on air in 1950, while at the same time bolting it on to the SABC and state structures. The financial egg was to be scrambled but without breaking the state shell. The old 'A' and 'B' programmes would lift the highbrow culture of white South Africans with the aid of funds newly raised in the marketplace. It would be the best of all possible worlds.[36]

But not everyone was convinced that it could work, and it prompted yet another South African plea for business favours in Mozambique. Smart thinking, or so it would seem, only reached the southern shores long after it sported legs in the country's northern industrial heartland. In 1948, nearly fifteen years after McHarry first aired the notion of a commercial channel focused on the Rand to the Lourenço Marques administration, and seven years after IW Schlesinger had made his unsuccessful wartime approach to the Portuguese state for a second channel, the exhausted idea finally crawled into sleepy Cape Town.

Roy Stark of Sea Point put together a consortium that, he told the colony's Cabinet Secretary, had £100 000 at its disposal (about £3.5 million in today's money) to purchase a modern and more powerful transmitter. Of course, he wrote, it would not interfere in any way with the 'already small transmitter in your territory', and the new group had its 'own advertising clientele ready to participate'. The Lourenço Marques administrators did not bother to reply to his postal probing.[37]

Stark, Schoch or Schlesinger – it made no difference – the astute Gabby McHarry, sensing the coming of a new age in commercial radio, had made the necessary pre-emptive market adjustments to leave him well ahead of the pack. When his LMR concession was successfully renewed, in 1946 – just as Dr Schoch began examining his hands more carefully – McHarry locked his licence into a new special-purpose vehicle, GJ McHarry (Pty) Ltd, leaving sufficient space for a long-standing partnership with RCM.[38] There was nothing too special about that legal manoeuvre, but what followed was inspirational and provided him with a marketing advantage that lasted three decades.

'Think globally, act locally' – an exhortation repeated ad nauseam by 21st-century business-school drones – is about as banal as it is ahistorical. It was a pattern of thought that the East India Company had mastered centuries earlier but was still far from common in the thinking of small- to medium-sized enterprises on the Witwatersrand in the mid-1940s. McHarry had got the point at least a decade earlier when he first spotted the potential of offshore broadcasting in Europe, and in 1946 he followed through rigorously on the same logic. If LMR was to continue to grow and prosper in an expanding market for commercial radio, it would require repositioning. He needed to separate the ownership of the station not only from its management but from the marketing of its advertising offerings, and to present listeners with an even better, lighter and more professional product. LMR was going into a war and would need experienced troops to fight behind the lines.

Who or what it was, back in mid-decade, that attracted John Davenport and Richard Meyer to South Africa now lies beyond the reach of historians. But the firm of Davenport & Meyer (Pty) Ltd (D&M), registered in the seminal year of 1946, became so closely linked to LMR, and for so long, that it is difficult to escape the conclusion that McHarry must have been closely involved in luring them south. It could only have been he who persuaded them to open an advertising agency that would deal exclusively with LMR from Johannesburg.[39]

In terms of inspiration and early management, D&M was a direct descendant of that eccentric English pioneer of offshore commercial radio, Captain Leonard Plugge, Radio Normandie and the recently victorious British Army. The company, set up before the Broederbond and the nationalists had even thought about coming up with a strategy for national broadcasting, served both McHarry and LMR quite brilliantly.

John Davenport (1912–2006) was destined to go to Oxford, but disastrous speculation by his City financier father saw him diverted into office work, where he acquired a liking for stylish – 'foppish' – dressing and a passion for market intelligence and travel. In 1939, when war broke out, he was doing market research for the BBC, but he then obtained a commission in the army's Intelligence Corps and was sent to the Middle East. In Cairo and Beirut he 'analysed the radio-listening habits and opinions of British soldiers' and enjoyed having access to privileged information to the point where the highest compliment that he could pay a man was to say that he was 'discreet'. A *bon vivant* with liberal views and 'sensual tastes', in South Africa he soon linked up with and then married Gezina Albertyn, a Dutch national with equally refined tastes who worked for 'progressive causes'. He retained an interest in D&M, but the political trajectory of the Afrikaner nationalists jarred. In 1951, he left for the UK where he became a legendary commissioning editor for the *Reader's Digest*.[40]

RL Meyer (c. 1903–1972) was the son of successful Birmingham journalist of Polish-Jewish origins and received a fine education at London's famous St Paul's School for boys. Like Davenport, Meyer did not find South African politics to his liking and, like him, retained an interest in D&M. By the late 1950s he too was back in England, and went on to become the successful owner of Radio Manx, which he later sold to the Isle of Man government. He was also one of the moving forces behind the introduction of television to Rhodesia in the early 1960s. Little is known about Meyer's earlier career. Reputedly 'a short man with a short fuse', he was nevertheless of cheerful enough disposition and his close friends called him 'Dickie'. What *is* known is that, in the late 1920s, Plugge had made him manager of Radio Normandie, where he was based in the 1930s. The war found him in the Cairo headquarters of the British Army's Forces Broadcasting Service (FBS), alongside John Davenport, and by 1945 Meyer had reached the rank of colonel. On returning to London Meyer was made manager of the well-established IBC and later settled in the south of France. Meyer was happiest when exploiting the weaknesses of ponderous states.[41]

It was a McHarry masterstroke that persuaded D&M to take control of the business side of LMR. But it was another inspirational appointment by D&M – drawn from the same pool of talent – that deepened the transformation and commercial success that ensued at LMR. David Davies, so financially and managerially adept that he eventually became chairman of the board at D&M after the senior partners retreated from South Africa, was a charismatic and unusually gifted presenter and a notable mentor of young disc jockeys, as well as being a promotional wizard. He, too, had been an announcer for IBC at Radio Luxembourg and Radio Normandie before being sent to Beirut and Cairo to work in radio and audience research for the FBS. In 1947, he became the chief announcer and station manager in Lourenço Marques, where he took up residence in the Polana Hotel with his wife, Brenda. And, to complete the complement, Davies brought along yet another FBS recruit, David Gordon, as part of a dynamic new team.[42]

McHarry and D&M thus had a transnational business fortress and a market intelligence-gathering capacity run by former army officers

Press campaign, 1950–1953, backing LM Radio, the cultural and financial scourge of Afrikaner nationalists.

for LMR in place years before the SABC – shuffling along in Reithian slippers – could find its way into the studio to turn on the microphones at Springbok Radio. Worse was to follow. D&M were specialists in offensive, not defensive, operations, and their troops poured out of the base to take up every strategic position of importance they could find.

The terrain had been well prepared by McHarry. Listeners had been complaining for years about the heavy doses of classical music on the SABC's 'A' programme and the mind-numbing boredom of the Calvinist lockdown over the week's end. 'The result', 'Very Lowbrow' informed the editor of the *Rand Daily Mail* in 1940, 'is that promptly at 5.30 pm we tune into that ever-popular Lourenço Marques which realizes that Sunday is the only time that a working man or woman can make use of the radio.' The grievance remained in place for most of the decade but, within 12 months of D&M's taking over management of the station, LMR extended its Sunday-evening coverage of light music, on shortwave, from 9 pm to 11 pm. That, in turn, laid the foundations for what became the popular 'LM Hit Parade', for decades the station's unmistakable signature.⁴³

But D&M were never content to restrict the fight for an expanded audience to the number of hours broadcast. Perhaps they took their cue from live entertainment provided to the armed forces during the war. From the outset, the company focused on personalising radio in ways that allowed listeners to develop a direct, more meaningful relationship with LMR and its youthful presenters. They wanted members of a mass audience to rise above hearing a disembodied voice coming out of loudspeaker in their living room, and to enable the sound to conjure up a mental picture of a person or radio announcer that they had seen.

If France and Normandy gave the D&M directors the template for transnational invasion by air, then it was the British Army in the Middle East that taught them that soft power could be derived from a ground assault in enemy territory by focusing on winning the hearts and minds of the people. And focus they did. By the late 1940s, a series of 'variety shows', pre-recorded in Johannesburg on Sundays between 6 pm and 7.30 pm at the 20th Century Cinema, had become a feature for many young English speakers with a love of popular culture. On one memorable occasion, a large plate-glass window was broken when an enthusiastic crowd, estimated to be 4000 strong, surged forward in the hope of gaining entry. The Sunday slots, it was claimed by the fanatical and faithful alike, pitted variety concerts against church services and further underpinned an old saw in Calvinist binary thinking that would be trotted out for decades to come.⁴⁴ The young, it was argued, could either be true believers or followers of popular music – but not both. The variety shows were only the forerunner of many other live events.

As with an unfolding campaign to sell advertising on the 'new' LMR, which, unlike under McHarry's former regime, allowed agencies to charge commission, D&M interventions were underpinned by intensive, ground-breaking research.⁴⁵ British wartime intelligence-gathering and monitoring techniques – pioneered by the FBS in Cairo – were recast to develop and expand professional market research in South Africa. Initially, the company had little data to work with and used the volume of fan mail directed to radio announcers, or responses to competitions, to gauge the depth and reach of LMR. But within 36 months the investment and sophistication of D&M's market research – along with that of Market Research Africa – was attracting the attention of many business analysts and an awed print media. The staid SABC, by contrast, spurned all market research and surveys.[46]

The SABC's indifference came at a time when, as one analyst noted, D&M and LMR were 'spending thousands of pounds a year on listener research' and making serious inroads into the market for advertising. By 1949, 12 months before Springbok Radio went on air, the success of the east coast aerial invasion was becoming ever more apparent. A survey revealed that at some point or other on every day of the week, 45 per cent of South Africans were tuning in to LMR, and by Sunday evening, when a church-and-state induced stupor made even the chronically idle yearn for the coming of Monday, the figure rose to 48 per cent. Other, anecdotal, evidence pointed in the same direction. The sales of radio sets capable of receiving shortwave signals from Lourenço Marques, it was said, were outpacing those of sets capable only of receiving the 'A' and 'B' programmes. More alarming was the growing realisation – one that the ultra-nationalists eventually picked up on to use for political leverage – that the success of LMR and RCM was evidence of the 'drainage' of South African finance into Mozambique. An occasional earache on Sundays was one thing, chronic pain in the wallet another.[47]

When Springbok Radio first took to the air, on 1 May 1950, there were whisperings in the market that the 'competition' was going to force LMR to close. Dickie Meyer dismissed the rumours as 'fantastic', as well he might have. McHarry and D&M had been preparing for the arrival of Springbok for years and welcomed it. A mature ballerina, in pointes grown familiar and supple with use, had little to fear from a novice in crispy *chaussons de ballet*. 'We are glad that the success of the Lourenço Marques station has helped the Government's decision to start its own commercial service', Meyer announced, saying that it was 'going to make South African listeners much more radio-conscious than ever before.'[48]

Colonel Meyer had good reason to be confident. So financially successful did the company prove that twice within 48 months – in late 1950 and then again in early 1954 – D&M approached the courts to reduce its working capital, returning sizeable sums of the original investment to its principal shareholders, who never numbered more than half a dozen.[49]

True to character, D&M welcomed Springbok with a series of pre-emptive strikes on radio and in the print media that were carried through over the 36 months after 1950. LMR extended its Saturday-night service until midnight, and on Sunday evenings all the way to 11 pm, putting Messrs Calvin & Reith on the back foot. For those having trouble finding their way around their radio dials, adverts – designed to be clipped from newspapers – offered a guide as to what the best frequencies were to follow LMR on by day or night.[50]

Sweeping across a broad front, D&M brought a light, modern touch to an extensive press campaign that kept LMR listeners feeling close to, and comfortable with, the music and familiar voices coming out of the lounge or kitchen. Amusing cartoons, crisp caricatures and short readable biographies of established or new presenters shortened the psychological distance between far-off LMR and its audience in ways that the around-the-corner SABC could only aspire to.[51] Exhibition appearances, roadshows and talent contests completed the assault.

News on the Rialto, too, was less than promising. The SABC, locked into state machinery and beholden to a nationalist government that needed to nod approvingly in the direction of creative artists who were also voters, was having trouble positioning itself in the market – lots of trouble. The SABC could not produce sufficient radio features, plays and serials at competitive prices to fill the programmes, and Springbok Radio was forced to import most of its early material from Australia.

Unlike influential English speakers in South Africa, who had been saved from Afrikaner nationalist hegemony by the British Army in the Anglo-Boer War, and therefore had an enduring loyalty to the BBC, the crown and England, Australians had less of the colonial cultural cringe about them. High-minded Reithian philosophy failed to take root on a gigantic barren island wasteland masked by its attractive, circumscribing coastal strip. By 1950, when South Africans were still toying with the novelty of having two commercial stations, Australia was served by more than 100 commercial stations, producing features and scripts for radio at a fraction of the cost possible on the Witwatersrand. By then, LMR was said have won over more than 30 per cent of all potential listeners in the Cape Province, Natal and the rural Orange Free State.[52]

Newspaper clip-out wavelength guide to LM Radio, c. 1952.

To prime the pump for more local radio productions and finance them through advertising revenue, the SABC manipulated import controls to fix prices that local sponsors – prevented from importing directly – found prohibitive. LMR, unencumbered by nationalist considerations, surged ahead of the supposedly fleet-footed Springbok. 'Some programmes which would cost £15 [in Johannesburg] had been bought by sponsors over Lourenço Marques Radio for £10 [per quarter of an hour] and 'thousands of pounds are involved in these deals.'[53] The nationalists learnt a hard lesson: the market put price above patriotism.

In Mozambique, the sumptuous new Radio Palace provided material evidence as to just how profitable the South African advertising industry was becoming for D&M, GJ McHarry (Pty) Ltd, LMR and RCM. For sceptics there were other career and lifestyle indicators pointing in the same direction. D&M was becoming less dependent on the direct, hands-on management of its two principal partners, who were already looking to the northern hemisphere for new opportunities. Gabby

McHarry, too, was becoming less involved in and more relaxed about the future of his company as the family settled in to their Saxonwold home. In 1955, he and Irene completed the journey he had begun in 1919 when they embarked on an extended sea voyage to, and vacation in, Argentina. A few months later, he handed over the business to his son Trevor, and the McHarrys then 'retired' to their cottage at Uvongo. LMR had won some battles, if not the war.[54]

By the mid-1950s, it appears to have been grudgingly conceded by the press and a sleepy public that LMR had outmuscled the SABC's two principal stations, as well as its ponderous commercial stepson. The gravity of the immediate and long-term situation, and the potential political implications of not arming the state with the resources to compete across the African continent, seem to have been brought home to the government and the ultra-nationalists by a maverick MP in the course a remarkable speech in the House of Assembly in May 1956.

What else could you expect from a man whose given name was Baarzilia but who was better known as 'Blaar' Coetzee? Three years earlier, he had had the whip withdrawn from him by the United Party for rejecting its choice of leader to replace Smuts. It was in character; he had suffered from a serious political itch for most of his life. For many decades a charismatic free spirit with a talent for publishing fringe newspapers and magazines, Coetzee moved from the far left of the political spectrum – as a student – and ended his days in the comfortable embrace of the National Party. At the time of his speech, however, Coetzee was an 'independent' MP with an ongoing interest in the media and the increasing power of broadcast radio.

Coetzee launched a wide-ranging attack on the government with a few home truths. The SABC had been outgunned by LMR in the market for advertising, as well as in technical terms, and 'more and more people were tuning in to Lourenço Marques'. A new 20-kilowatt popgun of a transmitter, erected at Bloemfontein, was no match for the long-range artillery of RCM and LMR, which, like others up and down the continent, was about to be powered by an impressive 100-kilowatt transmitter.[55]

The refrain about the appeal of LMR failed to raise the eyebrows, let alone the hackles, of most members of the ruling party. It was old hat. But what *did* get to them, and to those influential in the nongovernmental ultra organisations, was Coetzee's blunt warning that powerful transmitters in Egypt, India and Ceylon were beaming out programmes and messages from fully independent nations run by people of colour – into Africa.[56]

For nationalists intent on entrenching white minority rule, statist to the core, the thought of border-crossing whispers bearing subliminal messages about dignity, independence and self-determination to a black majority was of considerable concern. Among those sitting up and taking notice was *the* rising star in the Afrikaner Broederbond. Piet Meyer was readying himself for the fight, not only in the marketplace, where a win was not guaranteed, but one behind the shield of the state.

The Ascent of the Brotherhood Made Manifest, circa 1959–1965

The arrival of a state-controlled commercial radio station and the possible inroads that it might make into the advertising revenue of the print media aroused the Unseen Elect from a slumber that dated back to Hertzog's courtship of Reith. Two years after Springbok Radio first took to the airwaves, in 1952, the AB canvassed its branches, countrywide, for their opinion about the strengths and weaknesses of a new dispensation for press and radio.

There was a range of responses, some of them idiosyncratic and revealing, others offering pointers as to where the AB executive committee might best attempt to intervene and protect the Calvinist cultural and language preferences of those it purported to represent. All replies crossed the desk of Assistant Secretary PJ Meyer, and a few of the ideas appear to have stayed with him. As befitted a secretive, top-down organisation that prided itself on doing the nation's more serious cerebral work, many branch responses reflected the contempt in which, behind closed doors, AB members held most of the citizenry: 'People do not think for themselves, but that cannot be attributed only to the press and radio. The masses have never thought for themselves. Only individuals are capable of thinking.' Unfortunately, 'the press and radio must give the masses what they want'. It followed that 'care must be taken to ensure that radio remains in control not only of Afrikaners, but of those who *understand* what the nature and struggle of our people and their culture should be'. Part of that struggle might involve mastering technology in ways that isolated 'unhealthy' influences that did not accord with national aspirations, including stricter licensing and control of wavelengths so that 'only South African broadcasts could be received'.[57] In keeping with the thinking of modern Afrikaner intellectuals, Calvinism, science and urbanisation could be reconciled in ways that did not clash.[58] But not all the members had eyes front; old stalwarts looked backwards just as easily.

Predictably, several branches wanted to see the entrenchment of venerable Afrikaner cultural and religious features, while others muttered about the supposed dangers of Roman Catholicism. And, as ever in South Africa, some branches wanted to see more of an effort from the 'Americanised' Springbok Radio when it came to the need for 'nation-building', which, translated, meant the advancement of 'society' but on terms dictated solely by the racial grouping currently in power.

For the most part, the branch replies were framed broadly around the familiar tenets of Afrikaner civil religion. Many were of the view that commercial radio was doing much to erode the spiritual well-being of the nation, and that the youth were particularly vulnerable. In retrospect, the 1952 survey did two things. It alerted the AB executive to the fears and misgivings of middle-class Afrikaners about a broadcasting system that was still largely beyond their reach and relatively independent. The survey also helped set the agenda for a new dispensation and provided the executive with the mandate to push ultra militants into strategic positions within the SABC. The writing was on the wall, but the print was so small that Gideon Roos, the old-school nationalist incumbent Director-General, had difficulty reading it.

The executive of the Unseen suffered from no such problem. Calligraphers and readers of note, the ultras could bring any issue with an ethnic tinge to it into the sharpest focus at very short notice. Within months, the AB produced a memorandum on 'Developments in Radio'. Much of the document was devoted to an examination of the financial problems of the SABC's 'cultural services' – the 'A' and 'B' programmes – and the vexed question of what a more appropriate radio licence fee might be for a country as large as it was thinly populated by listeners.

But, as with a scorpion, the poison was not in the body of the memo but in its tail, which was disingenuously marked 'Other Issues'. Only three of the nine heads of SABC departments were 'convinced' Afrikaners, which meant that they were always in a minority when it came to day-to-day managerial issues. The chairman of the Board of Governors, Dr SH Pellissier, was hopelessly even-handed in meetings and failed to understand the importance of commanding the detail. The AB executive needed to pay the closest possible attention to who his successor might be, as well as to the future composition of the board.[59]

In November 1955, after the AB executive failed to secure a face-to-face meeting between Dr Piet Meyer and the Minister of Posts and Telegraphs, Brother JJ Serfontein, at short notice, it sent the Minister a letter outlining its preferences. It wanted the next vacancy on the board filled by a Rand-based 'steadfast young Afrikaner' whose proximity would ensure that he was totally au fait with all developments in radio. The name suggested was that of advocate and Brother J van Wyk de Vries, years later an obediently conservative if not wholly reactionary judge.[60]

Over the months that followed, the AB executive gave ever more attention to the capacity, financing, management and structure of the SABC in memoranda notable for their professionalism and depth of research, proving that gross incompetence and nationalism were not necessarily handmaidens. But the big prize, the chairmanship of the Board of Governors, continued to elude the brotherhood, which had to move at the pace of the prime minister and designated cabinet minister.

On 8 May 1956 – two weeks *before* Blaar Coetzee delivered his speech in the House announcing that the SABC had lost the continental as well as the regional radio war with LMR – the AB executive received an early warning of government shortcomings when it came to funding the SABC. Via its own channels within the SABC, the executive obtained a copy of a memorandum written by Gideon Roos drawing attention to precisely the same issues that were soon to surface in parliament. It is difficult to avoid the conclusion that a copy of the Director-General's memorandum had somehow also found its way to Blaar Coetzee, or that perhaps Roos himself had briefed

Coetzee so as to force the government to sit up and pay attention to the challenges that the SABC was facing. Problems included a lack of sufficient advertising slots on Springbok Radio, financing, the threat posed by transnational broadcasts and – significantly – how Calvinist Sundays and the marked imbalance between talk and music hamstrung the SABC. It all underscored the need for the AB to intervene at the state broadcaster.⁶¹

But a government obsessed with the need to enforce the physical separation of Africans from whites in every way conceivable struggled to make space for less pressing issues, even if the SABC remained firmly on the agenda of the AB and its militant moralising faction. Then, as sometimes happens, the failure of one man's heart gave another his head. When Prime Minister JG Strijdom died, in August 1958, he was succeeded by HF Verwoerd, whose cabinet rejigging found space for Dr Albert Hertzog as Minister of Posts and Telegraphs.

Brother JAM Hertzog, like his confidant and friend, PJ Meyer, was a cultivated and well-educated Afrikaner boasting several degrees that, somewhere along the line, like Meyer's, included a major in ethics. It was Hertzog who needed and wanted Meyer – who, within months became the chairman of the Broederbond – at the SABC. After Meyer had made Verwoerd eat a slice of humble pie, for the elbowing he had dished out to No. 787 back in 1943 and request that Meyer agree to becoming the chairman of the Board of Governors, the Brotherhood had a rediffusion system plumbed directly into the highest offices in the land. The sentiments expressed in the 1952 AB survey and other memoranda were about to be elevated to the status of official practice. The 'national' policies of the 'two-stream' white South Africa, which during the interwar wars had shown signs of coalescing, were set to take on the increasingly separatist nationalist trajectory favoured by the ultras and then broadcast across the country.

Meyer assumed office at the SABC in June 1959, remaining in charge of the corporation for 20 years until his retirement in May 1981. A determined, focused and outcomes-driven individual, Meyer dominated almost every cabinet minister he reported to formally. For the same reason, he occasionally had to be brought to heel by the prime ministers that his minister served.⁶² Prime ministers, for their part, were aware of Meyer's powerful covert role as chairman of the

Unseen Elect, in a decade notable for technological advances in FM radio and later television. But his covert influence in the party was soon matched overtly by his partly self-created role as Tsar of the Airwaves. On one occasion, as we will come to note, he got a cabinet decision reversed.[63]

On taking office, Meyer set himself three tasks that, collectively, turned him into the undisputed supremo of the reconstituted organisation. As the full-time salaried chairman of the Board of Governors he moved into the SABC headquarters, converting his role from one of policy oversight to that of chief executive, overseeing the day-to-day operations of the corporation. He then redesigned the managerial structures and processes in a manner that complemented his new role. Finally, he used the unfolding dispensation to gradually diminish and undermine the authority and status of the by then increasingly nominal director-general to the point where Roos eventually took a voluntarily negotiated financial settlement by way of compensation, and resigned.[64]

With the inner pathways of the doddering corporation's nervous system reconfigured to serve enhanced control, Meyer set about strengthening the SABC's outer shell, its physical infrastructure. A smallish man, he was accustomed to the relatively low profile that came from working for a secretive political organisation at a modest salary. But at the age of 50, Meyer was getting into full stride, and was at pains to make certain that his office reflected his stature as a public persona of increasing note.[65] In a decade notable for its economic buoyancy, he and the Brothers Ultra were intent on creating an imposing cluster of iconic physical structures along the western skyline of an otherwise ideologically hostile city devoted almost exclusively to the pursuit of profit.[66] Collectively, the new encrustations they designed would bear witness to the presence of a modern, insurgent Afrikaner nationalism.

Meyer boasted that when the new radio and television complex at Auckland Park – built in part on property expropriated by the state – was officially opened, in 1976, it occupied the largest consolidated area in the world devoted to mass communication.[67] The SABC building, a 34-storey concrete erection, dominated a longed-for cultural stronghold that comprised a transmission tower, a hospital, a teachers' training college and a new Afrikaans university, which Meyer, once dismissed as an 'intellectually pretentious crank', became chancellor of.[68]

Dr PJ Meyer, chairman of the Broederbond and the SABC, with a model of the buildings at Auckland Park, Johannesburg, which he claimed constituted the largest consolidated centre for mass communication in the world.

From deep within his urban cultural fortification Meyer set about expanding the countrywide FM radio network by placing various African-language stations into silos. Ethnicised outlets were used to advance apartheid policies and inhibit the growth of black political solidarity across ethnic lines in a decade marked by the growth of African nationalism across the continent.[69] The introduction of television, an expensive exercise replete with exotic influences, was deliberately delayed until such time as the SABC's radio stations had habituated listeners, including those conservative Africans locked into racially segregated rural reserves, to fine-tuned presentations of drama, current affairs, news and traditional music rendered in the vernacular.[70]

With the economy roaring along and Meyer's political influence reaching its apogee in a morally flawed state that was becoming isolated internationally, there was no stopping the SABC from peddling propaganda to a largely quiescent white electorate. The corporation put on weight faster than a porcine schoolboy hogging custard and malva pudding. Between 1960 and 1967 the corporation's assets increased by 452 per cent, to R50 million. A *Financial Mail* survey noted that, when measured in terms of total assets, only ten South African companies were larger than the SABC.[71]

With so impressive an infrastructure, the SABC was prepared for a war of the airwaves inside and outside the country. But, as Afrikaner nationalists – of all people – might have known, not all conflicts are settled by access to superior weaponry; hearts and minds count too.

Lourenço Marques Radio and South African Popular Culture, circa 1959–1972

One of the problems that come with having attained the pinnacle of achievement is that it has, by definition, to be followed by a descent that can be equally demanding. By the mid-1960s, Meyer and the AB were in full control of the SABC and wielding enormous influence within the cabinet and ruling National Party. But the passage of time and the same dynamic economy that had facilitated their rapid ascent of the ridge at Auckland Park had had other, often unintended, social consequences that did not yield easily to the law or political power.[72]

Besides being elitist and secretive, as befitted a Calvinist people entrusted by God with special custodial duties at the southern tip of black Africa, members of the AB were exclusively male, patriarchal, unilingual by chance or by choice, and mainly middle-aged if not positively elderly. The brotherhood was, by definition, not drawn from a generation well-suited to nurturing or understanding the changing aspirations, behaviour or lifestyles of the Afrikaner youth in a decade underpinned by the increasing affluence of white South Africans. Across the West, the decade was labelled 'the Swinging Sixties'.[73]

Most young adults in the 1960s were born after World War II. In the case of young Afrikaners, they were part of a third or fourth generation of city dwellers, well clear of their 'poor white' forebears of yesteryear. They were often better educated, more literate and modern in outlook, stylishly dressed and, not infrequently, more experienced travellers than were their parents or grandparents.[74] They also carried fewer of the cultural scars inflicted on previous generations of Afrikaners by condescending, taunting Anglophiles who would sing 'God Save the King' lustily at the conclusion of every cinema show, concert or other public performance. Crucially, young Afrikaners were also more likely to be bilingual than any of their formerly rural kin. While it was true that they remained largely tone-deaf when it came to their political beliefs and voting behaviour, they were present in growing numbers and open to exploring the airwaves on the ubiquitous transistor radio sets. In cultural terms, they were increasingly accessible, and the McHarrys, Davenport & Meyer and a clutch of new disc jockeys at LMR knew it.

So, just as Commissar of Culture Meyer installed new managerial systems at the corporation to bring his narrowing policies into greater alignment with what he saw as the nation's broadcasting aspirations, his counterparts at D&M set about broadening LMR's appeal by further modernising and internationalising the station's music presentations.

By the mid-1960s, mirroring the migration of its founders back north, D&M's financial interests had become more diversified. Colonel Dickie Meyer, true to the company's offshore tradition, had acquired a valuable concession from the government of the Isle of Man, with Radio Manx's advertising and music reaching deep into northwestern England, while John Davenport, based in London, was well in tune with Carnaby Street culture. In South Africa, the innovative David Davies, who undertook frequent trips to London, presided over the board, while the company's day-to-day operations were managed by David Pinnell, recruited from Radio Caroline, one of the 'pirate' stations operating from ships anchored in the North Sea.[75]

Between them, Davies and Pinnell recruited a set of legendary young disc jockeys who not only enjoyed the relaxed lifestyle in the more tolerant atmosphere of 'continental' Lourenço Marques but also received salaries significantly better than those of their more staid South African counterparts.[76] The new crop of presenters at LMR were introduced to the South African public via D&M events, including talent shows, outside broadcasts and personal appearances, until several of the more eligible bachelors among them assumed the proportions of minor pop stars in their own right. D&M was also instrumental in introducing a transatlantic imprimatur at LMR via another signature of the 1960s – maddeningly effective, mind-adhering advertising jingles – specially commissioned from the Pepper-Tanner Company in Memphis, Tennessee, and then re-recorded in Johannesburg.[77]

At the same time, McHarry (Pty) Ltd and RCM came up with yet another creative, profit-seeking initiative by extending the parallel use of any studio equipment and transmitters surplus to immediate requirements. Through the Pan American Radio Company (PAR), which handled much of the broadcasting business of evangelical churches in the United States, Gabby McHarry, although nominally retired, developed valuable contacts with several of the PAR's most popular preachers.[78]

Shortly before LMR shut down for the day, the station started simultaneous broadcasts of pre-recorded sermons – replete with the usual appeals for funds – to late-night and early-morning listeners. The Americans were said to have 'profited very handsomely from their purchase of airtime' in a continent seemingly created for the foolish and gullible. One or two of the evangelicals, McHarry discovered, perhaps had more in common with Elmer Gantry than Saint Peter. Whenever in Johannesburg to renew their contracts with LMR, the pastors, mindful of expenses, shared hotel rooms with their secretaries.[79]

The near round-the-clock broadcasting formula profited McHarry (Pty) Ltd and RCM to the point where the Portuguese government eventually acquired the dominant share of the Rádio Clube's holdings in the original partnership. A former financial manager at D&M noted that, by the mid-1960s, Rand advertisers were queuing up for a rare vacant slot in prime time and that 'LMR was an extremely profitable station'.[80]

As in the 1940s, during the run-up to the launching of the SABC's commercial radio service, D&M's slickly managed adjustments to new trends in advertising and international broadcasting in the 1960s left the sadly named Springbok Radio looking flat- rather than fleet-footed. New, more powerful medium-wave transmitters augmented the old shortwave service, giving LMR a more accessible and clearer signal that made yet more inroads into Springbok Radio's limp listenership.[81]

The assault on SABC stations was relentless. LMR's target of choice when it came to finding the time best suited to seducing South African listeners remained the hours of the living dead – the Calvinist-Reithian weekends and Sunday nights. For the young and young at heart – schoolchildren, students, newly married couples, working men and women – the pop music that came from the 'Top 20' and iconic 'LM Hit Parade' helped bury the week that had passed and lifted the spirits for what lay ahead. The competition was blown away.

Direct confrontation in the marketplace was D&M's weapon of choice when it came to attracting weekend listeners, but it hardly exhausted their repertoire. Any attempt at reprisals by competitors hobbled by Sunday observance legislation risked being met with a burst of deadly sniper fire. When, in 1960, Springbok Radio dared to play music into the wee hours of Saturday mornings, the response was as brutal as it was swift. LMR began piping dance music and jazz into parched Union ears until 1 am on Sundays. As the liberal *Rand Daily Mail* explained to readers, 'no radio station in South Africa is allowed to continue its programme for a second after midnight each Saturday'. But LMR could and did. 'And there is nothing the South African authorities can do to stop it.' 'Mozambique is a Catholic country and as such, regards Sundays as a day of rejoicing and fiesta.'[82]

By 1960, McHarry's pioneering broadcasting initiative had been a source of cultural irritation and financial loss to the SABC for close on three decades. But, as the decade wore on and the South African state sank deeper into authoritarian, neo-fascist, racist practices and policies, the nature of the irritation experienced by 'the authorities' began to turn from social and economic to political. With the government's legitimacy increasingly being called into question by a few internal and many external organisations, the ultras – many of them older white males out of touch with a new generation – could ill afford to lose the battle for the hearts and minds of either the established electorate or a new cohort of young males destined for national service. What citizens needed more of, according to the elderly conservatives, was high culture, ethnic heritage, patriotism and tradition, and less of the detested liberalism, modernity and pop music coming out of LMR.

Unfortunately, 'the youth', always an elusive category, included not only young English speakers – dismissed as cultural agnostics by the ultras – but others drawn from within the wider nationalist family. It included some Afrikaner men and women with one ear tuned to old political mantras and the other to modern music streaming into the country from across the border. Some folk, it seemed, were capable of being both modern and nationalist. By the mid-1960s, LMR was attracting about two per cent more young Afrikaans-speaking listeners than their English-speaking counterparts. The 'problem' never went away. An SABC survey revealed that, by the end of the decade, the Sunday-night 'LM Hit Parade' was attracting about 187 000 young Afrikaners, while its culturally constipated competitor – the staid 'B' programme – drew a paltry 40 000 listeners from the same youthful cohort. In the concrete fortress of Auckland Park it was the stuff of a recurring nightmare – that the genre of music played by LMR would somehow eventually force Springbok Radio to 'fall into line' and thus 'lower' standards.[83]

In the marketplace, LMR reigned supreme, but by then Brother No. 787 and the South African government's priorities were no longer solely about shoring up the economy or its electoral base. For some time, they had been grappling with a few 'new' concerns – concerns that Gideon Roos and Blaar Coetzee had hinted at a decade earlier, in 1956, and which Harold Macmillan had then underscored in his 'Wind of Change' speech to a bemused National Assembly in February 1960.

The Dirty Wars and Lourenço Marques Radio, circa 1961–1975

In the 1960s, South Africa was trapped between two opposing forces – economic advance and political decay. White prosperity signalled progress, encouraging innovation and the adoption of new technologies, while a growing challenge from black nationalists inside the country and beyond the national borders accelerated the unravelling of an already threadbare white 'democracy'. The modernisers of the Unseen Elect within the SABC urged improvements in material conditions, while a conservative rump beyond bleated on about Christianity and the need to maintain cultural traditions. Meanwhile, the governing National Party struggled to batten down the hatches of repression in the face of a gathering black political storm.

The Sharpeville massacre, in March 1960, followed by hundreds of acts of sabotage and the Rivonia treason trial of Nelson Mandela and others, in 1963–1964, helped shift the political climate in southern Africa. It led to the passing of the Defence Amendment Act of 1967, which saw young white males conscripted for an initial period of nine months, later extended to two years.[84] The National Party, accustomed to setting and enforcing the political agenda for 'the nation', was placed in a defensive posture, having to contend with an ideological, political battle *and* an armed struggle within and beyond the country's borders.

By railing against change and putting the dampers on managerial adaptations at the SABC and Springbok Radio, Afrikaner conservatives played into the hands of D&M and LMR. The more that Calvinists insisted on maintaining the status quo, or on reverting to 'tradition', the greater the disjuncture between a largely mythical past and the realities of the modern world grew. As the decade unfolded, LMR's need to find additional marketing ammunition waned simply because the AB and SABC were intent on firing a double-barrelled shotgun into their own palpably flat feet. In 1969, a special synod of the NGK in the rural northern Transvaal not only took exception to advertisements being aired on Springbok Radio on Sundays and Christian holy days, but also to the fact that alcohol was marketed at all.[85]

For some country folk and old-timers in the National Party, the

'Boer War' and the struggle against the English had never quite ended. At the Free State provincial congress in 1967, complaints about English being advantaged over Afrikaans on Springbok Radio were so heartfelt and insistent that Prime Minister John Vorster was forced to take up the issue with the SABC. It was only after certain advertising and marketing realities had been put to him, privately, that he reluctantly backed off the issue. Other old-order stalwarts on the SABC board fretted about how LMR and Springbok Radio seemed to be 'anglicising' coloureds, who were becoming harder to reach via mother-tongue Afrikaans.[86]

But the angst of rural conservatives, who craned their necks when peering into the mists of culture in the hope of dispatching the last of the retreating redcoats, paled in comparison with the pain experienced by those who had sneaked a glimpse of a future that indicated the coming of a multicultural, if not a multiracial, hell. For them and the SABC management, the entire decade was ruined by popular music – everything from jazz to rock and roll – with lyrics in the language of their one-time conquerors and the modern masters of the urban marketplace. The executive of the FAK wanted to know from the SABC board why preference seemed to be given to American rather than more tolerable European jazz, and what percentage of 'beat music' played by the SABC was American.[87]

Small-scale cultural skirmishes led by a few noisy ideologues did little to unsettle the 'modernists' in control of the Auckland Park fortress, who simply listened respectfully to their complaints, waved them on and then effectively ignored them. But then, late in 1966, a cultural storm of global proportions buffeted the SABC belfry in a way that just could not be ignored and demanded a full-blown authoritarian response.

John Lennon's suggestion that the Beatles were 'more popular than Jesus' drove the chairman of the SABC and his Board of Governors bats precisely because, subliminally, it linked the corporation's puritan approach to the genre of music that appealed most to LMR listeners – the station that had been stealing the state broadcaster's lunch for close on three decades. Lennon's challenge was so profound and so well publicised that polite deflections of the usual sort were out of the question. The churches, the conservatives and even Brother Piet Meyer, ultra-modernist that he was, demanded the raw red meat of revenge.

The board banned the playing of any Beatles music on any of its radio stations. The following year, in another gesture to those withdrawing into the laager of white civilisation in what felt like the coming of the Black Death, the SABC extended the ban to what it could not define but nevertheless termed all 'hippy music'.[88] And, in the offices of D&M and the LMR studios, teams of surgeons could not remove the knowing grins that followed instantly. The state broadcaster, supposedly set on maintaining its niche in the marketplace via Springbok Radio, had, yet again, executed the old nose-and-face trick to largely muted applause.

Piet Meyer and his senior managers at the SABC remained preoccupied with the allegedly deleterious effect of 'hippy culture' and popular music on 'the youth' throughout the 1960s and well into the 1970s. LMR's output, drawing on a musical repertoire that appealed to the young in a supposedly decadent Western world, was increasingly at odds with the political climate in the country. 'South Africa' – that mythical entity – was intent not on relaxing and enjoying its growing affluence but on mobilising young and old alike for the coming war between black and white nationalists. LMR was seen as part of a fifth column operating from beyond the border and, more than ever before, its demoralising pop output needed to be reined in, if not stopped entirely.

But the seriousness of the position in greater southern Africa had long since moved beyond a conflict of cultures, and Meyer knew it. In late 1964, Frelimo formally committed itself to military operations against Portuguese forces in northern Mozambique. Within weeks, in early January 1965, Meyer informed the SABC governors of his need to conduct 'urgent talks' on certain – unspecified – matters 'in Lisbon'.

It was around that time that Rudolf Hess's one-time skiing partner, hitherto content with being cultural commissar of an imagined 'nation', placed himself on a full war footing. Meyer promoted himself to the informal, self-created positions of censor-in-chief for inland broadcasting and minister of radio warfare throughout southern Africa. His new roles were at the cutting edge of the unfolding situation and well in keeping with the radically changing times – an undeclared civil war around competing ideologies at home, and a hot war developing along the country's borders. As fine a reader of the personal power relationships within the upper echelons of the ruling National Party as ever there was, Meyer, in his own way, was merely anticipating the significance of the promotion of another strongman, PW Botha, to the key Ministry of Defence, in 1966. The two men were peas in a pod.

No longer confined to cultural issues but responsible for more wide-ranging decisions, Meyer sensed the need to beef up the SABC's Board of Governors with a credible, senior appointee who did not come from within the ranks of the Unseen Elect.[89] What he needed most, now that not only the Afrikaner nation but the entire country was at risk, was an English-speaking heat-seeking missile who could be deployed in the political struggle among the whites. His new man would help sniff out the witting, or unwitting, proponents of 'communism' along with their handmaidens – floppy, university-based liberals. Together, he and a latter-day Joe McCarthy would keep the airwaves safe for 'the nation'.

Professor Brian Bradshaw was a publicly committed ideologue with conservative views that bordered on the daft. Based in the small university town of Grahamstown, 12 miles from the village of Salem, in the eastern Cape Province, Bradshaw could sniff out 'leftist' and 'liberal' witches at a rate that would have been the envy of any activist in 17th-century rural Massachusetts. Born in Bolton, Lancashire, and the head of fine arts at Rhodes University, Bradshaw enjoyed a distinguished career as an artist. He had attended the Royal College of Art, won the prestigious Prix de Rome and, in 1955, been appointed vice chairman of a British parliamentary committee on art education. Disillusioned with art education in leftish post-war Britain, he had emigrated to the politically more congenial South Africa. But it was not his artistic prowess that had first attracted Meyer to Bradshaw but rather his paper on 'Communism in Western Culture' presented to the 'People's Congress' on 'Christianity vs Communism' in Pretoria in 1964.[90] The Bible was up against any hidden Bolsheviks.

Bradshaw, as bold and charismatic as he was devious and treacherous, did his mentor and the SABC board proud as he set about defending his adopted country from what he saw as whites undermining the status quo. Minutes of a meeting held in March 1968 recorded his proclivities:

> Proceeding, Prof. Bradshaw said he had in the past submitted the names of personalities he was convinced, because of evidence, were working against South African interests – and therefore should not be given the use of the broadcasting channels. Some of these people had been involved in political subversive activities which had necessitated investigation by the Security Police.

Some of those he had named had nevertheless managed 'to get themselves on the Corporation's channels', including a member of his own department at Rhodes, the watercolourist Alfred Ewan.[91]

The SABC regional manager, Buncher, had slipped up, and then, a year later, damn, he did so again. Ewan had somehow managed to gain access to the local channel. Bradshaw, clearly irritated, reminded the board that the unfortunate Ewan was 'a very peculiar personality' whom he 'considered to be 100% undesirable'. It took one of Meyer's managerial enforcers, Douglas Fuchs, to explain why a paperless system sometimes failed, and to remind the good Professor of how blacklisting worked: 'For obvious reasons, the Corporation does not issue a list of banned persons. A word of caution was usually passed on verbally to the official concerned. He would certainly follow up on the matter and would privately speak to Mr Buncher.'[92]

Bradshaw never wanted for company. Meyer, a graduate in ethics, liked being surrounded by pliant academics who shared his philosophy of robust patriotic nationalism. Professor PFD Weiss, past chair of the South African Academy for Science and Arts, was another hand-picked culture warrior willing to share what he had picked up through an ear trumpet pressed up firmly against the door of the modern world. After listening to a play by Günter Grass that had somehow sneaked through the fine mesh that by then covered all microphones in Auckland Park, Weiss suggested that it would probably be better if none of the clearly 'leftist' German's works were aired.[93]

By the mid-1960s, the corporation had been carefully piloted into a position about as far away from Reith's original moorings as the *Titanic* was from a safe berth in the western Atlantic. But the bottom was still some way off, and just in case anybody was confused about the direction in which things were moving, a new sign pointing in the direction of authoritarian centralism loomed out of the murky depths.

The idea of a 'Board of Governors' guiding the corporation's fortunes smacked of an old-style, gentlemanly British imperial structure. It was out of keeping with the nature of the new war machine Meyer was busy forging. The lightweight paper remains of the old 'Board of Governors' were stashed away somewhere in a safe room, and the 'Board of Control' was born.[94] Control was all-important if the sort of purified unity of purpose between body and mind that the ruling Afrikaner Christian nationalists aspired to was ever to be achieved.

Ministers of religion in churches – mostly English – who dared link Christianity to liberalism or, God forbid, non-racialism were placed on a watch list and prevented from broadcasting allegedly subversive sermons.[95] Any fuzziness in the thinking of untutored secular minds was dispelled by broadcasting 'editorials' on 'Current Affairs' that faithfully reflected nationalist policies.[96] And, within the tower block at Auckland Park, younger female employees who failed to see the link between dress and decadence were saved from a moral implosion when the panoptical Board of Control banned the wearing of miniskirts.[97]

Important as they were, Carnaby Street skirt lengths were not the most serious threat the republic had to face through the 1960s, and Meyer and Minister of Defence PW Botha knew it. The cultural and political struggle being waged against 'communists' and 'liberals' – part of an ideological contest between unevenly matched forces on the home front – was one thing; a mounting guerrilla war being fought along the country's long borders and against Portugal, in Mozambique, was another.

But not everyone agreed with Botha. In 1971, Colonel van der Hoven of the 'Military Medical Institute' delivered a hellfire lecture at a Dutch Reformed church on the evil influence that 'psychedelic music' had on the minds of the young. He encouraged ministers of religion to protest about it, in writing, to the SABC, which apparently remained unaware of the hidden dangers. The Board of Control was not convinced but, to stay on the right side of the Church, issued a press statement reiterating its policy on pop music and reminding ideological militants that it had put a stop to all SABC stations playing any music from *Jesus Christ Superstar*.[98]

Meyer, however, was closer to van der Hoven on the music issue than he was to PW Botha. For Meyer, the war within and the war without called for a united effort to defend 'the nation' against all its enemies. The civil war included arm-wrestling with LMR about pop culture and the fate of the 'nation's' white youth. And, yes, the Border War was possibly about body bags and the survival of the republic, but, because the conflicts could not be separated that easily, Meyer saw the opportunity of linking the corporation's 30-year struggle against LMR to the war along the borders of the republic and in neighbouring Mozambique. The Board of Control might not beat LMR in the marketplace, but if the SABC advanced behind the shield of the South African Defence Force (SADF), it would leave GJ McHarry (Pty) Ltd and his infernal machine, D&M, weakened and vulnerable to a takeover bid. It was not a question of the military or money; it was the military *and* money.

Within weeks of Frelimo's going to war in Mozambique in 1964, Meyer signalled to the South African government the need for the republic to guard against the possibility of LMR's falling into the hands of an ideologically hostile force, and the need to prevent it from gaining access to the airwaves via a backdoor. But Prime Minister Verwoerd, aware of Meyer's assertiveness and influence within the Broederbond, and of the danger of compromising existing defence and military agreements with Portugal, would not allow Meyer to deal directly with the government in Lisbon. All he was willing to allow was for Meyer to conduct negotiations directly with GJ McHarry (Pty) Ltd and RCM.

Meyer approached the head of RCM – a military man – and asked him to forward an offer of undisclosed financial proportions to the nominally retired Gabby McHarry. But D&M and LMR, riding the crest of an economic wave driven by the winds of popularity and profitability, were in an exceptionally strong position. Senior partners at D&M and LMR were unenthusiastic about an SABC takeover and, according to Piet Meyer, began making 'excessive' demands of the corporation. Always more of a stick than a carrot man, Meyer then broke off negotiations and, taking his lead from Europe, began toying with the idea of a Radio Amendment Act aimed at curbing the activities of so-called pirate stations, even though LMR itself was hardly an offshore station, like Radio Caroline, but was located in a neighbouring state.

Complying with the letter of Verwoerd's instruction not to negotiate directly with the Portuguese government, Meyer found a way of getting his head halfway out of the noose. On a visit to Lisbon, in early 1965, he had a lengthy discussion with the well-connected Dr Solar Allegro, a former secretary of Salazar's, then in charge of radio. Meyer put to him the same proposition that he had peddled in Mozambique – that the two countries should cooperate and run LMR in a way that would ensure that RCM would not incur any financial loss and control its output of popular music. Allegro said neither yea nor nay, deflecting the discussion, pointing out that Portugal was contemplating new legislation that would govern broadcasting throughout its empire.[99]

Back home, Meyer pushed for a 'Radio Pirate Bill', as he was wont to refer to it, with renewed vigour. Prime Minister Verwoerd, like John Vorster, who succeeded him in 1966, continued to keep Brother Meyer, whose appetite for control knew few bounds, and who had already bullied his minister, Albert Hertzog, into convening a select committee of parliament to consider the proposed legislation, at arm's length.[100]

In the months that followed, the select committee sat twice. On each occasion it took evidence from Meyer, who by now was haunted not only by the possibility of LMR eventually falling into the hands of a 'communist' Frelimo. He also dreaded the prospect of being encircled by politically 'hostile' broadcasting emanating from the former British crown colonies that were about to become independent, as they duly did – Botswana and Lesotho in 1966 and Swaziland in 1968.[101]

Verwoerd and Vorster, increasingly hard-pressed when it came to challenging domestic and regional political developments, were irritated by Meyer's insistently contrived interventions that stemmed from the inability of ministers to control him effectively. So, whenever they got the chance, they rapped him across the knuckles just to refresh his memory as to the pecking order. Verwoerd complained when the SABC aired the national anthem during a programme on Louis Botha without having received prior clearance from his office. Vorster told Meyer that he needed to re-examine his ambitious plans to expand the SABC's external service to promote apartheid policies abroad.[102]

Meyer did everything in his power to push first Verwoerd and then – after Verwoerd's assassination in September 1966 – Vorster to get the 'pirate radio' legislation onto the statute books as speedily as possible.¹⁰³ The Prime Minister and a stream of influential cabinet ministers were entertained at lavish official lunches on the ridge, where they were invited to inspect the facilities and listen to SABC stations speaking in tongues, to almost as many 'nations' within the country's borders as there were across the entire African continent, about the supposed advantages of racial separation.

At select committee hearings, flanked by fellow Broederbonders and other politicians, Meyer – in keeping with the style of white South Africa's 'hard men' like PW Botha – was all realpolitik, blazing away about the potentially poisonous soundwaves that threatened to infiltrate the republic not only from across the country's borders but, apparently, from even beyond its territorial waters!¹⁰⁴ Back on the ridge, however, in the boardroom and before trusted academic supplicants, Meyer was happier to release the private demons that danced away to LMR's hated 'beat music' beneath the topmost floor of his Calvinist consciousness.

The unofficial minister of radio warfare – hoping to match what the Minister of Defence was doing by putting ever more agents on the ground across borders – longed to stem the nation's aural vulnerability by stuffing its ears with parliamentary order papers. But he appeared to be making little, if any, progress. Back at Fort Auckland Park his embarrassment and frustration were becoming increasingly palpable. 'The Corporation', he informed his all-male choir, in 1968, 'had on two different occasions given evidence to a select committee of Parliament and the reasonableness of its case had been appreciated.' But clearly not by the party's whips. 'The bill', he lamented, 'had been introduced and for two successive years had only got as far as a first reading.'¹⁰⁵

Weeks later, Meyer set out on a European tour, attempting primarily to cultivate as many political and professional men of standing as possible in the world of broadcasting and to expand the reach of the SABC's ambitious 'external services'. At a time when apartheid policies were slamming closed more office doors than they ever opened, he preened and prattled his way through ten besuited capitals, including London. But, restrained by his hated prime-ministerial leash, he could not get as far as Lisbon. Back in the boardroom the gap in his itinerary was so obvious that even Prof Weiss felt the need to hum a tune that he did not really know the words of.[106] The board reminded Meyer, who needed no reminding, that all roads to military and political realities, and his unwavering determination to control LMR's pop music, led to Lisbon.

But it was not only the SABC's Board of Control that was tracking Meyer's movements across the northern hemisphere with interest. Davenport & Meyer, with its long-standing presence in London, and LMR, with connections of its own in Lisbon, knew almost instantly what was afoot. Piet Meyer was preparing the way for Portugal to revoke the McHarry concession and bring LMR under direct government control.

Military and political developments unfolding in Angola, South West Africa and Mozambique – in particular Frelimo's war of liberation – had become the minister of radio warfare's principal argument for revoking LMR's licence. But, as we will see shortly, there was an important secondary consideration that was never far from his mind – his obsessive dislike of the 'beat music' that tilted the Sunday-night war in LMR's favour. It was Ringo Starr and others of his ilk from Britain and the US that bashed away at Piet Meyer's exposed eardrums until he felt like a victim of tinnitus.

At LMR, where Meyer's earlier attempt to buy the station had simply been brushed aside, news of an impending diplomatic-political onslaught to get the McHarry concession revoked gave rise to new and deep-seated concerns. Fending off Auckland Park nonsense about pop music and the fall of Western civilisation was amusing. But talk of LMR one day – soon – handing Frelimo the key to the back door of black South Africans' political consciousness was not. Only a fool would confuse the SABC and the SADF. So unspoken new guidelines sidled into place. LMR presenters remained free to present the tops of the pops as they saw fit, but there was never to be so much as a badly chosen word, or a stray comment, that even hinted at the fact that Pretoria presided over a morally indefensible, deeply repressive racist regime.

When GJ McHarry's grandson Patrick arrived at LMR to try his luck as a disc jockey, in late 1968, the fog of fear had already permeated every corridor in the Radio Palace. 'There was', he later recalled, 'a paranoia among the broadcasting staff to avoid any reporting or commenting on news or current affairs.' It was already 'part of the corporate culture' and it was not 'imposed from the top'. He simply 'picked up on the practice through conversations with my peers'.[107] South African-style censorship was stretching out across the border.

By then, however, it was not only the menace posed from beyond by Meyer that threatened the concession and the company that managed it. There were internal problems as well. Like many privately owned family businesses, GJ McHarry (Pty) Ltd had to deal with the problem of succession as the company's founder aged and a change of leadership loomed. Gabby McHarry was slowing down, and the holding company was already being partly run by his son Trevor. Trevor did his best for several years, but he was an alcoholic and he and his father both died in 1975.[108] LMR was becoming more vulnerable, and in the Broederbond barracks on the hill they sensed it.

In the early part of the 19th century, a Prussian general who had once engaged Napoleon's troops at Borodino came up with an observation that was eventually to become a classic of its kind. 'War', Carl von Clausewitz famously suggested, was 'a mere continuation of politics by other means.' The general might as well have been writing about southern Africa. The wars in Angola and Mozambique gave Meyer what two prime ministers had pointedly denied him – direct, high-level access to an increasingly hard-pressed government in Lisbon.[109]

The Hertzog Tower was the unusual setting for what seemed like a most unlikely gathering, on 11 February 1969. Minister of Defence PW Botha, who did not attend the lunch, had asked Meyer and four senior generals drawn from the South African Air Force and Army to host a meeting with General Horácio José de Sá Viana Rebelo, Portugal's influential Minister of Defence (1968–1973). Rebelo and entourage were so puzzled by the strange choice of venue and Piet Meyer's role in military business that curiosity trumped the need for diplomacy. Lunch had barely commenced when Rebelo asked Meyer why the SABC had been asked to host the meeting. And in that instant, the door to Lisbon, long closed to the unofficial minister of radio warfare, creaked open.

Chairman Meyer, presiding over a team of house-trained academic dogs capable of sniffing out domestic 'communism' and 'liberalism', strode in. Meyer told Rebelo about how closely the SABC cooperated with the SADF. He then elaborated on how such work could form part of a coordinated, international effort throughout a region beset by anti-colonial struggles. Starters dispatched, Rebelo clearly relished the ideological main course but hardly had time to settle back into his chair before dessert was pressed on him.[110]

Meyer raised the issue of LMR and the McHarry concession, suggesting that Portugal use any revised broadcasting legislation to turn RCM into a statutory body falling directly under state control. Rebelo, far more interested in Angola, was not much taken with the idea of controlling LMR. It seemed like a side issue, but he had heard enough to invite Meyer to address a cabinet committee when next he visited Lisbon. Within days Meyer, delighted by what he described as the potentially 'fruitful' talks with Rebelo, informed the SABC board of his intention of going to Portugal to build on what had been achieved.[111]

But Meyer realised that going to Lisbon bearing only the gift of cooperation with Portugal's army in the southwestern Africa theatre would not give him the leverage needed to prise the McHarry concession off RCM. Carnations were all well and good for Angola, but what was needed in Mozambique was a crowbar, the one the government had been denying him for years, the 'pirate radio act'. So, six weeks later, in April 1969, he had another go at the party whips, who agreed to amend the Broadcasting Act so that the SABC could erect transmission stations 'outside the borders of the Republic'. But they remained unwilling to pass legislation that would allow cross-border stations to be deemed 'pirate stations' and subjected to sanctions.[112]

Shortly thereafter, Meyer drafted, in English, the awkwardly worded but remarkably forthright 20-page document that formed the basis of his opening exchange in Lisbon, in mid-1969.[113] The outline, although incomplete, was important enough for Meyer to keep a copy in his personal papers, but a record of the secret negotiations that followed appears not to have been preserved anywhere in South Africa. It also earned him a sharpish rebuke, from Dr Hilgard Muller, the Minister of Foreign Affairs, that he should take care not to get involved in any issues best dealt with through regular diplomatic channels.[114]

Meyer opened the discussion with a brief history of the SABC, only mentioning, much later, the original oversight that 'led to the private station Lourenço Marques, beginning to direct a commercial service on [sic] the Republic in 1936, when an advertising service was still illegal in South Africa'. The consequences were significant since the 'SABC has no shareholders and acquires its income from licence fees and advertising'. The exception was Radio Bantu, aimed at black South Africans, which was underwritten by a subsidy from the government because 'military and police action has little or no meaning unless the indigenous population accept that the rulers of the country are there to protect them and to lead them to greater maturity'. It stood to reason that cooperation around military and police operations was also of importance regionally. External services, too, were most important and South Africa had 'already gained a lead on Moscow and Peking'.[115]

The SABC had a clear duty to safeguard the country's people 'against physical attacks or attacks on the mind'. South Africa was a 'bastion of the west' and its contribution to the preservation of culture and the economy had to be acknowledged. Among white South Africans those ideas had 'already taken root', but there was no room for complacency. More disciplined thought was necessary when it came to 'the struggle between the liberalistic and conservative schools of thought for the control over the minds of the people'. Radio helped gain the 'approval, sympathy and active participation of the population for the preservation of the way of live [sic], form of government etc. of our country'.[116]

Having unveiled a philosophy that, he believed, was shared by Portugal's beleaguered imperialists, Meyer launched a direct assault on the independence of RCM and LMR, coupling old diplomatic and legal agreements to his current political nightmares. At an international conference in Geneva, in 1936, it had been agreed that countries would refrain from broadcasting 'false information' calculated to incite neighbouring populations, thereby undermining 'good international relations'. In essence, that agreement, he argued, had been reconfirmed by the United Nations General Assembly, in 1954, and supplemented by the International Telecommunications Convention agreed upon in 1972 to which both Portugal and South Africa had been signatories.[117]

According to Meyer, who cited no jurisprudence, it meant that 'no private undertaking [could] erect transmitting stations outside the borders of the country concerned and broadcast programmes to that country', and that should it do so, it qualified as a 'pirate station'. The South African government was contemplating passing legislation to deal with precisely such cases. It was true that LMR currently focused 'on entertainment only', but the potential for trouble was heightened by the fact that the station derived almost all its income from South African advertisers and was managed by 'a firm in Johannesburg'. That company accounted to neither the government of Portugal nor that of South Africa, and when its 'programme presentation' (was) 'analysed soberly and objectively' it was quite clear that it would 'not necessarily agree with the policy of the SABC'. Decoded, LMR's playing of pop music that offended white South African Calvinist sensitivities, including the Sunday-night broadcasts, might jeopardise pending loan agreements, joint military operations and political cooperation between two countries already locked into wars of liberation.

For Meyer and the Unseen Elect the way round the impasse was clear. RCM and its shareholding partner, the Mozambican administration, could not be asked to make any financial sacrifices, but LMR needed to be placed firmly under the control of the government in Lisbon:

> [I]t stands to reason that it would be logical that an agreement between the official Portuguese Radio authorities and the SABC, which is responsible for all public broadcasts in South Africa, should be entered into. In this manner, Radio Lourenço Marques can be assured of a fixed income, but not under the control of a concessionary and a private firm in Johannesburg, but on the contrary, to the benefit of the Portuguese radio in co-operation with the SABC, in a manner which is agreeable with the programme policy which is accepted for listeners in South Africa.[118]

It was an outrageous suggestion. International conventions and laws were cited, and twisted, to allow for a financial arrangement to be entered into, not between governments but between radio 'authorities' in the two countries. It would occur without the prior consent of either the concession holder or the company managing its business, both privately owned. And all that to accommodate the aspirations of a man so fixed on the idea of controlling all the airwaves across southern Africa that two prime ministers had refused to provide him with the enabling legislation, backed by sanctions, that would allow for direct government-to-government negotiations against the backdrop of war.

If any such agreement were reached, in addition to addressing the political concerns that would inevitably arise, it would pander to a bullying, obsessive and sinister individual. Meyer presided over a powerful secret brotherhood and chaired a state-owned corporation dominated by a board richly endowed with informers and enforcers. Between them, they took it upon themselves to stifle legitimate political opposition to apartheid policies. They indulged fears about the dangers posed by 'beat music' and the real or imagined deficiencies of Western culture and 'liberalism' that bordered on the cranky, if not delusional.

The Portuguese government had bigger fish to fry than LMR's output of popular music. But it was unwilling to dismiss Meyer's offer of cooperation on other fronts out of hand. In any case, what did it stand to lose by offering RCM a steady stream of income in a strong currency in return for reining in LMR's output of supposedly offensive music? But more important, by far, was the fact that the push from the South Africans could not have come at a more awkward moment for Portugal, and Botha and Meyer both knew it. Indeed, the timing of their combined assault on LMR was most unlikely to have been entirely coincidental. There was a bit of history to Meyer's 1969 grab for RCM.

By 1968, after a hesitant start that had included a visit to Lisbon by PW Botha during the previous year, the Portuguese military had become increasingly willing to accept South African air support for a war in southern Angola that it was in danger of losing. And a year after that, in March 1969, the South African Minister of Defence was back in Lisbon arguing for increased military cooperation in southern Africa.[119]

Equally telling, however, was Portugal's need to accept financial aid from Pretoria, a development that dated back to a loan for a hydro-electric project in Angola in 1966. What was most revealing about Botha's 1969 visit, however, was how closely a proposed loan of R50 million was tied to military assistance and other South African support that included the development of the Caborra Bassa dam project in Mozambique. But, in May 1969, round about the time that Meyer was urging Portugal to take control of RCM and LMR, Botha had told his Portuguese counterpart, Meyer's one-time guest in the Hertzog Tower, General Rebelo, that South Africa could only provide Lisbon with half the sum originally agreed upon.[120] Portugal was on the back foot.

Nor – one now suspects – was it merely by chance that, in the memorandum used as the basis for his presentation in Portugal, in 1969, Meyer cited the Caborra Bassa project and the dealings of the Bank of Lisbon as fine examples of 'co-operation' between the two countries.[121] In truth, Meyer's biggest assault on the McHarry concession, D&M and LMR came at a moment when Portugal was financially and militarily most vulnerable, and he rode into battle on the coat-tails of PW Botha.

The Pyrrhic Victory and Financial Implosion of LMR, circa 1969–1975

Tracing the negotiations that took place between the government of Portugal, the Radio Clube de Moçambique, Davenport & Meyer and GJ McHarry, on the one hand, and the SABC, on the other, well into the year that followed upon Meyer's aggressive presentation in Lisbon, in 1969, is difficult. It may not be important beyond noting, as we already have done, that the talks did not take place among equals.

The government of Portugal – financially vulnerable and weak – was the majority shareholder in RCM. David Davies, the formidable entrepreneurial and financial force who chaired the board of D&M, had retired to England in 1969 where he died of cancer, aged 59, in 1974, while Gabby McHarry no longer managed his company fully. Meyer and the SABC, backed by the threat of the 'Radio Amendment Bill', which, if passed would outlaw 'pirate stations' – loosely interpreted and across southern Africa – still had access to the financial largesse of the 1960s as well as the ear of the government and a dog-whistle board.

By late 1970, Lisbon, unable to hold the line in a dirty little commercial war amid the all-too-real liberation struggles taking place in its African colonies, including Mozambique, had drawn all the interested parties on its side of the fence into line and was ready to concede. It was a potentially embarrassing and humiliating defeat, and all Portugal asked of the victor was that it agree to contain the political damage by maintaining as much secrecy as possible in the deal that would follow.

Meyer, for his part, had little to take credit for personally, or to be particularly proud of. The prizes he lusted after most – additional advertising revenue and, more especially, control of popular culture, which in his eyes threatened to soften the ideological resilience of Afrikaner youth fighting to protect apartheid – had been presented to him not by his beloved National Party but by black liberation fighters. It was only in 1970 that, for the first time in its history, the SABC's revenue from advertising was greater than that from licence fees.[122]

When negotiations for the takeover of LMR were at an advanced stage, Meyer reluctantly began sharing information with the SABC board, but only marginally more openly. 'The Portuguese government', he told members, 'would like to avoid unjustified and harmful publicity, particularly from other African countries, to the effect that Portugal will allow South Africa to take over a radio service in Portuguese territory.' The income from LMR, subject to the approval of the cabinet minister the board reported to, would be divided, on a percentage basis that he did not disclose, with GJ McHarry (Pty) Ltd for a period of ten years.[123]

Given Lisbon's sensitivities amid the anti-colonial struggles it was facing, the lack of detailed information about the way that politics and economics were shaping a tacky deal was perhaps unsurprising. Board members certainly felt no need to press the chairman for particulars about the possible financial implications of the revenue-sharing aspect of the proposed contract – an omission that they may later have had reason to regret. Meyer was, however, much more forthcoming about the bee that had been buzzing in his bonnet for decades – how to exercise greater control over the musical dimension of popular culture.

Meyer said that the corporation was pushing for an agreement, the terms of which would include

> full control of the programme content of the service and over the staff of Lourenço Marques [being] granted to the SABC so that without changing the basic nature of the service, a channel for pop music would be available to the SABC. The agreement must also be written in such a manner that by way of mutual consent control could be exercised over standard of acceptability, selection of records etc. [124]

If the evolving, secretive terms were agreed to in full, Meyer would preside over a variant of the Calvinist radio heaven that he had long dreamt of. And if the details of the agreement could be fully or partially concealed, neither the advertisers nor the listening public need be any the wiser about the mutation in character that the station would undergo. LMR would, hopefully, be politically neutered for a decade, and such pop music as did reach South Africa would have been subjected to prior censorship. It was neocolonialism of a type that might fool the deaf and the truly dumb.

Three months later, in February 1971, Meyer was ready to share a few titbits of information about the impending deal with the academic wise men and patriots who constituted a board that supposedly served as the nation's broadcasting watchdog. Board members were fed morsels of contradictory information that did not appear to trouble them unduly.

After an opening prayer, they were told that negotiations with RCM were going well and that the 'final contract will naturally be submitted to the Board for approval and then be forwarded to the Minister of National Education [to whom Meyer then reported] for confirmation by the cabinet'. The board members, it seemed, were to be charged and trusted with making the decision. In what passed for a democracy, all appeared to be in order.[125]

But, within minutes, the tone of the meeting, as well as the process being proposed, mutated in surprising fashion. Exempted from sniffing out communists and liberals for the day, the board dogs were in relaxed mood. They were content with a pat on the head and a promise from the chairman that, once all was done, they would be fed 'a detailed report as well as copies of the final contract for their information'. The relevant supporting documents and final contract would be 'for their information' rather than for their prior approval. 'In the meantime,' Meyer said, 'information and documents will be made available to Senator van der Spuy [his minister] to finalise the matter and make the appropriate announcements.' There was no barking, just tails wagging in unison, and all was well within white South Africa's 'democracy'.[126]

Emboldened, Meyer pushed on. The deceit and secrecy surrounding a deal that, in the final analysis, would be agreed between the governments of Portugal and South Africa, though fronted by the SABC and

RCM, would be maintained: 'The announcement that Springbok Radio will, in future, act as commercial manager for LMR, should prevent the Portuguese government being forced into an embarrassing position by international publicity.' The board should not be too concerned about the financial aspects of the deal since 'initially the SABC [would] guarantee the income from advertising and the corporation could expect approximately R100 000 per annum'.[127]

A month later, in March 1971, the South African cabinet agreed to Meyer's scheme but wanted no further official part of the business, other than to be reassured that he had secured the written agreement of the government in Lisbon. He had, a month earlier. Van der Spuy went public with the fiction about the management by Springbok Radio, and 'No further information needed to be made known.'[128] But it was. Within weeks a journalist was on to the story, plotting, as best he could, the semi-public dimensions of what clearly was a very secretive deal.

Both McHarry and D&M, if they were to be believed, were caught completely by surprise, simply taken aback, by RCM's handing over the concession for the functioning of LMR to 'Springbok Radio' – in reality, the SABC. David Pinnell and Leslie Bonnell, resident directors of D&M, claimed that van der Spuy took 'them completely by surprise' but 'declined to answer any inquiries'. They were also at pains to hide the extent of the profits that D&M derived from LMR – estimated to be around R750 000 per annum (about R50 million in today's terms). The blanket of silence smacked of Piet Meyer-enforced secrecy.[129]

The apparently 'sudden' marginalisation of D&M by the Portuguese authorities gave the SABC and Springbok Radio effective control of LMR's managerial and operational functions, something that Meyer had been lusting after for close on a decade. What it did not do, however, was immediately terminate D&M's profit-sharing arrangement with Gabby McHarry, then 78, who was cast as a multimillionaire 'tycoon'. In a rare interview, when asked whether he had made R5 million or R10 million out of LMR over the years, he said, 'I would rather not give any figure.' He also appeared to be strangely sanguine about recent developments. 'Well,' he said, when pushed, 'I have had a good run for my money.'[130] The founder must have known that GJ McHarry (Pty) Ltd would be the next item on Meyer's state-funded shopping list; all he had to do was to wait for the right offer.

However, within days of the SABC's takeover of LMR being made known, the full financial implications of the deal began to creep through the lofty tower perched on the Auckland Park heights. RCM remained responsible for all infrastructural and maintenance costs at the Radio Palace, but there were new developmental costs that would have to be met from the South African side of the border. Meyer got Pretoria to agree to fund an FM transmitter that would allow the SABC to broadcast LMR to a wider audience, the understanding being that a clearer signal spread across the country's commercial heartland would produce a matching rise in advertising revenue.[131]

But the economically buoyant 1960s were largely a thing of the past. By the end of 1971, it was becoming ever clearer that the SABC was unable to generate as much advertising revenue for LMR as had been produced by D&M, which itself had seen a decline in sales over the past three years. That decline had taken place during the very period when Meyer had been pushing so hard to acquire the station while, simultaneously, being parsimonious with the financial information that he was willing to share with his politically compliant but economically semi-literate board. A possible solution, as he saw it, would call for a little more chicanery:

> [T]he SABC would have to continue or intensify [the D&M] effort if sales were to be maintained. For this reason and in order to maintain an impression of independence as far as advertising agents were concerned, and in order to preserve the continuity in the sales effort, it would be highly desirable for the SABC to employ some of the sales staff presently working for Lourenço Marques Radio.[132]

But the problems did not end there. LMR's commercial success had not gone unnoticed in the former British protectorates. Botswana, Lesotho and Swaziland were already looking around for ways of funding their own, potentially militantly African nationalist and wretchedly independent broadcasting services. Meyer had just extinguished what he saw as a spark capable of starting a fire in Lourenço Marques that might threaten civilisation and proper order in South Africa when new dangers began flickering from across other borders. He began to fret about the possibility of Gaborone, Maseru and Mbabane becoming bases, using advertising revenue drawn from the same white commercial heartland of the subcontinent, not only to play decadent, morale-sapping pop music but to underwrite inflammatory propaganda directed at black nationalists operating in South Africa.[133]

For Meyer, the problem of 'hostile' broadcasts from neighbouring states was irritating twice over. He had foreseen the problem and provided a possible solution years before the National Party appreciated it. Now, more than ever, his far-sighted but whip-delayed Radio Amendment Bill needed to be passed.[134] By mid-1972 he was back at his own minister, van der Spuy, and the Minister of Foreign Affairs, Hilgard Muller, and through them the Prime Minister, to get the bill enacted.[135]

Amid deteriorating financial circumstances Meyer now chose to underscore the commercial rather than the political logic of a bill that had been largely of his making. 'Naturally, the intention was not to enforce the Radio Act Amendment bill [*sic*] immediately but rather to discourage advertisers from buying advertising time on such radio stations as Radio Swazi', he told the board.[136] A few weeks later, he was more forthright with his happy hounds and a bit readier to acknowledge the deeper motivation behind what he still often referred to as the 'Piracy Act'. 'The primary objection to radio stations outside the borders of South Africa', he reminded them, 'was not that they derived advertising revenue from South Africa but that they lacked sufficient understanding of the political climate in South Africa.'[137]

But, either way, the Prime Minister was having none of it. Vorster, like Verwoerd before him, remained deeply suspicious of Meyer's hidden agenda and political manoeuvrings. As the leader of the Unseen Elect, and a force both within the cabinet and among the rank and file of the National Party, Meyer involved himself in initiatives that cut across the defence, finance and foreign affairs portfolios in ways that had potentially embarrassing consequences for all. So, when Meyer attempted to set van der Spuy up to visit 'various organizations abroad', Vorster put the plan on hold, allegedly only for logistical reasons.[138]

Meyer, sensing that GJ McHarry (Pty) Ltd, by then managed by troubled son Trevor, was increasingly vulnerable after the death of the original concessionaire, moved to further extend the SABC's control of LMR. In June 1972, seemingly without prior notice, he informed the board that the 'SABC had undertaken to buy out the interests of GJ McHarry and that it would involve a sum of R110 000' (about R7 million in today's terms). If previous estimates of McHarry's wealth were anything to go by, it was cheap at the price. Yet again, there was no barking from board members but perhaps less tail-twitching.[139]

The chairman's fixation on acquiring and controlling the entire LMR supply chain was, however, becoming increasingly expensive just as funding was becoming more difficult to acquire via advertising, licence fees and a state subsidy. At that same board meeting, Meyer informed his rubber-stamps that 'the SABC' had guaranteed RCM a monthly income of R60 000, which meant that – by the end of 1972 – about R450 000 would have to be transferred to Lourenço Marques. For a sum of that size to be moved, authorisation from the Reserve Bank was necessary. Meyer needed some additional cover and was granted the board's permission to seek the necessary authorisation.[140]

In good times there is often far more room for flexibility when it comes to reconciling the complementary worlds of economics and politics. Throughout the prosperous 1960s, the cabinet and the treasury had indulged Meyer's expansionist visions because radio licence fees had held steady and the National Party, just like Meyer's docile board, was happy to accommodate the SABC as an apartheid propaganda machine headed by a man it had reason both to fear and to respect. But by the 1970s, with the economy slowing, the gap between politics and economics was narrowing, leaving less room for manoeuvre and pragmatism, and Meyer was in danger of overreaching himself. Vorster and his compliant cabinet began to feel the need to rein him in further.

Some of the minister of radio warfare's self-created problems dated back to the previous year. In May 1971, during a trip to Europe, an SABC colleague phoned Meyer at his hotel in Vienna and informed him that, during his absence, the cabinet had granted a licence – along with the right to erect transmitters independently within South African borders – to Trans World Radio (TWR). In essence, TWR was not all that different from the Pan American Radio Company, which McHarry and RCM had, in the 1960s, authorised to broadcast evangelical church sermons and raise funds via LMR's twin transmitters in the wee hours after commercial operations had ceased for the day.[141]

Meyer, authoritarian and controlling to beyond his wisdom teeth, was furious. The timing of the TWR decision could not possibly have been fortuitous, 'I was never further than five minutes from a telephone', he thundered, 'and moreover, not all of the SABC was with me.' Yet again, as with the neighbouring, newly independent African states, his primary objection to the decision was not monetary – although the decision was probably not without financial consequences for the state – but was born of his need to ensure hegemonic ideological control of the airwaves in the apartheid state. TWR, said Meyer, provided a service financed and operated by a number of American churches 'not one of which supported our policies'. Here, then, was a watchdog with teeth.[142]

He took the first flight home, and within hours was in the offices of the relevant cabinet ministers. Meyer forced van der Spuy and Marais Viljoen, the Minister of Posts and Telecommunications and the man ultimately responsible for the issuing of licences, into conceding that, in terms of the existing Broadcasting Act, no new licence could be issued without the prior approval of the SABC. Suitably chastened, the ministers then accompanied Meyer to see Vorster, who, having listened to the trio and done the relevant political sums, agreed that the decision to grant TWR a licence be overturned, and it was. But it was yet one more instance of Meyer bullying the National Party cabinet into a line that complicated its position in increasingly fraught foreign affairs.[143]

The TWR debacle was not only costly in political terms for Meyer personally, but it came at a real price for the SABC. Yet again, part of the problem could be traced back to Meyer's fixation on LMR. How, having just put a stop to the TWR evangelicals doing good business in South Africa, could he look Vorster and his minister in the eye while LMR's own finances continued to be bolstered by PAR broadcasts, which included a good number of American churches that had not been subjected to strict political vetting by the SABC? It had to be set right.

So, in June 1972, the board decided that the SABC should forfeit most of the income earned from LMR via PAR because 'religion could not be viewed as a tradeable commodity' despite its deeper 'meaning and value' to so 'many listeners'. The McHarry family's personal commitment to religious broadcasts slowed down PAR's disengagement from LMR, but Meyer reassured them that the SABC would continue to allow those churches it 'found suitable' – that is, not ideologically opposed to apartheid – to retain access to its after-hours service. The board's censorship and control were extended, but it came at a price.[144]

Costly as these decisions and interventions undoubtedly were, in truth Meyer remained politically almost untouchable. The Prime Minister and ministers overseeing the SABC remained largely in the thrall of the man even as they started to apply more pressure to him.[145] Just days after the PAR decision, Meyer's power was again manifest. He wrote to Minister van der Spuy requesting an increase in radio listeners' licence fees, often a ticklish issue when it came to the white electorate. Meyer also wanted the finance for his FM-LMR scheme to be regarded as a 'fixed loan' and requested 're-imbursement for the operating expenditure of the External Services'. More troubling still, he included an outline of the capital requirements of the corporation. In short, the SABC was feeling the financial pinch and looking for more direct and indirect funding. It was enough to cause a convulsion in the cabinet.[146]

Trapped between fires closing in on him from Meyer on the one hand, and Vorster on the other, van der Spuy did not know which was the more menacing, or what to do to prevent his trousers from bursting into flames. The Vorster heat, he decided, would be hardest to bear, so he turned away from the Prime Minister and approached the SABC, going down on all fours and then crawling towards it. Meyer, as accustomed to being supplicated to as he was desirous of it, smelt the fear and quickly applied his foot to the small of van der Spuy's back. The board minutes recorded Meyer's retort to the minister's wavering approach.

Chairman Meyer explained to the board that van der Spuy 'had asked whether the SABC would permit a special committee to examine the financial position of the SABC'. 'The Chairman said that he had acceded to this request on condition that the corporation might appoint the committee.' Van der Spuy, chin to floor, agreed. A committee consisting of five members was eventually appointed – two of whom were Meyer himself and a trusted SABC sidekick, JN Swanepoel.[147]

The committee, unsurprisingly, then submitted its report to the 'Chairman of the Board of Control of the Corporation', merely underscoring all the initial financial requests and suggestions made to the minister. Thus, Meyer was a member of a committee that, with his minister's approval, reported to himself. In the end, nothing much came of the report and the SABC's finances continued to drift slowly south.

At that same meeting where, in good part, he reported to himself, Meyer – possibly sensing that he may have been overplaying his role as Tsar of all southern African broadcasting – decided that what had once been the 'Board of Governors' and then become the 'Board of Control' should in future be referred to more modestly as 'The Board'. It was not as if anyone on the board or in the government was in any doubt in whose office the ultimate source of power in the SABC resided.[148]

But there is no rest for a Tsar. It was not long before Vorster and the cabinet were again reminded that it was their patriotic duty to protect the citizens of South Africa against that poison that seeps into the mind through the ears. By 1973, it was 'Radio Freedom', the exiled outlet of the banned ANC, broadcasting from Lusaka, Zambia, that gave the Tsar the most sleepless nights. The station was not only polluting the minds of black South Africans with the idea of political freedom but, as with LMR – before it was partly SABC-neutered – it was playing music by artists such as Abdullah Ibrahim and Miriam Makeba that could not be heard on any of the domestic channels of Radio Bantu because of censorship.[149]

Radio Freedom was the old LMR nightmare come true with bells and whistles, and it sent Meyer scurrying back to his minister with the same old idea that by then he had been peddling for a decade – the 'Radio Amendment Bill', his dust-laden, much longed-for 'Piracy Act'. And it elicited the same old response from the National Party establishment. 'Apparently only two government departments had reacted against the introduction of the Radio Act Amendment Bill', Meyer informed the board, 'namely, the Department of Commerce and the Department of Foreign Affairs.'[150] Saving white South Africa from the democratic impulses of the 20th century was frustrating enough without access to the necessary funding; being thwarted politically was just depressing.

Unable to silence LMR via the 'Piracy Act' denied him by his political partners, the Tsar had eventually won control of that station with the complicity of the Portuguese political elite in the shape of RCM and the SABC's cheque book. But a dish painstakingly put together over several years to appeal to a client in Lourenço Marques would never make it to Lusaka. Zambia not only lacked a comparable class structure, with an outgoing colonial bourgeoisie, but also a broadcasting history that intersected in any way with South African interests. Moreover, the cost of having acquired the LMR chain was becoming painfully apparent.

Within the SABC's internal structures, Meyer reluctantly had to come to terms with the embarrassing fact that in LMR he, with the help of a board comprised largely of narcoleptics, might have bought a pig in a poke. Little wonder that the minister had wanted a 'special committee' to take a much closer look at the corporation's finances. At a meeting in June 1974, JN Swanepoel, Meyer's director general and trusted in-house financial wizard, disclosed the extent of the unfolding financial mess at LMR as the corporation announced a new and, it hoped, more competitive 'package basis' for advertising fees on the clearly ailing station.[151]

Between late 1972 and June 1974 – that is, 'for the past 20 months' – 'L.M. Radio's daily audience [had] dropped by 50%'. Most of that fall might, no doubt, be attributed to gradually deteriorating economic circumstances across the country, but the censorship of pop music and the dropping of many of the PAR religious programmes on LMR would not have helped. Also, having previously hiked the advertising fees on 'Radio Bantu and the Regional Services' in an ongoing search for additional funds for the SABC, commercial agents and clients had also cut back on what they had previously spent at LMR. Even Meyer must have felt the chill as Swanepoel announced that 'L.M. Radio is no longer cost-efficient and in most cases is a very uneconomical buy'.[152]

The goose that just a few years earlier had been laying golden eggs for D&M and GJ McHarry was, if not dying, showing little interest in nesting. The board by then had given the SABC 'standing approval for a bank overdraft of R500 000 [approximately R26 million today] for very short periods' – a sign of the times.[153] Meyer, who 24 months earlier had been on the financial offensive, then attempted to stage a measured retreat from the SABC's agreement with RCM/LMR, which guaranteed it a monthly income, payable in rands.

But his penchant for intervening in the affairs of the cabinet – once done out of political strength – now came back to haunt him just as the SABC's financial muscles atrophied. The Ministry of Foreign Affairs, alarmed by what it saw as the increasingly uncertain future of Mozambique, requested that the SABC not act unilaterally or be over-hasty in its attempt to cut ties with the now beleaguered RCM.[154]

The truth was that, by the early 1970s, it was no longer Portugal – with or without the assistance of South Africa – that determined the future of Mozambique, RCM and LMR but Frelimo. Village by village, district by district, and province by province, African liberation forces were reclaiming the elongated, economically emaciated, central-eastern coastline of one of the continent's oldest colonies. And, as the Frelimo forces advanced southward, the days of Mozambique acting as a frontline buffer state for the oppressive regime in Pretoria, too, were becoming numbered.

Among the first to privately acknowledge, if not publicly pronounce, that the wars in Lisbon's African colonies were no longer militarily, let alone economically or politically, sustainable, were the generals in Portugal's army. Between 1961 and 1974, the cost of the wars on the continent grew to absorb a third of Portugal's annual budget.[155] Body bags by the thousand were having to be offset against balance sheets.

Prime Minister Marcello Caetano – who had inherited the arthritic Estado Novo from his predecessor, Salazar, in 1968 – failed to understand fully how the progressive stiffening in the state's economic joints was impairing political mobility domestically or in the colonies. On 25 April 1974, the Armed Forces Movement, led by General António de Spínola, overthrew the venerable right-wing dictatorship. One of the principal objectives behind what became popularly known as the 'Carnation Revolution' was to free Portugal from its African chains.

By chance the SABC board met on the morning after the Lisbon coup, and its members looked to their politically connected, philosophically inclined and widely read chairman to inform them as to what might be in the offing in Lourenço Marques. Meyer was in a sanguine frame of mind and provided them with the necessary counsel at some length.

There was, he said, no reason to be unduly concerned. There was no sign of a civil war breaking out in Portugal, and from De Spínola's book *Portugal e o Futuro*, arguing for an end to the country's colonial wars, it was evident that he was a conservative military man who would not readily capitulate to any pressures coming from 'terrorists'. In Meyer's opinion, the solution to the country's problems lay in granting the colonies a greater measure of independence. If that happened, the local administration should be able to develop more acceptable relationships between different population groups. The SABC would therefore adopt a positive attitude as regarded the coup, and members needed to bear in mind that the Tsonga service of Radio Bantu could readily be followed and understood in several parts of Mozambique.[156]

South Africa's minister of radio warfare, hitherto on goodish terms with the Portuguese military, had offered his analysis of Lisbon's prospects and, at least as far as the SABC's Tsonga service was concerned, personally determined what the state's attitude would be when it came to the Carnation Revolution. It was not difficult to see why the Minister of Foreign Affairs and a few others were often content to 'request' and not suggest – let alone instruct – Meyer to consider their interests before taking up positions almost entirely of his own making.

But prophecy, even for a man who had once happily swapped notes with Martin Heidegger, could be a hard taskmaster, so Meyer proceeded with caution. When the Portuguese army took control of the radio transmitters in Lourenço Marques several days later, the chairman sent the corporation's advertising manager to the coast to determine to what extent the SABC's share in LMR was at risk. It was difficult to know what exactly was happening, but the board agreed that the SABC should continue 'to reflect developments in Portugal, Angola and Mozambique in a calm and balanced way'.[157] It was the SABC way.

By August 1974, however, the only thing holding together the SABC's increasingly tenuous broadcasting agreement in deeply unsettled Mozambique was the request from the Minister of Foreign Affairs for the corporation not to back out of its contract with RCM-LMR unilaterally. And then history stepped in. Mozambique's remaining European settlers, and more especially those in the Sul do Save, felt that Lisbon had betrayed them, leaving them at the mercy of

African nationalists who, for good historical reasons, had little reason to be well-disposed to most white colonists.[158]

At the economic heart of the country, in Lourenço Marques, disaffected whites, although formally leaderless and part of a glaringly inchoate mass without any clear-cut class interest, included hundreds of former security officials and soldiers who had, until recently, been responsible for enforcing the colonial order. By September 1974, this politically directionless, ill-disciplined, statist constituency was intent on declaring 'independence' from both reason and reality and mobilising for a struggle against common sense.

A long-fermenting but largely 'unorganised insurrection' started on the evening of 6 September as pamphlets 'attacking the Lourenço Marques newspapers and radio [RCM] for traitorous conduct were distributed'. The initial disturbances occurred outside the offices of the newspaper *Noticias*, which, in an attempt to reconcile the old reality of remaining profitable within a new political order, had adopted a pro-Frelimo stance. The following day, in a move smacking more of chance than conspiracy, a small crowd took control of the poorly guarded Radio Palace, using it as the base from which to promote the just-launched 'Free Mozambique Movement'. The countercoup, which saw the loss of more than 3 000 lives, mostly African, lasted just three days until the armed forces regained control of the city's command centres.[159]

LMR, a nominally apolitical English-medium extension of RCM, continued broadcasting throughout the occupation of the Radio Palace. Yet the political future of Mozambique was by then so clear that even the Ministry of Foreign Affairs, in Pretoria, understood the message. Within days, Meyer was told that the minister's long-standing objection to the SABC withdrawing from its contract with RCM no longer applied.[160] But in the end the SABC was pushed before it could jump.

For many years, certain LMR programmes had been pre-recorded in the Johannesburg studios, but the number had increased substantially in 1974. There was also a good deal of reallocation and switching of broadcasting loads – including some carrying LMR – between the new FM and older medium-wave transmitters in South Africa.[161] By January 1975, a shadowy new operating system for LMR was in place and functioning reasonably well, anticipating, by some months, the fact that Mozambique would become fully independent on 25 June 1975.

Meyer's original nightmare of a 'hostile' radio station broadcasting political propaganda to black South Africans from a neighbouring state – father to his idea of a 'Piracy Act' – had long since become a reality. But by then the ideological poison was seeping into the country from Radio Freedom, in far-off Lusaka, as well as from nearby Lourenço Marques. Like good businesses everywhere in the world, RCM – in any case, largely state-owned – was already flicking its tongue in preparation for the new round of bootlicking that would be required of it by its incoming black political masters. It was the way of Africa.

African governments, like chameleons, could adjust their skin colour to fit in with the changed electoral background relatively quickly. But their eyeballs, capable of scrolling backwards, almost invariably fixed on the flies closest to their sticky tongues – ethnic nationalism. In March 1975, RCM, paving the way for impending changes in regional power, broadcast a programme commemorating one of white South Africa's most notorious apartheid massacres, one that the SABC board was content to refer to in its minutes only as the 'Sharpeville incident'.[162] The RCM initiative – business leading from behind – was, Meyer knew, merely a trailer for what was likely to follow. So the SABC, building on the precautions that had steadily been put in place since the beginning of the year, prepared for what it termed an 'emergency takeover' by a station with a new name should LMR be shut down. The new station was to be named 'Radio 5' – later still to be renamed '5FM'.[163]

Meyer was prepared, but Independence Day celebrations in Mozambique in June 1975, to which the SABC sent official representatives, came and went without so much as an on-air cough or splutter in the famed Radio Palace. The new Samora Machel-led government, or so it seemed, was content to move, if at all, at the pace that characterised so much of the continent – slowly. But the attempted countercoup of the previous year had not been forgotten and Frelimo was intent on nationalising all the media in the former colony. The wish was translated into law on 2 October 1975, as Decree No. 16/75. The new Frelimo minister lost no time writing to Meyer informing him that, since Frelimo was embarking on a programme of mass political mobilisation, its transmitters would no longer be at the disposal of the SABC:

> As you are aware, Sir, Springbok Radio has been using leased transmitters from the former Radio Clube de Moçambique to broadcast commercial programmes beamed to the Republic of South Africa, a practice which, I am afraid, can no longer continue under the forementioned circumstances. I would therefore like to request you to advise the Manager of the English Section of Radio Clube de Moçambique (known as LM Radio) to cease broadcasts as soon as applicable. I would also like to add that the time limit for such termination should be not later than 15th October 1975.[164]

On 12 October 1975, 40 years after GJ McHarry gave birth to the idea, LMR expired, and at 5 am on Monday 13 October, Radio 5 took its first breath. It would, an SABC press statement reassured white South Africans who had in large measure already abandoned LMR in its new censored SABC format, 'conform to the same music formula and general programming style which was developed by LM Radio and appeals so successfully to young South Africans and with the same familiar broadcasting personalities'. Radio 5, the illegitimate child of the Meyer and the SABC, was born a liar.

If the history of 20th-century Europe – the crucible of colonialism and imperialism – is about anything, then it is, in good part, about the primacy of the enabling ethnic and racist ideologies that drew on the hubris and supposed sanctity of nation-states underwritten by real or imagined notions of cultural homogeneity and superiority. The global contestations that followed World War I were increasingly informed by rapid advances in radio technology that allowed for the mass transmission of ideas and interpretations capable of underwriting not only social cohesion but also conflict and genocide on a scale without precedent.

In Africa, old colonial enclaves that only acquired recognisable boundaries in the late 19th century, and then went on to aspire to political autonomy as their economies developed between the two world wars, were plagued by all the ambiguities built into mass communication. Radio technology was employed to help transform yesterday's cartographical scribbles into something approximating nation-states.

But broadcasting in youthful, ex-colonial administrations, intent on furthering racially exclusive 'nation-building' projects, differed radically from those in the fortresses of old imperial Europe, gradually extending class- and gender-restricted franchises into broader-based democracies, often in settings of comparative cultural homogeneity. The logic driving broadcasting in Africa, where the object was to confine the franchise to the racially privileged, was inherently different.

Nowhere in Africa were the contradictions that underlay colonialism and mass communication by radio more evident than at its southern tip, site of the continent's only (and deeply flawed) industrial revolution. In South Africa, riven by class, ethnic, linguistic, racial and social complexities, the state did not emerge until 1910, and then only after the most brutal anti-colonial war ever fought against British imperial forces by white settlers. Among many other factors that contributed to this relatively late emergence of a state that still aspires to nurturing a unified 'nation' was the depth and strength of African primary resistance to colonial intrusions and a European elite divided by differences in culture and language, and an adherence to Calvinist dogma.

It is difficult to conceive of a former colony with a strong emerging economy less suited to adopting, largely uncritically, a British template designed to govern public broadcasting than was South Africa. But that was precisely what the United Party government did when, hoping to further reconcile political differences between its Afrikaans- and English-speaking white constituencies, it invited Sir John Reith to investigate and report on how best to structure and govern public broadcasting in 1934. It was the Reith report that formed the basis of the Broadcasting Act 22 of 1936.

But the Reith report – foundational to broadcasting policy in South Africa for more than half a century – was flawed in several important respects. Some of those deficiencies should have been evident to Reith and his hosts in the mid-1930s; others, more deeply hidden, would become evident only with the benefit of hindsight and the passage of time.

Spawned at a time when the politics of Afrikaans and English speakers held the promise of moving whites closer together, Reith and the United Party were aware of the need to nurture a bilingual broadcasting system. Indeed, that became an overriding consideration when the Broadcasting Bill was debated in the House of Assembly.[165] What the legislators and the report did not, and probably could not, foresee, however, was the need for a far more broadly based, deeply rooted representative structure for the governance of the state broadcaster. The board needed to be able to withstand the political pressures that might emanate from a narrower, ethnically based form of nationalism capable of giving rise to de facto one-party dominance in a multicultural and multiracial country always prone to social myopia and self-interest. It proved to be the curse of the 20th century and promises to linger well into the 21st.

Even when allowing for Reith's cultural conservatism and penchant for state control, less understandable by far was his unwillingness to make any concessions to the possibility of commercial broadcasting. His aversion to popular entertainment and modern music coming from independent radio stations within the country or from beyond its borders was already well known. There were three weaknesses in Reith's report that South African nationalists, often more focused on the country's Calvinism and exceptionalism than on situating social development within a wider context, failed to spot.

First, even as Reith was compiling his report on what the future of public broadcasting should look like in South Africa, the BBC's hegemony of the airwaves in the United Kingdom was being challenged. A few continental radio stations were already beaming commercial services into parts of coastal England. But '[n]o man is an island entire of itself', even if Reith refused to come to terms with the idea of radio transmissions bringing continental Europe closer to Britain, and vice versa. The muffled sounds that he reacted to indecisively, outside the back door of his own domain, in England, proved to be perfectly inaudible in southern Africa. For him, South Africa too might as well have been an island kingdom, one separated not only from neighbouring British protectorates without a political future but also from the nearby Portuguese colony of Mozambique.

Second, like Canute, Reith believed that he could command the rising tides of commercialism sweeping over much of the world not to swamp the island radio of his blighted vision. It is true that, by the mid-1930s, South Africa had only one set of commercial radio outlets, owned by the monopoly-loving IW Schlesinger. This made Reith's task of strengthening the public broadcaster by buying out IWS's interests a bit easier, but other parts of the sprawling British Empire were already awash with commercial radio stations signalling the arrival of the future.

In 1932, during the Great Depression, Australia already had 43 commercial radio stations and Canada 77. Reith might have read his South African hosts' conservatism and suspicions about big business correctly, but he appears to have been singularly out of touch with the trajectories of capitalism elsewhere in the Empire, let alone the United States. In many countries, the licence fees and taxes provided by market-based commercial stations contributed to the fiscus, helping to cross-subsidise public broadcasting services unable to survive on modest, self-generated income streams. If that was broadly true for a few monolingual countries, then it was doubly true of bilingual white South Africa, which needed to double up on the expenses for its services.

Third, the deadly combination of Calvinism and enforced Sunday observance, to which Reith and the South African government both subscribed, left the public broadcaster at a further disadvantage. It provided any future commercial radio station with a competition-free, ring-fenced time and space in which to broadcast popular entertainment and music. The government's decades-long religious conservatism helped create and protect precisely what it abhorred – airtime for the broadcasting of commercial advertising, jazz and popular music on the Sabbath.

It was not as if Reith was confronted by a shortage of tea leaves to read at the time. McHarry had been printing *The African Radio Announcer* since 1932, and during 1935–1936 obtained a concession to develop Lourenço Marques Radio as a commercial station. Predictably, many years later, broadcasting the 'LM Hit Parade' on Sunday evenings became one of LMR's most attractive lures when fishing for younger, middle- and working-class white South African listeners. Not only were Reith and his Calvinist hosts dead set against making any concession to commercialism and the rhythm of the working week in an industrialising state with a significant white working class, but they failed to understand that LMR was locked into an adjacent Catholic dispensation that had a very different view of how to spend Sundays.

The Reith report, the broadcasting bible for South Africa for decades thereafter, contained several verses that, upon closer examination, raised more questions than the report ever answered. It was flawed not only by errors consciously committed but by errors of omission, which, over time, became increasingly difficult to deal with in commercial, cultural, financial, political and religious terms in a country where whites-only governments always denied the realities of living in Africa.

But the world is governed by more than constitutions, ordinances and regulations. It is presided over by those who oversee guidelines, those who not only read what is prescribed by the black-letter law but feel free to interpret the ambiguities and silences around and between them with greater or lesser wisdom. The mental health, personalities and political proclivities of men – and they usually are men – appointed to head public broadcasting corporations around the world, no doubt, follow the outlines of the familiar bell-shaped curve. Some will be exceptionally well qualified, but most will fall comfortably within the range of what passes for 'normal' and do a reasonably good job of controlling institutions that are, in the final analysis, accountable to the electorate and the government of the day in states manifesting greater or lesser degrees of political maturity, stability and tolerance.

By the same token, however, there will be a minority of men, seriously deficient in one or more respects, who are unsuited to leading public broadcasting institutions. It is true that those who show an unsettling desire to control or manipulate men and machines, an intolerance born of religious conviction, or other obsessive traits, can be checked if people of principle and open to reason form a majority in the governance structures of the institution. The real danger, however, arises when governments in complex, multicultural societies, located in partial, or skewed, 'democracies', and driven by narrow cultural, racial and/or divisive religious agendas, appoint individuals showing excessive ideological rigidity or profoundly anti-social excesses to chair weak boards of governance served only by the party faithful, or 'patriots'.

This menacing configuration, where consciously enfeebled structures of governance are deliberately used to accommodate persons lacking in integrity and/or mental health to advance ethically questionable actions capable of advancing exclusive or manipulative political agendas, is seldom of purely theoretical interest. In Africa, where in the latter part of the 20th century crimes against humanity in seriously flawed 'democracies' have, by chance or design, ranged from apartheid to genocide, such contrived and inappropriate appointments have resulted in dire social consequences.

In Rwanda, where, it is said, Hutu and Tutsi lived in comparative amity in pre-colonial times, serious ethnic clashes dated back to 1959. But it was the wholesale slaughter of Tutsis, in the infamous genocide of 1994, that shocked the world and gave birth to political tensions that continue to bedevil the region. Central to the mass mobilisation of the Hutus, some prosecutors attached to the International Criminal Tribunal for Rwanda believe, was a privately owned radio station – Radio Télévision Libre des Milles Collines – set up to rival the state-owned Radio Rwanda and 'conceived, from the outset, as a vehicle to fan ethnic hatred and exterminate the Tutsi population'.[166]

It is true that, in colonial southern Africa, LMR was never directly involved in fanning ethnic or racial tensions. But, lest we forget, its development – the subject of long and intense commercial contestation – its takeover by the SABC and its dismal end were all historically linked to African resistance within southern Africa, the subject of contestations between white political parties and outright warfare. Like colonialism and racism, radio and war are an ugly couple.

In Europe, the very idea of private radio stations, some of which in later years were deemed to be offshore 'pirate' stations, was spawned by experiences gained during two world wars and could be directly linked to the rise of D&M as a management company and LMR. It was former British Army officers experienced in audience research who provided the managerial drive and inspiration for the commercial success of LMR well into the 1960s, right up to the point where, by 1950, the SABC was forced into competing via its own limply commercial, state-owned version – Springbok Radio.

In similar vein, it should be recalled that it was African resistance to apartheid policies that, in 1960, precipitated the Sharpeville massacre. After that, with growing urgency, the SABC, through PJ Meyer, sought – unsuccessfully – to have parliament approve a 'Piracy Act'.

The corporation tried to forestall the possibility of radio stations in neighbouring territories, and especially the long-resented LMR, providing a platform capable of further priming the political consciousness of black South Africans intent on ushering in a democratically elected government. And it was the liberation war in Mozambique, and an attempted countercoup by settlers there, that helped precipitate the abrupt closure of LMR.

As elsewhere on the continent, popular resistance in the streets, armed struggles inside and outside the country, and outright warfare through much of the region formed the backdrop to changing broadcasting policies in southern Africa from the mid-1960s into the early 1990s. South Africa and Portugal found common political ground on the battlefield through their commitment to maintaining white rule, but it was an alliance that also benefited from the way in which radio was used to facilitate military and police operations. This, in turn, contributed to the willingness of RCM to secretly dispose of part of LMR to the SABC.

Why exactly the acquisition and control of LMR became so important to South Africa by the 1960s can, as we have seen, be traced back largely to the Reith report and the flawed Broadcasting Act of 1936. Both the deficiencies in the original Act and the ways in which it informed the SABC's quest to gain control of LMR, however, owed almost as much to the public moralising and privately deceitful proclivities of the two men most responsible for the subsequent ethical shortcomings of 20th-century broadcasting in southern Africa – John Reith and Piet Meyer – as they did to the weaknesses in the 1936 Act.

Reith, the Calvinist, engineer, soldier, arms contractor and man, is of only passing interest here. But it might be noted that, according to his daughter, his public persona as the embodiment of fairness and moral rectitude was wholly out of keeping with his private life when observed from close up. Ambitious, authoritarian, contemptuous of all commerce, hypocritical and self-interested, Reith was a serial adulterer noted for his prudish attitude about sexual matters while at the BBC. A one-time admirer of Hitler, he had an intense dislike of jazz and was always keen to bookend the religious obligations of public broadcasting. His military career and philandering aside, there is something of Reith's make-up to be found in PJ Meyer too.

Meyer may have been a feared and respected man in public life, but it cannot readily be claimed that he was much loved. Academically inclined and intellectually pretentious, he wrote several books about his career and how it intersected with the struggle of the *volk* he devoted himself to, but for all his undoubted importance to the nationalist cause – and perhaps significantly – he has not been the subject of a definitive biography. It is a lamentable omission. Meyer was central to transmitting apartheid ideas and policies during the decades that the country was closest to becoming a fully fascist state. Meyer may not have been a soldier, but he was an ardent ideological warrior.

His ostentatious Calvinist zeal exceeded even that of Reith. Meyer insisted that each day's broadcasting cycle on corporation stations – including LMR – commence and end with a religious meditation. The SABC not only declined to broadcast Sunday sporting events but refused to carry the results of any such encounters in its news bulletins. The corporation imposed an antiquated dress code on its female staff. Meyer opened all SABC board meetings with a prayer. Given what sometimes transpired during the proceedings that followed, a call for ethical or moral guidance from on high was probably most appropriate.

Chairman Meyer made certain that the SABC's Board of Control was dominated by his nominees – titled academics, sycophantic yes-men largely incapable of independent thought, let alone tolerance. His obsessive dislike of 'beat' or 'pop' music as signifiers of decadence and godlessness, along with the supposedly pernicious influence they exercised over the minds of youth, enjoyed the wholehearted support of the learned men and far transcended Reith's own contempt for jazz.

Nor was the corporation's board distinguished by its business acumen. As chairman, Meyer fed board members only such morsels of financial information as he saw fit while pursuing the acquisition of LMR for political and cultural rather than commercial ends – a costly adventure that ended extremely poorly. Indeed, Meyer's enthusiastic pursuit of apartheid policies, which continued to be applied to African audiences through separate ethnic channels right up to the 1990s, probably contributed to the progressive decline in the SABC's financial position over the decade that followed.

Meyer's all-male board members, supposedly chosen for their ability to act impartially in a quest for fairness and even-handedness in a complex society enforcing increasingly authoritarian racist policies, actively identified the government's political opponents, ensuring that they did not gain access to the regional or national airwaves. In some cases, for example that of Professor Brian Bradshaw, such political victimisation was, on occasion, informed by envious personal vindictiveness. The SABC board may not have been an instrument of terror in an authoritarian state, but it certainly was a source of political oppression.

As with Reith, Meyer's admiration for right-wing extremist groups in the 1930s, including those with a liking for Hitler and Nazism and a penchant for wartime sabotage, are well known.[167] Clandestine and conspiratorial politics, conducted within the confines of the privileged and powerful circles, were formative influences in the way that Meyer conducted both his own and the SABC's board's affairs. It was an elitist form of engagement that held most of its own ethnic constituency, along with the white public at large, in contempt – part of a self-anointed vanguardist political organisation dismissive of democratic procedures and processes. It was also a form of political socialisation that left Meyer well suited to becoming chairman of a secret organisation of nationalists, the Afrikaner Broederbond, and the executive head of the SABC – high offices that, for many years, he held simultaneously.

As the head of the Broederbond and the SABC, Meyer was capable of powerfully influencing, if not delivering, an important northern constituency within the ruling National Party. He effectively bullied and controlled virtually every cabinet minister he ever reported to. For much the same reason, he was feared by prime ministers, who had to find ways of working around Meyer, whose ideological proclivities and ambition to control radio throughout the region gave rise to interventions that cut across several cabinet portfolios at a time when apartheid policies were subject to increasing criticism internationally. Never were these realities more evident than in 1972, when Meyer, after a long personal campaign, eventually forced Portugal and South Africa to agree to the highly secretive takeover of LMR by the SABC.

A capacity for manipulation, secretiveness and the exercise of power intentionally concealed fed into Meyer's increasingly arrogant and bellicose behaviour during the 1960s and 1970s – conduct that, in part, was further facilitated by the fact that the white governments were engaged in armed struggles with African liberation forces. Meyer, ever the ideological warrior, thrived, as he always had, within the context of warfare. It did not, however, make for deep or lasting political friendships.

There appears to have been a feeling of 'mutual disdain' between Meyer and several of the political leaders of the National Party. Neither Meyer's nor Verwoerd's children recall there being close personal ties between the two men, which, given a tetchy professional relationship that dated back to World War II, is no surprise. Vorster and Meyer clashed on at least one occasion about the SABC's lack of what the Prime Minister considered adequate coverage of his electioneering. Meyer, in turn, was willing to fight fire with fire. He once suggested to a few senior members of staff that he was 'flying down to Cape Town to see John Vorster, to tell him to get out of bed and start governing the country'. Meyer's doctrinal rigidity and ideological impermeability were poorly received by Cape-based editors and journalists such as PJ Cillié and Schalk Pienaar, intent on probing all the parameters of apartheid policies.[168]

Meyer's personality and position slotted comfortably into the domestic and regional political context at a time when white dominance was experiencing an increasingly serious challenge at the hands of African nationalists. Together, the man and the moment gave rise to the perfect storm that provided Portugal and South Africa with the political cover needed to address the Reithian flaw dating back to the Broadcasting Act of 1936 and take over LMR in 1972. The SABC's acquisition of a controlling share of LMR cannot be ascribed to the free interplay of market forces.

The capture of LMR was the result of a long-standing, dirty commercial and political campaign drive by Afrikaner nationalists and was conducted over very many years – a struggle punctuated by contradictions and rich in irony. It was the outcome of a conflict, one in which the 'LMR Hit Parade', deliberately aired on Sunday nights when much of white South Africa was in the deepest part of its self-inflicted, Calvinist-induced coma, constituted only a tiny part. The rise and fall of LMR forms an important part of the history of the decolonisation of nominally Calvinist and Catholic enclaves in southern Africa, and cannot be reduced to a matter of peripheral interest for those interested only in the history of 'the media'.

Sometimes it is the silences in history that speak loudest to those historians willing to listen. It is significant that, in all of Meyer's narcissistic autobiographical ramblings and the existing histories of Afrikaner nationalism, the progressive subversion of LMR gets very little attention or none at all. And when silences prevail unchallenged, they allow those men and women who are party to shaping ethically reprehensible domains to occupy the vacated spaces and consciously corrupt the historical record. The lesson was not lost on PJ Meyer.

In October 1981, Meyer, a recipient of an honorary doctorate from the Rand Afrikaans University, which he helped found and was chancellor of, was invited to present the 11th Hertzog Memorial Lecture. He chose as his subject 'General JBM Hertzog, Sir John Reith and the Broadcasting Act of 1936'. As was to be expected at such an occasion, Meyer used the opportunity principally to pay homage to Hertzog and Reith and to praise the foresight and wisdom of both men, whom he had met over the course of his career. But the secondary objective of his lecture was to draw out the underlying continuities in public broadcasting in the country and, more particularly, to show how he and the SABC were the direct descendants of the vaunted Reithian traditions.

In his talk, Meyer flaunted the Reithian maxim – which the SABC does to this very day – about the primary duty of the public broadcaster being to educate, inform and entertain. But that was not enough for Meyer. He drew attention to Reith's injunction to use radio 'in the service of wisdom, beauty and peace', which, he insisted, the SABC board 'has followed faithfully since its inception up to the present'. It was important, Meyer argued, that the public broadcaster remain 'a free, autonomous cultural entity and not become, as in communist and third-world countries, either a state-controlled body that could be used for political ends, or a commercial organisation used for financial gain'.

But it was Meyer's lengthy and unchallenged peroration that did – and does – most to foul the footpaths that historians need to tread as they attempt to approach accuracy and truth as circumspectly as possible:

> Mr Chairman, the fact that all the basic views and purposes of the Hertzog government and General Hertzog's advisor, Sir John Reith, as stipulated in the Broadcasting Act of 1936, have, up to

the present, remained without noteworthy revision and that the SABC board, as constituted then and later, has adopted the same views on autonomy in regard to the cultural role and calling of the Corporation, and as envisaged and underwritten by the lawmakers of 1936, is, without doubt, the lasting foundation on which we pay homage tonight to two great men in history of broadcasting in our country, General JBM Hertzog and Lord Reith.[169]

In this way, complicit white South Africans were mocked by the travesty of broadcasting history they were presented with, one evening back in 1981. A new generation of scholars needs to scrape the muck from the soles of their shoes before striding out in new directions as we attempt to move gingerly towards a more complex and nuanced history of broadcasting in southern African than we currently have.

SELECT BIBLIOGRAPHY

Articles

Browne, D.R. 'Radio Normandie and the IBC Challenge to the BBC Monopoly', *Historical Journal of Film, Radio and Television*, Vol. 5, No. 1 (1985), pp. 1–7.

Correia, P. and Verhoef, G. 'Portugal and South Africa: Close Allies or Unwilling Partners in Southern Africa during the Cold War', *Scientia Militaria: South African Journal of Military Studies*, Vol. 37, No. 1 (2009), pp. 50–72.

Foster. J. '"Land of Contrasts" or "Home We Have Always Known"? The SAR&H and the Imaginary Geography of White South African Nationhood, 1910–1930', *Journal of Southern African Studies*, Vol. 29, No. 3 (September 2003), pp. 657–680.

Foster, J. 'Northward, Upward: Stories of Train Travel and the Journey towards White South African Nationhood, 1895–1950', *Journal of Historical Geography*, Vol. 31 (2005), pp. 296–315.

Gordimer, N. 'South African Riviera', *Holiday* (Philadelphia), Vol. 22, No. 6 (1957), pp. 166–168.

Grundlingh, A. '"Are We Afrikaners Getting too Rich?" Cornucopia and Change in Afrikanerdom in the 1960s', *Journal of Historical Sociology*, Vol. 21, No. 2/3 (June/September 2008), pp. 143–165.

Gupta, P. 'Consuming the Coast: Mid-century Communications of Port Tourism in the Southern Indian Ocean', *Communição Midia e Consimo*, Vol. 12, No. 35 (2015), pp. 149–170.

Harvey, A. 'Counter-Coup in Lourenço Marques: September 1974', *International Journal of African Historical Studies*, Vol. 39, No, 3 (2006), pp. 487–498.

Lekgoathi, P.S. 'The African National Congress's Radio Freedom and its Audiences in Apartheid South Africa', *Journal of African Media Studies*, Vol. 2, No. 2 (August 2010), pp. 139–153.

Maharaj, B., Pillay, V. and Suchen, R. 'Durban a Subtropical Paradise? Tourism Dynamics in a Post-Apartheid City', *Études caribéennes*, Nos. 9–10 (April 2008) [online, no page numbers].

Moreira, C.O. 'Portugal as a Tourism Destination: Paths and Trends',

Méditerranée: Journal of Mediterranean Geography, No. 130 (2018) [no page numbers].

Nance, F.J. 'A Holiday in Lourenço Marques', *South African Railways & Harbours Magazine* (December 1920), pp. 466–467.

Peleggi, M. 'The Social and Material Life of Colonial Hotels: Comfort Zones in British Colombo and Singapore, c. 1870–1930', *Journal of Social History*, Vol. 46, No. 1 (Fall 2012), pp. 124–153.

Pirie, G.H., 'Elite Exoticism: Sea-Rail Tourism in South Africa, 1926–1939', *African Historical Review*, Vol. 43, No. 1 (June 2011), pp. 73–99.

Power, M. '*Aqui Lourenço Marques!!* Radio Colonisation and Cultural Identity in Colonial Mozambique, 1932–74', *Journal of Historical Geography*, Vol. 26, No. 4 (2000) pp. 605–628.

Prinsloo, D. 'Dr. Piet Meyer in Johannesburg, 1936–1984', *Historia*, Vol. 32, No. 1 (May 1987), pp. 44–54.

Roque, P. 'Notas Para a História da Radiodifusão em Moçambiue: O Caso do Rádio Clube de Moçambique, 1933–1973', *Arquivo, Boletim do Arquivo Histórico de Moçambique*, No. 3 (April 1988), pp. 47–60.

Teer-Tomaselli, R. 'The Contradictions of Public Service and Commercialisation in Mid-century South African Broadcasting; A Case Study of the Schoch Commission and Springbok Radio', *Media History*, Vol. 25, No. 2 (2019), pp. 225–243.

Book chapter

Grundlingh, A. 'Holidays at Hartenbos: Sand, Sea and Sun in the Construction of Afrikaner Cultural Nationalism, c. 1920–c. 1961', in Grundlingh, A., *Potent Pastimes: Sport and Leisure in Modern Afrikaner History* (Pretoria, 2013), pp. 34–53.

Books

Alexander, D. *Holiday in Mozambique* (Johannesburg, 1971).

Clarence-Smith, G. *The Third Portuguese Empire, 1825–1975: A Study in Economic Imperialism* (Manchester, 1985).

De Klerk, W.A. *The Puritans in Africa: A Story of Afrikanerdom* (London, 1975).
Duffy, J. *Portuguese Africa* (Cambridge, Mass., 1959).
Giliomee, H. *The Afrikaners: Biography of a People* (Charlottesville, 2002).
Katzenellenbogen, S. *South Africa and Mozambique: Labour, Railways and Trade in the Making of a Relationship* (Manchester, 1982).
Kennedy, D. *The Magic Mountains: Hill Stations and the British Raj* (Los Angeles, 1996).
Matisson, J. *God, Spies and Lies: Finding South Africa's Future Through its Past* (Vlaeberg, 2015).
Merrill, D. *Negotiating Paradise: U.S. Tourism and Empire in Twentieth-Century Latin America* (Chapel Hill, 2009).
Meyer, P.J. *Nog Nie Ver Genoeg Nie: 'n Persoonlike Rekenskap van Vyftig Jaar Georganiseerde Afrikanerskap* (Johannesburg, 1984).
Moodie, T.D. *The Rise of Afrikanerdom: Power, Apartheid, and the Afrikaner Civil Religion* (Berkeley, 1975).
O'Meara, D. *Volkskapitalisme: Class, Capital and Ideology in the Development of Afrikaner Nationalism, 1934–1948* (Johannesburg, 1983).
Penvenne, J.M. *African Workers and Colonial Racism: Mozambican Strategies and Struggles in Lourenço Marques, 1877–1962* (London, 1995).
Povinelli, E.A. *The Empire of Love: Toward a Theory of Intimacy, Genealogy, and Carnality* (Durham, NC, 2006).
Rosenthal, E. *You Have Been Listening: The Early History of Radio in South Africa* (London, 1974).
Said, E.W. *Culture and Imperialism* (London, 1993).
Spence, C.F. *The Portuguese Colony of Moçambique: An Economic Survey* (Cape Town, 1951).
Vaughan, G.E. *Portuguese East Africa: Economic and Commercial Conditions in Portuguese East Africa (Moçambique)* (London, 1952).
Van Onselen, C. *New Babylon, New Nineveh: Everyday Life on the Witwatersrand, 1886–1914* (Cape Town, 2001).

ACKNOWLEDGEMENTS

Writing history is the outcome of a paradoxical process. It occurs when creative, mildly explosive ideas are made to rely on discipline to help free them from the confines of the mind. Once out of the head and down on paper, ideas can assume the more ordered release of energy required of a convincing narrative. Without disciplined ideas there can be no narrative, and without a narrative informed by agency, chronology, process and structure, there will be no readers. For most of us this is so difficult to accomplish that 'good' writing remains an aspiration rather than an achievement. I have found it to be so. For social historians, the task is rendered more complex by having to deal with historical actors, characters manifesting the full range of attitudes, beliefs and behaviours that human beings are capable of. And, since all readers and writers believe themselves to be uniquely qualified when it comes to a 'real' or 'true' understanding of the inner motivations of a person, a group or a class – as made evident through action or utterance – success remains elusive, if not impossible. Historians, like all other writers, must simply accept that it is the way that things are, ever has it been thus.

But an author can take out some insurance along the way – group cover of a sort that feels good, but which will not save him or her cometh the reviews. That is why writers must emphasise that colleagues, fellow historians, friends and family, along with many generous collaborators and informants, are not responsible for any egregious errors of fact or interpretation that occur in a book. Lucky them. Luckier still the historian who has had the benefit of so many considerate and kind people who have saved him from the worst of howlers or other shortcomings through their generous assistance with the primary research or drafts that resulted.

The late Cecilia Bailie and Tozio Mugabe helped gather a great deal of the raw data and assisted in processing the large volumes of research material that this book rests on. I can no longer thank them personally, and only hope that they would both have approved of a work that, in many ways, they did much to help shape.

'The Sunday Night Wars' could not have been written without the assistance of persons directly or indirectly associated with key personnel at the South African Broadcasting Corporation, on the one hand, and with Davenport & Meyer and Lourenço Marques Radio, on the other. They, more than academic colleagues, need to be distanced from my descriptions and interpretations of people and events in Auckland Park, Johannesburg, or the Radio Palace in Lourenço Marques. I can only thank them for them for their assistance and understanding.

I am greatly indebted to Dr Dioné Prinsloo (née Meyer) of the Suid-Afrikaanse Akademie vir Wetenskap en Kuns for providing me with easy access to the published works of the late Dr PJ Meyer of the SABC. Her willingness to come to the assistance of a fellow historian with whose views she is most unlikely to agree was exemplary. She has my sincerest thanks for agreeing to assist me.

Perhaps I am even more indebted to my friend John Matisson. He knows more about broadcasting history than I ever will. Some years ago, when common sense, good citizenship and mental health were taken seriously as requisites for public office – but only for a brief period – John was appointed to the board at the SABC. Through his good offices, I gained access to the minutes of the meetings of the corporation's Board of Control/Governance that were not, and probably still are not, available for scrutiny to members of the public. It is a South African rule: the more 'public' the institution ostensibly is, the more confidential/private/secret the documents are, and the less likely they are to find their ways into the 'national' archives, where, in any case, they may be lost, mislaid or neglected. It is our way.

Likewise, were it not for a few exceptional individuals I would have experienced the greatest difficulty in understanding what little I do about the workings of Davenport & Meyer and Lourenço Marques Radio. Foremost among those whom I am indebted to is the late Patrick McHarry, grandson of GJ McHarry. I tracked him through that neglected source of social history, the telephone directory, and, via a few phone calls and many letters, he provided me with invaluable insights into the history of the remarkable founder of LMR and its managing company. I would also like to record my thanks to Gary Edwards and the late John Berks, famous disc jockeys at LMR, and to Keith Giemre, a former financial manager at D&M. All three of those gentlemen could not have been more helpful or encouraging.

The Director of the Centre for the Advancement of Scholarship at the University of Pretoria, Prof James Ogude, and the Vice Chancellor of the University, Prof Tawana Kupe, have been unfailingly accommodating and supportive of my ever more reclusive mode of working over several years and during an exceptionally difficult time in my life. Like others named here, they will have to do with a mere 'thank you', but truly, as that awful but accurate cliché has it, 'without them' etc.

The 'group insurance' came from the usual academic suspects, some of whom I am also privileged to call friends. They helped provide the advice and guidance necessary to try and control the research and writing needed to complete an overly ambitious project such as this. Blame them for their taste in friends and intellectual company but for nothing else. My debt to them is extraordinary. I wish to thank, most sincerely, Joel Cabrita, Hermann Giliomee, Albert Grundlingh, Karen Harris, Paul la Hausse, Andrew MacDonald, Marlino Mubai, Kathy Munro, Jeanne Penvenne, Ian Phimister, Deryck Schreuder and June Sinclair. Readers and reviewers may think that they know the culpability of publishers when it comes to producing a book. I think they do not know the half of it. I have long been deeply in the debt of Eugene Ashton and Annie Olivier of Jonathan Ball Publishers, along with my editor, Alfred LeMaitre. They know how to encourage the hard of hearing. I would also like to thank Phil Stickler for the maps, and Cecilia Kruger for assistance in procuring suitable photographs.

But the biggest prize of all, as ever, goes to those with the godsent gift of being able to withstand lengthy bouts of depression, grumpiness, impatience, chronic unreasonableness and a deep-seated loathing of nationalisms past and present. Where would I, or this project be, were it not for the unconditional understanding, love and support that I got from Cherie, Gareth, Jessica and Matthew? There was a time when I could have added one more, unforgettable, name to that short list.

Charles van Onselen

NOTES

Part I

1. As quoted in J. Duffy, *Portuguese Africa* (Cambridge, Mass., 1959), p. 339 [hereafter Duffy, *Portuguese Africa*].
2. E.W. Said, *Culture and Imperialism* (London, 1993), p. 36.
3. See Duffy, *Portuguese Africa*, p. 95; and United States of America (USA), Stanford University Library, Despatches from United States Consuls in Lourenço Marques, Mozambique, Roll 4, Vol. 2, June 2, 1900–April 19, 1902, S. Hollis to Assistant Sec. of State, Washington, DC, 5 August 1900 [hereafter USA, Stanford, Despatches].
4. Republic of South Africa (RSA), Johannesburg, Standard Bank Archives and Historical Services (A&HS), Inspection Report of the Lourenço Marques Branch as at 13 Aug. 1930 [hereafter RSA, JHB, SBA & HS].
5. C.F. Spence, *The Portuguese Colony of Moçambique; An Economic Survey* (Cape Town, 1951), p. 89 [hereafter Spence, *Moçambique*].
6. Spence, *Moçambique*, p. 88.
7. Contrast Spence's gloomy prognostications with D. Alexander's chirpy *Holiday in Mozambique* (Johannesburg, 1971), a decade later [hereafter Alexander, *Holiday*].
8. Schreiner, as quoted in C. van Onselen, *The Fox & The Flies: The Criminal Empire of the Whitechapel Murderer* (London, 2007), p. 145 [hereafter van Onselen, *Fox & Flies*), and Pratt, as cited in C. van Onselen, *New Babylon, New Nineveh: Everyday Life on the Witwatersrand, 1886–1914* (Cape Town, 2001), p. 3 [hereafter van Onselen, *New Babylon, New Nineveh*].
9. F. Wilson, *Labour in the South African Gold Mines, 1911–1969* (Cambridge, 1972), p. 9.
10. See van Onselen, *New Babylon, New Nineveh*, p. 36, as well as for essays on alcohol and prostitution.
11. See van Onselen, *New Babylon, New Nineveh*, p. 36.
12. See, for example, holiday rates for the Cardoso Hotel as advertised in the *Rand Daily Mail*, 16 December 1911.
13. See F.J. Nance, 'A Holiday in Lourenço Marques', *South African Railways & Harbours Magazine* (December 1920), pp. 466–467 [hereafter Nance, 'Holiday'], and N. Gordimer, 'South African Riviera', *Holiday* (Philadelphia), Vol. 22, No. 6 (1957), pp. 166–168 [hereafter Gordimer, 'South African Riviera'].
14. Gordimer, 'South African Riviera', p. 167. For those interested in the theory that underlies capitalism, space and time, there is a useful introduction in K. Goldman, 'Bodies on the Edge: Representing Urban Nightlife and Corporeality in New York's Coney Island, 1900–1945', undergraduate thesis, Department of Sociology and Anthropology, Swarthmore College, May 2015, pp. 9–31.
15. Nance, 'Holiday', p. 965.
16. On the early reputation of the hotel, see B. Goudvis, *South African Odyssey:*

The Autobiography of Bertha Goudvis (Johannesburg, 2011), p. 78 [hereafter Goudvis, *South African Odyssey*], and 'O Commandante Augusto Cardoso', blog post, *The Delagoa Bay World*, 14 January 2017. Cardoso sold the hotel to Giuseppe Sorgentini, of Italian descent, in 1925; see Alexander, *Holiday*, p. 47.

17 The quotes are taken from Goudvis, *South African Odyssey*, pp 75 and 82; and USA, Stanford, Despatches, Hollis to Assistant Secretary of State, Washington, DC, 11 October 1900.
18 The changing fortunes of the Royal Hotel can be traced in Goudvis, *South African Odyssey*, pp. 78–90.
19 Van Onselen, *New Babylon, New Nineveh*, pp. 19–20, and van Onselen, *Fox & Flies*, pp. 145–180.
20 See, especially, Rabbi M. Silberhaft, 'The Jewish Community of Lourenço Marques, 1899-2000', unpublished essay. For Rabbi Hertz's post-Boer War ongoing struggle against the white slave traffic, see van Onselen, *New Babylon, New Nineveh*, pp. 150–151.
21 There is a fine description of the 'inevitable barmaid', mostly with tinted blonde hair, 'looking as though she had just arrived from Piccadilly Circus' and 'leans across the counter simpering at her attendant swains' in W.C. Scully, *The Ridge of the White Waters: Impressions of a Visit to Johannesburg, with Some Notes of Durban, Delagoa Bay, and the Low Country* (London, 1912), p. 34 [hereafter Scully, *Ridge of White Waters*].
22 Paragraph based on Goudvis, *South African Odyssey*, p. 82, and, more problematically, L.G. Green, *Harbours of Memory* (Cape Town, 1982), p. 138.
23 Goudvis, *South African Odyssey*, p. 82. See also Scully, *Ridge of White Waters*, p. 41.
24 Nance, 'Holiday', p. 965.
25 Scully, *Ridge of White Waters*, p. 36, and Nance, 'Holiday', p. 965.
26 Alexander, *Holiday*, p. 4.
27 On 'sporting men', see, for example, J. Sterngrass, *First Resorts: Pursuing Pleasure at Saratoga Springs, Newport & Coney Island* (Baltimore, 2001), p. 153 [hereafter Sterngass, *First Resorts*].
28 On the Savoy, see *O Africano*, 22 November 1913; on police and liquor licences, see *Rand Daily Mail*, 3 June and 5 July 1912.
29 See *Rand Daily Mail*, 16 May 1910, and *O Africano*, 22 November 1913.
30 *Rand Daily Mail*, 29 March 1912.
31 See S.M. Correa, 'Heterotopia e vilegiatura em Lourenço Marques (1890–1930)', *Revista de História* (São Paulo), No. 178 (2019) [hereafter Correo, 'Heterotopia'].
32 In this sense, one could do no better than to follow E.A. Povinelli, *The Empire of Love: Toward a Theory of Intimacy, Genealogy, and Carnality* (Durham, NC, 2006), at p. 10: '[L]ove, intimacy, and sexuality are not about desire, pleasure, or sex per se, but about things like geography, history, culpability, and obligation; the extraction of wealth and the distribution of life and death; hope and despair: and the self-evident fact and value of freedom.'
33 See, for example, 'Billets at Delagoa', *Rand Daily Mail*, 23 August 1913. For an excellent overview of white prostitution in the port at the time and, more especially in the 1930s and 1940s, see A. MacDonald, 'Colonial Trespassers in the Making of South Africa's International Borders, 1900–c. 1950' and, more

especially, Chapter Four, 'The Dançerinas of Lourenço Marques: Sexuality, Merry-making and Women Travellers', pp. 165–203, unpublished DPhil thesis, Faculty of History, Cambridge University, August 2012 [hereafter MacDonald, 'South Africa's International Borders'].

34 Republic of South Africa (RSA), Pretoria, National Archives of South Africa (NASA), SAB, South African Police, Confidential, Conf 6/160/13, HBM Consulate-General, Lourenço Marques, to the Secretary for the Interior, 7 August 1913 [hereafter RSA, Pretoria, NASA].

35 See van Onselen, *New Babylon, New Nineveh*, pp. 156–164, and, for the wider context, F.A. van Jaarsveld, *Die Afrikaners se Groot Trek na die Stede* (Johannesburg, 1982).

36 See RSA, Pretoria, NASA, CS 924/18503, HBM Consulate-General, Lourenço Marques to the Secretary for the Interior, 7 August 1913; and pertinent reports in the *Rand Daily Mail* of 28 August 1913, 7 April 1916 and 21 June 1916.

37 RSA, Pretoria, NASA, SAP Confidential, 6/160/13, E. MacDonnell to the Acting Secretary for Justice, 23 October 1913.

38 RSA, Pretoria, NASA, SAP Confidential, 6/160/13, Under Secretary for the Interior to the Chief Commissioner, South African Police, Pretoria, 20 Aug. 1913.

39 RSA, Pretoria, NASA, SAP Confidential, 6/160/13, Under Secretary for the Interior to the Chief Commissioner, South African Police, Pretoria, 20 August 1913. MacDonnell's actions in this regard should be read within the wider context of British imperialism in the Indian Ocean region, where the employment of British barmaids was being curtailed from Burma to Hong Kong in the first decade of the 20th century. See M. Peleggi, 'The Social and Material Life of Colonial Hotels: Comfort Zones in British Colombo and Singapore, c. 1870–1930', *Journal of Social History*, Vol. 46, No. 1 (Fall 2012), p. 139 [hereafter Peleggi, 'Colonial Hotels'].

40 RSA, Pretoria, NASA, SAP Confidential, 6/160/13, Inspector in Charge, C.I.D., to Deputy Commissioner of Police, 18 August 1913.

41 *Rand Daily Mail*, 26 February 1914, 8 July 1915 and 5 June 1916.

42 See *Rand Daily Mail*, 16 June 1916, and Nance, 'Holiday', p. 966.

43 Based on information drawn from Mozambique (MOZ), Maputo, Arquivo Histórico de Moçambique (AHM), Arquivo da Repartição Central da Secretaria da Colónia (ARCSC), Pasta No. 2, Processo No. 29, Alinea a, and, especially, A. Cardoso to the Governor General, 5 May 1916 and other documents [hereafter MOZ, Maputo, AHM].

44 See, especially, two essays by J. Foster, '"Land of Contrasts" or "Home We Have Always Known"? The SAR&H and the Imaginary Geography of White South African Nationhood, 1910–1930', *Journal of Southern African Studies*, Vol. 29, No. 3 (September 2003), pp 657–680, and, slightly more tangentially, 'Northward, Upward: Stories of Train Travel and the Journey Towards White South African Nationhood, 1895–1950', *Journal of Historical Geography*, Vol. 31 (2005), pp. 296–315.

45 As reported in the *Beira Post*, 9 December 1916.

46 For a broader, comparative view, see also, for example, C.S. Aron, *Working at*

Play: A History of Vacations in the United States (New York, 1999), pp. 69–77.
47   See van Onselen, *New Babylon, New Nineveh*, pp. 257–268.
48   See also V.D. Zamparoni, 'Entre Narros & Mulungos: Colonialismo e paisagem social em Lourenço Marques, c. 1890–1940', PhD thesis, Faculdade de Filosofia, Letras e Ciências Humanas, Universidade de São Paulo, 1998, pp. 330–331; and *O Africano*, 29 November and 6 December 1916.
49   This paragraph draws on the following sources: G. Clarence-Smith, *The Third Portuguese Empire, 1825–1975: A Study in Economic Imperialism* (Manchester, 1985), pp. 136–138 [hereafter Clarence-Smith, *The Third Empire*]; *Rand Daily Mail*, 23 January 1923; and R. Williams, 'Creating a Healthy Colonial State in Mozambique, 1885–1915', PhD thesis, Department of History, University of Chicago, 2013, at pp. 236–237.
50   B. Ngqulunga, *The Man Who Founded the ANC: A Biography of Pixley ka Isaka Seme* (Cape Town, 2017), p. 229.
51   See, for example, the blackballing of prospective members of the Polana golf club, in Correo, 'Heterotopia'.
52   And did so well into the 1960s; see Alexander, *Holiday*, p. 14.
53   See T.M. Costa, *Cartas de Moçambique: De Tudo um Pouco* (Lisbon, 1934), pp. 205–219; and J. O' Hara's entry on 'Rupert Theodore (Rufus) Naylor (1812–1939)', in B. Nairn and G. Searle (eds.), *The Australian Dictionary of Biography* (Melbourne, 1981).
54   The Johannesburg end of the lottery operations can be traced in the *Rand Daily Mail* of 11 May 1917 and 27 January 1925, and in *The Star* of 13 and 14 February 1919.
55   See Nance, 'Holiday', p. 965, and, on the 'Naylor Express', RSA, Pretoria, NASA, JUS, Vol. 955, File 1/840/26/1, A. Trigger, C.I.D., to the Deputy Commissioner, South African Police, Witwatersrand Division, 21 January 1927.
56   See van Onselen, *Three Wise Monkeys*, Volume 1, Part III.
57   See the report on this acquisition by the syndicate (though not named as the DBLS), Annual Series No. 1904, *Report for the Year 1896 on the Trade and Commerce of Lourenço Marques*, p. 18. See also 'A Delagoa Bay Lands Syndicate em 1904 e Lourenço Marques', blog post, *The Delagoa Bay World*, 1 June 2019. See also the report on the annual meeting of DBLS shareholders, 'Polana Beach Possibilities', *Rand Daily Mail*, 29 March 1913.
58   S. Joel, *Ace of Diamonds: The Story of Solomon Barnarto Joel* (London, 1958), p. 52. I am indebted to Kathy Munro for bringing this source to my attention. On Imroth, see also Alexander, *Holiday*, p. 48.
59   See 'Delagoa Lands', *Rand Daily Mail*, 13 March 1914.
60   In 1896, Cohen was described by his bankers as being 'respectable, hard-working and energetic', but by 1910 he was characterised as being 'hopelessly insolvent' although 'smart and plausible'. See RSA, JHB, SBA & HS, Lourenço Marques Inspection, 31 August 1896; and Inspection Report, Lourenço Marques Branch, 8 July 1910.
61   For the winter-season attractions arranged by the CDT, which included various excursions, concerts, a regatta and a tennis tournament, see, for example, *Rand Daily Mail*, 15 June 1916.

62 See B.J.N. Marçal, 'Um império projectado pelo "silvo da locomotiva"', PhD thesis, Department of History, Universidade Nova de Lisboa, July 2016, p. 209; and A.B. de Melo's comprehensive 'A Polana e O Hotel Polana', blog post, *The Delagoa Bay Review*, 15 February 2010, which is partly based on original documents and a complementary article, not cited, by José Maria Mesquitela [hereafter ABS, 'A Polana e O Hotel Polana'].
63 See Peleggi, 'Colonial Hotels', pp. 125–126.
64 Paragraph based on ABS, 'A Polana e O Hotel Polana'; A. Carvalho and J.M. Henriques (eds.), *O Estoril e as Origens do Turismo em Portugal* (Cascais, 2011); C.O. Moreira, 'Portugal as a Tourism Destination: Paths and Trends', *Méditerranée: Journal of Mediterranean Geography*, No. 130 (2018) (no page numbers); and G. Verheij, 'The Aesthetic of Lisbon', unpublished PhD thesis, Faculty of Arts, University of Barcelona, April 2017, p. 118.
65 See ABS, 'A Polana e O Hotel Polana'.
66 See RSA, Pretoria, NASA, GOV, Vol. 1407, PS 13/114/07, 1907, Appointments Maia – Portuguese Curator and, in the *Rand Daily Mail*, items on 27 April and 10 May 1907.
67 See ABS, 'A Polana e O Hotel Polana'; and Anúncios na Revista Colonia', 4 November 2017.
68 On the differences between aspirant 'patriotic' capitalists and others in Lourenço Marques, see, for example, J.M. Penvenne, *African Workers and Colonial Racism: Mozambican Strategies and Struggles in Lourenço Marques, 1877–1962* (London, 1995), pp. 30–31.
69 The most likely connection was Giuseppe Sorgentini, who purchased the Cardoso Hotel in 1935. See Alexander, *Holiday*, p. 47.
70 See MOZ, Maputo, AHM, *Govérno Geral de Moçambique*, CX.163, *Aruivo da Repartição do Gabinet* (ARG), *Pasta B/5, Exmo. Sr. Director Geral das Alfandengas*, signed by J.J. Chalus, 30 July 1922.
71 ABS, 'A Polana e O Hotel Polana'.
72 See ABS, 'A Polana e O Hotel Polana', and United States of America, *Bureau of Foreign and Domestic Commerce, Commerce Reports 1918* (Washington, DC, 1918), p. 778 [hereafter USA, *Commerce Report* 1918].
73 The finest description of the newly opened Polana Hotel – which still makes for impressive reading – is to be found in the *Rand Daily Mail* of 5 July 1922. Not coincidentally, the *Rand Daily Mail* was owned by JCI, which was heavily invested in the DBLS, which owned the Polana Hotel.
74 See *Rand Daily Mail*, 8 November 1922, and ABS, 'A Polana e O Hotel Polana'. The Polana Hotel was still receiving a subsidy from the state into the 1940s; see MOZ, Maputo, AHM, ARG, 1925–1948, Pasta C/39, A. de Souza Moutinho to Governor-General, Commandante Gabriel Teixeira, Lourenço Marques, 11 December 1948.
75 See ABS, 'A Polana e O Hotel Polana'.
76 See, for example, ABS, 'A Polana e O Hotel Polana' or contemporary advertising for the 'Serena Polana Hotel'.
77 On the contract being awarded to AH & W Reid and Delbridge, see ABS, 'A Polana e O Hotel Polana'. For W.J. Delbridge, the principal designer, see the

obituary carried in the *Cape Times*, 22 October 1946; and on the role of Cyril W. Reid in assisting with the Polana design, the *Journal of the Association of Transvaal Architects*, Vol. 5, No. 11 (March 1917), p. 62.
78   See *Rand Daily Mail*, 5 July 1922.
79   See, ABS, 'A Polana e O Hotel Polana'.
80   See *The Times* (London), 29 December 1921.
81   For escalating costs see, among others, USA, *Commerce Report 1918*, p. 778; ABS, 'A Polana e O Hotel Polana'; *Rand Daily Mail*, 5 July 1922; and RSA, JHB, SBA & HS, Inspection Report on the Lourenço Marques Branch on 31 January 1924.
82   See *Rand Daily Mail*, 5 July 1922, and 22 November 1922.
83   See *Rand Daily Mail*, 22 November 1922.
84   See S. Katzenellenbogen, *South Africa and Southern Mozambique: Labour, Railways and Trade in the Making of a Relationship* (Manchester, 1982), p. 138.
85   It is significant that this, too, was the moment at which the short-lived, Johannesburg-dominated Delagoa Bay Turf Club was launched; see MOZ, Maputo, AHM, *Boletim Oficial*, 3a Serie, No. 49, December 1922.
86   *Rand Daily Mail*, 8 November 1922, and Correo, 'Heterotopia', p. 25.
87   See various proposals and tenders as contained in MOZ, Maputo, AHM, *Govêrno Geral de Mocambique, Arquivo da Repartição do Gabinete, Processo c/14*, which covers the period 1920 to 1950.
88   See, for example, *Rand Daily Mail*, 8 November 1922.
89   National Archives of Zimbabwe, Harare, Hst. Mss. Newton Papers, W.M. Leggate to Sir Francis Newton, 2 September 1925. I am indebted to Ian Phimister for drawing this item to my attention.
90   On illegal casinos, see, among others, Nance, 'Holiday', p. 965, and *Rand Daily Mail*, 30 November 1923. On the prohibition of casinos by the late 1960s, see Alexander, *Holiday*, p. 14.
91   See *Rand Daily Mail*, 17 March 1926 and 20 March 1928.
92   See *Rand Daily Mail*, 17 March 1926.
93   See an especially informative section in R.G. Forman's nonetheless sadly titled 'Randy on the Rand: Portuguese African Labor and the Discourse on "Unnatural Vice" in the Transvaal from the Early Twentieth Century', *Journal on the History of Sexuality*, Vol. 11, No. 4 (October 2002), pp. 570–609.
94   Gordimer, 'South African Riviera', p. 168 [emphasis in the original].
95   See Clarence-Smith, *The Third Empire*, pp. 154–155, and, for post-colonial decline, p. 208.
96   On disruptions, see, for example, P. Gupta, 'Consuming the Coast: Mid-century Communications of Port Tourism in the Southern Indian Ocean', *Communição Midia e Consimo*, Vol. 12, No. 35 (2015), pp. 165 [hereafter Gupta, 'Consuming the Coast'].
97   RSA, JHB, South African Railways Heritage Centre (SARHC), File 329.1.11, *Lourenço Marques: A Corner of Europe in S Africa* (1928) [hereafter SARHC, *A Corner of Europe*]. (The deliberately incomplete 'S' in the title – 'S Africa' – can, presumably, be read in several ways but, one assumes, was designed to be reassuring for Transvaal-based visitors.

98   SARHC, *A Corner of Europe*.
99   See *Rand Daily Mail*, 10 January 1927 and 8 August 1928.
100 See *Rand Daily Mail*, 9 April 1935.
101 On the Blue Train, see, for example, RSA, Pretoria, NASA, BTS, 01, File 37/17, EK Scallon, Consul General, Lourenço Marques to Controller of Censorship, Pretoria, 2 September 1941; on cruise liners, see Gupta, 'Consuming the Coast', pp. 151–170; and, for the wider context, G.H. Pirie, 'Elite Exoticism: Sea-Rail Tourism in South Africa, 1926–1939', *African Historical Review*, Vol. 43, No. 1 (June 2011), pp. 73–99 [hereafter Pirie, 'Elite Exoticism'].
102 Bullfights, held over the Easter break, became something of a lasting attraction and were underwritten by two farm enterprises that bred special 'fighting bulls'. See Alexander, *Holiday*, pp. 54–56.
103 SARHC, A Corner of Europe. On the short-lived Delagoa Bay Turf Club, launched on 22 November 1922 at the height of Polana Hotel fever, see MOZ, Maputo, AHM, *Boletim Oficial*, 22 November 1922, 3a Série, No. 49, December 1922.
104 SARHC, *A Corner of Europe*.
105 *Rand Daily Mail*, 9 June 1936. For the casinos being inserted into cruise liner itineraries, see Gupta, 'Consuming the Coast', p. 164. For more detailed histories of the casinos see MOZ, Maputo, AHM, Fundo Governo Geral, Caixa 209, Pasta c/21.
106 Resorts have, of course, long been seen as 'morally ambiguous destinations'; see Sterngass, *First Resorts*, p. 155.
107 SARHC, *A Corner of Europe* – the 1928 and 1929 editions.
108 See MOZ, Maputo, AHM, Fundo Governo Geral, *Arquivo da Repartição do Gabinete*, Caixo 209, Pasta 2/23, unsigned memo from Delagoa Bay Lands Syndicate to Governor General, November 1946.
109 This echoes how 'conflicting constructions of class, race, and gender produced a culture clash between visiting consumers and hosts but also spurred negotiation'; see D. Merrill, *Negotiating Paradise: U.S. Tourism and Empire in Twentieth-Century Latin America* (Chapel Hill, 2009), p. xiii.
110 See also Nance, 'Holiday', p. 908; Peleggi, 'Colonial Hotels', p. 22; and for the serried ranks of Portuguese taxi-drivers, SARHC, *A Corner of Europe* (no page nos.); Duffy, *Portuguese Africa*, p. 298.
111 Duffy, *Portuguese Africa*, pp. 298–299.
112 All of these can be illustrated from case studies to be found in the following files in RSA, Pretoria, NASA, SAB, SAP, Ref. 1/57/39, Vol. 2; TAB. CS, Ref. 924/18503; and SAB, SAP, Confidential, Ref. Conf 6/160/13.
113 See also Peleggi, 'Colonial Hotels', p. 18.
114 See the following files, RSA, Pretoria, NASA, SAB, SAP, Ref. 1/57/39, Vol. 2; TAB. CS, Ref. 924/18503; and SAB, SAP, Confidential, Ref. Conf 6/160/13.
115 See RSA, Pretoria, NASA, SAB, JUS, Vol. 955, File 1/840,26/1, Report of Det.-Sergeant J.J. Coetzee to Divisional C.I. Officer, Pretoria, 24 September 1926, and *Rand Daily Mail*, 8 July 1928, and, for earlier, as noted by Scully around 1912, note 21 above.
116 Nance, 'Holiday', p. 964.

117 MacDonald, 'South Africa's International Borders', pp. 193–194.
118 RSA, Pretoria, NASA, SAB/SAP1/57/39, 'Information on South African girls employed in Dance Halls, Lourenço Marques', Consul General, Lourenço Marques to Secretary for External Affairs, 22 September 1949.
119 See MOZ, Maputo, AHM, Fundo Governo Geral, *Arquivo da Repartição do Gabinete, Pasta B/5*, Consul General to Governor General, 8 October 1935, and Consul General to Governor General, 21 February 1935.
120 See RSA, Pretoria, NASA, SAB/SAP1/57/39, file on 'Information on South African girls employed in Dance Halls, Lourenço Marques' for post-World War II passport cases; and for the circulation of names, in the same file, Deputy Commissioner of Police, Witwatersrand Division to the Commissioner of Police, Pretoria, 21 October 1949.
121 *Rand Daily Mail*, 8 March 1928.
122 See RSA, Pretoria, NASA, SAB SAP, Vol. 4, File 1/57/39, Consul General to the Secretary for the Interior, Pretoria, 27 July 1953.
123 See MacDonald, 'South Africa's International Borders', pp. 198–201.
124 RSA, Pretoria, NASA, SAB/SAP1/57/39, 'Information on South African girls employed in Dance Halls', Circular No. 8 of 1946, J.S. Hurter, Secretary for the Interior; and Secretary for External Affairs to Minister Plenipotentiary of the Union of South Africa, undated.
125 RSA, Pretoria, NASA, SAB/SAP1/57/39, 'Information on South African girls employed in Dance Halls', Secretary for External Affairs to Minister Plenipotentiary of the Union of South Africa, undated.
126 See, for example, RSA, Pretoria, NASA, SAB SAP, Vol. 4, File 1/57/39, Major Spengler to Commissioner of Police, 2 March 1954.
127 RSA, Pretoria, NASA, SAB/SAP1/57/39, 'Information on South African girls employed in Dance Halls', Chief Inspector commanding Witwatersrand Division to Commissioner of Police, Pretoria, 11 July 1954.
128 RSA, Pretoria, NASA, SAB/SAP1/57/39, 'Information on South African girls employed in Dance Halls', Secretary for External Affairs to Commissioner of South African Police, 1 May 1954.
129 A. and B. Isaacman, *Mozambique: From Colonialism to Revolution, 1900—1982* (Boulder, 1983), p. 89.
130 Duffy, *Portuguese Africa*, p. 274.
131 Perhaps the best account of the recruitment and treatment of a coloured hostess, Caroline Harrison, is to be found in RSA, Pretoria, NASA, SAB, SAP, File 1/57/39, E.F. Horn, Consul General, Lourenço Marques, to Acting Secretary for External Affairs, Pretoria, 5 November 1946.
132 RSA, Pretoria, NASA, SAB, SAP, File 1/57/39, Deputy Commissioner of Police, Pietermaritzburg, to Commissioner of Police, Pretoria, 21 January 1947.
133 *The Guardian*, as quoted in RSA, Pretoria, NASA, File 1/57/39, E.F Horn, to the Acting Secretary for External Affairs, Pretoria, 9 November 1946.
134 Alexander, *Holiday*, p. 14.
135 *Rand Daily Mail*, 15 June 1936.
136 There is a potted history of the Polana Hotel in Alexander, *Holiday*, pp. 48–49, which suggests that the first manager was T. Kershaw.

137 On other modern 'exotic locales, fenced off from native populations, and far enough from home and at sufficient cost to eliminate those from the lower economic classes', see Sterngass, *First Resorts*, p. 273.
138 See MOZ, Maputo, AHM, Fundo Governo Geral, *Arquivo da Repart tição do Gabinete*, Pasta 3/23 1946 a 1947, I.W. Schlesinger to J. Dias Monteiro, 2 November 1944.
139 MOZ, Maputo, AHM, Fundo Governo Geral, *Arquivo da Repartição do Gabinete*, Pasta 3/23 1946 a 1947, I.W. Schlesinger to J. Dias Monteiro, 2 November 1944.
140 MOZ, Maputo, AHM, Fundo Governo Geral, *Arquivo da Repartição do Gabinete*, Pasta 3/23 1946 a 1947, I.W. Schlesinger to J. Dias Monteiro, 2 November 1944.
141 See Pirie, 'Elite Exoticism', pp. 73–99.
142 In the extreme case, that of Afrikaner nationalists, this is convincingly and imaginatively portrayed in A. Grundlingh's 'Holidays at Hartenbos: Sand, Sea and Sun in the Construction of Afrikaner Cultural Nationalism, c. 1920– c. 1961', in his *Potent Pastimes: Sport and Leisure in Modern Afrikaner History* (Pretoria, 2013), pp. 34–53.
143 As ever, there are exceptions to this objection. The extensive and imaginative choice of subjects by Albert Grundlingh has done much, over many years to deepen our understanding of the social history of Afrikaners from the South African War into the modern era. N. Roos's *Ordinary Whites in Apartheid Society: A Social History of Accommodation, Complicity and Transgression* (forthcoming) promises to set a new benchmark for such studies.
144 See B. Maharaj, V. Pillay and R. Suchen, 'Durban a Subtropical Paradise? Tourism Dynamics in a Post-Apartheid City', *Études caribéennes*, Nos. 9–10 (April 2008), para. 10. It is difficult to understand why South African coastal resorts have not attracted more interest from those South African historians capable of seeing beyond the beach and willing to ask more theoretically informed questions.
145 I have slightly modified this phrase, hijacked from D. Kennedy's *The Magic Mountains: Hill Stations and the British Raj* (Los Angeles, 1996).
146 W. May, *The Highest Peak* (London, 1967) offers the familiar story of a beautiful young lady from upper-class Johannesburg who meets, and falls in love with a handsome, mysterious uniformed Portuguese officer in Lourenço Marques of the 1950s. It no doubt mirrors the experience of some female visitors.
147 Gordimer, 'South African Riviera', p. 171.

Part II

1 Most of the factual material that follows relating to the foundational history of broadcasting – but none of the analysis or interpretations that precede or follow in this chapter – derives from E. Rosenthal, *You Have Been Listening: The Early History of Radio in South Africa* (London, 1974), pp. 1–159 [hereafter Rosenthal, *The Early History*]. Rosenthal provided much factual material but

never documented his sources.
2. The best account of the Reith invitation and visit is P.J. Meyer's *Genl. J.B.M. Hertzog, Sir John Reith en die Uitsaaiwet van 1936*, Genl. J.B.M. Hertzog-gedenklesing Xl, Pretoria, 8 Oktober 1981 (publisher and date of publication unknown) [hereafter Meyer, *Hertzog*].
3. See D.R. Browne, 'Radio Normandie and the IBC Challenge to the BBC Monopoly', *Historical Journal of Film, Radio and Television*, Vol. 5, No. 1 (1985), pp. 1–7 [hereafter Browne, 'Normandie'].
4. Browne, 'Normandie', pp. 5–7.
5. G.J. McHarry's interest in radio dated to 1919 when he printed an in-house magazine that later went public for Philips S.A. Ltd. When Philips decided that the cost of producing the magazine had become prohibitive, in 1930, during the Depression, McHarry bought it and renamed it *The African Radio Announcer* – from a timeline contained in a letter to the author from Patrick McHarry (grandson of G.J.M.), 11 May 2020; see also Rosenthal, *The Early History*, p. 148. On the origins of the Rádio Clube de Moçambique, see C. Miller, 'Focus on Africa: The Mozambique Radio Story', *Wavescan*, 21 July 2014, and G.E. Vaughan, *Portuguese East Africa: Economic and Commercial Conditions in Portuguese East Africa (Moçambique)* (London, 1952), pp. 3–4, 39.
6. As early as April 1933, McHarry was encouraging radio enthusiasts in Lourenço Marques to advertise their programmes in *The African Radio Announcer*; see the comprehensive review of early broadcasting in Mozambique in P. Roque, 'Notas Para a História da Radiodifusão em Moçambique: O Caso do Rádio Clube de Moçambique, 1933–1973', Arquivo, Boletim do Arquivo *Histórico de Moçambique*, No. 3 (April 1988), pp. 47–60 [hereafter Roque, 'O Casa de Rádio Clube'].
7. On G.J.M. first picking up an amateur signal from RCM during the Depression, see P. McHarry to the author, 25 April 2018. Preceding this were radio transmissions of telegraphic-style material that date back to the late 1920s. See, for example, 'The Radio Station at Delagoa Bay', *Rand Daily Mail*, 20 June 1927. On the early history of RCM, see M. Power, 'Aqui Lourenço Marques!! Radio Colonisation and Cultural Identity in Colonial Mozambique, 1932–74', *Journal of Historical Geography*, Vol. 26, No. 4 (2000), pp. 605–628.
8. For some of the early background to McHarry and the concession, see also 'SABC takes over LM Radio Deal from tycoon of 78', *Sunday Times* (Johannesburg), 30 May 1971.
9. From a timeline of the family history provided to the author by Patrick McHarry in a letter dated 4 May 2018.
10. GJM's childhood reconstructed from letters to the author by Patrick McHarry dated 4 May and 10 June 2018.
11. See 'Story of a Cheque', *Rand Daily Mail*, 30 September 1916, and *The South African Indian Who's Who 1936*, p. 67.
12. On the original five-year concession, see, for example, RSA, JHB, SABC Headquarters, Auckland Park, Minutes of a Meeting of the South African Broadcasting Corporation (SABC), Board of Governors (BOG) held on 25 August 1970, pp. 8–9 [hereafter all such minutes referred to as RSA, SABC, BOG Minutes].

13 Roque, 'O Casa de Rádio Clube', p. 53.
14 See MOZ, Maputo, AHM, Fundo Governo Geral, Caixa 288, undated and unsigned 'Memorial – Como se Fundou e o que é Rádio Clube de Moçambique', c. 1941, p. 12.
15 The best summary of the origin and nature of the SABC's financial predicament, arising from having more than one official language to cater for, is to be found in RSA, Bloemfontein, University of the Free State, Archive for Contemporary Affairs, Afrikaner Broederbond collection, File AB 10/68, 'Kommissie vs Radio, 1955/57' [hereafter RSA, Bloemfontein, UFS, ACA].
16 For the full range of these organisations and their modes of engagement, see T.D. Moodie, *The Rise of Afrikanerdom; Power, Apartheid and the Afrikaner Civil Religion* (Berkeley, 1975) [hereafter Moodie, *The Rise of Afrikanerdom*] and D. O'Meara, *Volkskapitalisme: Class, Capital, and Ideology in the Development of Afrikaner Nationalism, 1934—1948* (Johannesburg, 1983) [hereafter O'Meara, *Volkskapitalisme*].
17 Rosenthal, *The Early History*, p. 60.
18 J. Matisson, *God, Spies and Lies: Finding South Africa's Future Through its Past* (Vlaeberg, 2015), p. 62 [hereafter Matisson, *God, Spies and Lies*].
19 See Meyer, *Hertzog*, p. 5.
20 For complaints that predate the passing of the 1936 Broadcasting Act, see, for example, 'Wireless Fees', *Rand Daily Mail*; and on language issues, Letters to the Editor, *Rand Daily Mail*, 5 May 1937.
21 See Moodie, *The Rise of Afrikanerdom*, pp. 50, 99–100, and O'Meara, *Volkskapitalisme*, pp. 60–63.
22 Moodie, as cited in *The Rise of Afrikanerdom*, pp. 107–109, and G.D. Scholtz, as cited therein.
23 Matisson, *God, Spies and Lies*, p. 26.
24 Matisson, *God, Spies and Lies*, pp. 26–27.
25 See D. Prinsloo, 'Dr. Piet Meyer in Johannesburg, 1936–1984', *Historia*, Vol. 32, No. 1 (May 1987), pp. 44–54 [hereafter Prinsloo, 'Piet Meyer'].
26 Prinsloo, 'Piet Meyer', p. 47.
27 Prinsloo, 'Piet Meyer', p. 49, and O'Meara, *Volkskapitalisme*, p. 204.
28 See Prinsloo, 'Piet Meyer', p. 51, but, more especially, P.J. Meyer, *Nog Nie Ver Genoeg Nie: 'n Persoonlike Rekenskap van Vyftig Jaar Georganiseerde Afrikanerskap* (Johannesburg, 1984), pp. 80–81 [hereafter Meyer, *Nog Nie Ver Genoeg Nie*].
29 See, for example, Moodie, *The Rise of Afrikanerdom*, pp. 209, 221 and 256.
30 Between 1938 and 1942, the number of radio listeners licensed annually in South Africa increased by a double-digit percentage, but from that elevated platform growth slowed – to a single-digit percentage increase – between 1943 and 1946; see T.M. Mhlambi, 'Early Radio Broadcasting in South Africa: Culture, Modernity and Technology', DPhil thesis, South African College of Music, University of Cape Town, 2015.
31 See *Rand Daily Mail*, 16 May 1939.
32 See *Rand Daily Mail*, 26 June 1938,
33 Timeline and entry appended in a letter to the author from P. McHarry, 4 May 2018.

34   MOZ, AHM, Arquivo da Repartiçao do Gabinete, 1937–1948, Pasta y/12, O Chefe da 3a Divisão, Into, Pedido de Autorieação para a Montagem de Una Potenete e Moderna Estação Transmissora de Radiodifusão, em Lourenço Marques, 4 July 1915 [15-year concession], and O Chefe do Gabinete to Cônsul Geral de Portugal, Nova York, 10 July 1941.
35   See R. Teer-Tomaselli, 'The Contradictions of Public Service and Commercialisation in Mid-century South African Broadcasting: A Case Study of the Schoch Commission and Springbok Radio', *Media History*, Vol. 25, No. 2 (2019), p. 231 [hereafter Teer-Tomaselli, 'Mid-century South African Broadcasting']. On the composition of the commission and its reception, see *Rand Daily Mail*, 6 and 7 September 1946.
36   Teer-Tomaselli, 'Mid-century South African Broadcasting', pp. 232–236. But, from the outset, this unusual private-public/commercial-state model met with opposition in certain business quarters hoping that any new station would be firmly in the hands of free-market entrepreneurs. See, for example, *Rand Daily Mail*, 8 September 1948.
37   MOZ, AHM, Arquivo da Repartiçao do Gabinete, 1937–1948, Pasta y/12, O Chefe da 3a Divisão, R. Stark to Lieutenant Eugenio Fiereira de Almeida, 26 October 1948.
38   As McHarry told Carel Birkby of the *Sunday Times* in a rare interview on 30 May 1971, 'McHarry retained one-third of the net profits of commercial operations at LM Radio and Davenport and Meyer received two-thirds for their management'. This long-standing arrangement went on to leave McHarry a comfortable millionaire.
39   RSA, Pretoria, Commissioner of Companies & Intellectual Property Commission, Disclosure Certificate, issued 18 May 2018, Davenport & Meyer, registered on 11 December 1946, updated with newly active managers listed between 1948 and 1965 – firm later dissolved.
40   Obituary, *The Independent*, 21 November 2006.
41   This summary of Dickie Meyer's career is drawn largely from letters to the author from a former disc jockey at LMR, Gary Edwards, dated 23, 28 and 30 June 2018. Meyer's promotion in the army can be traced in the *Supplement to the London Gazette*, 21 September 1945. For additional information on him, see also the *Rand Daily Mail* of 2 May and 18 June 1950, and 27 October 1960.
42   This paragraph is based on the letters to the author from Patrick McHarry (briefly, in 1960, a disc jockey at LMR) dated 4 May and 11 May 2018.
43   Paragraph based on items drawn from the *Rand Daily Mail* of 29 September 1940, 4 November 1940, 17 January 1948, 16–26 March 1948, and on LMR's response, 16 June 1948, as well as a letter to the author from Patrick McHarry, 25 April 2018.
44   See, for example, letter to the Editor from 'Psalms', *Rand Daily Mail*, 20 May 1949.
45   Not all McHarry's advertising arrangements – which were monopolistic insofar as LMR was concerned – went uncontested; see, for example, 'Judgment for £223 in Broadcasting Dispute', *Rand Daily Mail*, 5 November 1946.
46   See 'Radio as I hear it', *Rand Daily Mail*, 2 February and 4 July 1949.

47 This paragraph is based on material drawn from the *Rand Daily Mail* of 5 January, 2 February, 31 May and 15 June 1948.
48 *Rand Daily Mail*, 2 May 1950.
49 RSA, Pretoria, NASA, TAB, WLD Ref. 1864/1950 and TAB, WLD Ref. 412/1954.
50 See *Rand Daily Mail*, 1 February and 11 September 1950; and *Sunday Times*, 5 November 1950.
51 For examples of these, see the *Rand Daily Mail* of 14 and 21 September and 30 December 1950; 31 January 1951; and 5 January, 6 February and 2 March 1952.
52 See *Rand Daily Mail*, 5 July 1950.
53 'SABC charging too much for Imported Programmes', *Rand Daily Mail*, 26 May 1950.
54 On McHarry's changing lifestyle, see items in the *Rand Daily Mail* of 30 April 1954, 22 October 1954, 18 June 1955 and 24 August 1957.
55 See also 'Powerful new Radio Tests in L. Marques', *Sunday Times*, 5 October 1956.
56 See 'Radio War in Africa Lost', *Rand Daily Mail*, 30 May 1956.
57 See RSA, Pretoria, Erfenisstigting, Afrikanerbond Archive, File AB 11/23, Ref. 7/1952/P&R/Alg. – the quotations are taken from the collection of responses from various branches. All translations from Afrikaans – here and below – are those of the author.
58 See W.A. de Klerk, *The Puritans in Africa: A Story of Afrikanerdom* (London, 1975), p. 196 [hereafter De Klerk, *The Puritans*].
59 RSA, Pretoria, Erfenisstigting, Afrikanerbond Archive, File AB 11/23, Ref. 7/1952/P&R/Alg. 'Ontwikkeling op Radiogebied' (1954).
60 RSA, Pretoria, Erfenisstigting, Afrikanerbond Archive, File AB 11/23, Ref. 7/1952/P&R/Alg., unsigned letter from VDS to J.J. Serfontein, Bryntirion, Pretoria, 8 November 1955.
61 RSA, Pretoria, Erfenisstigting, Afrikanerbond Archive, File AB 11/23, Ref. 7/1952/P&R/Alg. Unsigned SABC Memo by 'GR' 'Springbok-Radio – Kortgolf-Afdeling', 8 May 1956.
62 See the revealing chapter in Meyer's memoirs, *Nog Nie Ver Genoeg Nie*, pp. 103–159. On his ability to tame ministers, and for the tension in his relationship with the equally authoritarian Verwoerd, see, especially, pp. 110, 114–117, 120, 128, 134, 137–138 and 157; see also Prinsloo, 'Piet Meyer', pp. 51–52.
63 Meyer, *Nog Nie Ver Genoeg Nie*, p. 154.
64 For the reasons as stated by Meyer for Roos's resignation and the retirement package that was negotiated, see RSA, SABC, BOG Minutes, Meeting held on 28 October 1969, p. 1.
65 See Meyer, *Nog Nie Ver Genoeg Nie*, pp. 114–115.
66 See Prinsloo, 'Piet Meyer', pp. 51–54.
67 Meyer, *Nog Nie Ver Genoeg Nie*, p. 152.
68 The description of Meyer came in a review of one of his books carried in the *Cape Times*; see Meyer, *Nog Nie Ver Genoeg Nie*, p. 152, and, on the Rand Afrikaans University, pp 160–189; see also Prinsloo, 'Piet Meyer', pp. 52–54.
69 See Prinsloo, 'Piet Meyer', p. 51.
70 See Meyer, *Nog Nie Ver Genoeg Nie*, p. 143.

71　RSA, SABC, BOG Minutes, Meeting held on 29 May 1968.
72　Significantly, the period 1955–1968 also saw a doubling in the number of AB members, from 4749 to 8154; see I. Wilkins and H. Strydom, *The Super Afrikaners: Inside the Broederbond* (Johannesburg, 2015), p. 47.
73　See, especially, A. Grundlingh's seminal '"Are We Afrikaners Getting too Rich?" Cornucopia and Change in Afrikanerdom in the 1960s', *Journal of Historical Sociology*, Vol. 21, No. 2/3 (June/September 2008), and, as regards radio, more especially pp. 153–157 [hereafter Grundlingh, '"Are We Afrikaners Getting too Rich?"'].
74　See De Klerk, *The Puritans*, pp. 300–305.
75　Paragraph based on letters to the author from P. McHarry, 25 April 2018; J. Berks, 22 June 2018; and K. Giemre (Financial Manager at D&M, 1964–1967), 25 and 26 June 2018.
76　Letter to the author from P. McHarry, 22 May 2018. Among many others, disc jockeys included Darryl Jooste, Gary Edwards, Evelyn Martin, Robin Alexander, John Berks and David Gresham.
77　Letters to the author from P. McHarry, 25 April and 11 May 2018. Jingles included 'You'll wonder where the dullness went when you brush your teeth with Pepsodent!'
78　G.J. McHarry's personal and LMR's commitment to religious broadcasts – some on Sunday nights – dated back to at least the early 1950s. See, for example, the advert for 'How Christian Science Heals', *Sunday Times*, 27 December 1953.
79　Interview with J. Berks, 22 June 2018, and letter to the author from P. McHarry, 4 May 2018.
80　Letter to the author from K. Giemre, (Financial Manager at D&M, 1964–1967), 26 June 2018.
81　Letter to the author from P. McHarry, 17 May 2018.
82　See 'Jazz on Sunday Now', *Rand Daily Mail*, 2 March 1960.
83　See Grundlingh, '"Are We Afrikaners Getting too Rich?"', p. 154; and on 'the youth' and 'modern music' and the temptations of LMR, see also RSA, SABC, BOG Minutes, meetings held on 25 October 1966, 30 January 1968 and 26 October 1970. For the wider context, see S.D. van der Merwe, '"Radio Apartheid": Investigating a History of Compliance and Resistance in Popular Afrikaans Music, 1956–1979', *South African Historical Journal*, Vol. 66, No. 2 (2014), pp. 349–370.
84　On the 1960s, see G. Nattrass, *A Short History of South Africa* (Cape Town, 2017), pp. 186–198.
85　RSA, SABC, BOG Minutes, Meeting held on 27 August 1969.
86　See RSA, SABC, BOG Minutes, meetings held on 24 January and 27 June 1967.
87　RSA, SABC, BOG Minutes, Meeting held on 15 June 1967.
88　See RSA, SABC, BOG Minutes, meetings held on 23 August 1966 and 22 August 1967.
89　For Meyer's fulsome praise of Bradshaw upon introducing him to the board, see RSA, SABC, BOG Minutes, Meeting held on 23 February 1965.
90　See, for example, 'Rhodes man at talks on Reds', *Evening Post* (Port Elizabeth), 28 March 1964, and, for Meyer's own long-standing 'anti-communist' activism

and credentials, Prinsloo, 'Piet Meyer', p. 48.
91 RSA, SABC, BOG Minutes, Meeting held on 26 March 1968.
92 RSA, SABC, BOG Minutes, Meeting held on 22 April 1969.
93 On Weiss's introduction to the board by Meyer, see SABC, BOG Minutes, Meeting held on 27 June 1967.
94 See, for example, RSA, SABC, Minutes of the 63rd meeting of the 'Board of Control' of the SABC held on 23 February 1971.
95 See Bradshaw's criticism and suggestions in RSA, SABC, BOG Minutes, Meeting held on 29 May 1968.
96 See, for example, RSA, SABC, BOG Minutes, Meeting held on 26 September 1967. For Meyer's take on the necessity for such a programme, see Meyer, *Nog Nie Ver Genoeg Nie*, pp. 121–122.
97 See RSA, SABC, BOG Minutes, Meeting held on 22 August 1967.
98 See RSA, SABC, BOG Minutes, Meeting held on 26 October 1971.
99 See RSA, SABC, BOG Minutes, Meeting held on 22 June 1965.
100 RSA, SABC, BOG Minutes, Meeting held on 22 June 1965.
101 See, for example, RSA, Minutes of the Executive Meeting held on 2 May 1967.
102 See, RSA, SABC, BOG Minutes, meetings held on 22 March 1966 and 24 April 1967.
103 See, especially, RSA, SABC, BOG Minutes, Meeting held on 30 January 1968 and the 'various steps taken by the Corporation to counteract the activities of possible pirate stations'.
104 See, for example, RSA, SABC, BOG Minutes, Meeting held on 30 January 1968, item 11.
105 See RSA, SABC, BOG Minutes, Meeting held on 30 January, and, for more discontent, Minutes of a Meeting held on 26 March 1968.
106 RSA, SABC, BOG Minutes, Meeting held on 29 May 1968.
107 Letter to the author from P. McHarry, 7 May 2018.
108 The death of G.J. McHarry is recorded in the *Rand Daily Mail*, 21 July 1975.
109 1965–1969 formed the core years in the cautious but growing military cooperation between Portugal and South Africa, with the liberation war in Angola taking priority over that in Mozambique. See, especially, P. Correia and G. Verhoef, 'Portugal and South Africa: Close Allies or Unwilling Partners in Southern Africa during the Cold War', *Scientia Militaria: South African Journal of Military Studies*, Vol. 37, No. 1 (2009) and, especially, pages 59–60, 62, and 64–65 [hereafter Correia and Verhoef, 'Portugal and South Africa'].
110 RSA, SABC, BOG Minutes, Meeting held on 25 February 1969.
111 RSA, SABC, BOG Minutes, Meeting held on 25 February 1969.
112 RSA, SABC, BOG Minutes, Meeting held on 22 April 1969. Two months later, Meyer was still complaining about how the government was 'reluctant to designate Radio Lourenço Marques in terms of the proposed legislation with the result that neighbouring Lesotho or Swaziland might, and with justification, say that if the Portuguese could be given the "green light" why should they be excluded' – see Minutes of the Bantu Programme Control Board Meeting held on 17 June 1969. Regional politics, insofar as they shaped the emerging politics of radio, were clearly becoming increasingly difficult to manage.

113 RSA, Bloemfontein, UFS, ACA, ARCA-PV 720, Meyer Collection, undated 'Memorandum with a View to Discussions between the SABC and Portuguese Quarters'. The wording of the title of the document, drafted in mid-1969, underscores how anxious the governments of both South Africa and Portugal were to avoid allowing the negotiations any easily identifiable, formal standing in Pretoria or Lisbon.
114 RSA, Bloemfontein, UFS, ACA, ARCA-PV 720, Meyer Collection, Secretary, Department of Foreign Affairs to P.J. Meyer, Chairman of the Board of Control, SABC, 6 May 1969.
115 RSA, Bloemfontein, UFS, ACA, ARCA-PV 720, Meyer Collection, undated 'Memorandum with a View to Discussions between the SABC and Portuguese Quarters'.
116 RSA, Bloemfontein, UFS, ACA, ARCA-PV 720, Meyer Collection, undated 'Memorandum with a View to Discussions between the SABC and Portuguese Quarters'.
117 RSA, Bloemfontein, UFS, ACA, ARCA-PV 720, Meyer Collection, undated 'Memorandum with a View to Discussions between the SABC and Portuguese Quarters'.
118 RSA, Bloemfontein, UFS, ACA, ARCA-PV 720, Meyer Collection, undated 'Memorandum with a View to Discussions between the SABC and Portuguese Quarters'.
119 See Correia and Verhoef, 'Portugal and South Africa', pp. 59 and 64.
120 See Correia and Verhoef, 'Portugal and South Africa', pp. 55, 59, 60, 62 and 64.
121 RSA, Bloemfontein, UFS, ACA, ARCA-PV 720, Meyer Collection, undated 'Memorandum with a View to Discussions between the SABC and Portuguese Quarters'.
122 See *Sunday Times*, 30 May 1971.
123 RSA, SABC, BOG Minutes, Meeting held on 24 November 1970.
124 RSA, SABC, BOG Minutes, Meeting held on 24 November 1970.
125 RSA, SABC, BOG Minutes, Meeting held on 23 February 1971.
126 RSA, SABC, BOG Minutes, Meeting held on 23 February 1971].
127 RSA, SABC, BOG Minutes, Meeting held on 23 February 1971. On the government-to-government aspect of the deal see also, Minutes of the Bantu Programme Control Board, 24 February 1971.
128 RSA, SABC, BOG Minutes, Meeting held on 23 March 1971 and 27 April 1971. The assent, in principle, of the Portuguese government had been procured the previous month; see RSA, SABC, BOG Minutes, Meeting held on 24 February 1971.
129 See, especially, 'SABC take over LM Radio deal from Tycoon', *Sunday Times*, 30 May 1971.
130 *Sunday Times*, 30 May 1971.
131 RSA, SABC, Minutes of the Bantu Programme Control Board, 14 April 1971.
132 RSA, SABC, BOG Minutes, Meeting held on 25 January 1972.
133 See, for example, SABC, BOG Minutes, Meeting held on 22 February 1972.
134 RSA, SABC, BOG Minutes, Meeting held on 25 January 1972.
135 RSA, SABC, BOG Minutes, Meeting held on 28 March 1972.

136 RSA, SABC, BOG Minutes, Meeting held on 28 March 1972.
137 RSA, SABC, Board of Control Minutes, Meeting held on 23 May 1972.
138 RSA, SABC, BOG Minutes, Meeting held on 28 March 1972.
139 RSA, SABC, BOG Minutes, Meeting held on 20 June 1972.
140 RSA, SABC, BOG Minutes, Meeting held on 20 June 1972. On the growing twitchiness of the South African Reserve Bank about financial transfers to Portugal between 1972 and 1974, see, for example, Correia and Verhoef, 'Portugal and South Africa', pp. 69–70.
141 See 'Lourenço Marques Radio and South African Popular Culture' above.
142 Meyer, *Nog Nie Ver Genoeg Nie*, p. 155 [author's translation].
143 Meyer, *Nog Nie Ver Genoeg Nie*, p. 156 [author's translation].
144 See especially RSA, SABC, Report of the Management Committee of June 1972, which shows that the issue of determining the bona fides of various churches – including that of the Billy Graham Evangelistic Association – dated back to January of that year; see RSA, SABC, BOG Minutes, Meeting held on 20 June 1972.
145 Vorster had renewed Meyer's contract for a further period of five years at the SABC, in 1971, but such was Meyer's political reach that, even after the stormy years of 1971–1972, Vorster again renewed his contract for a further period of five years in the year of the Soweto shootings, 1976 – to the continued amazement of so-called enlightened elements within the National Party. See, especially, Meyer, *Nog Nie Ver Genoeg Nie*, pp. 151–154.
146 RSA, SABC, BOG Minutes, Meeting held on 23 August 1972.
147 RSA, SABC, BOG Minutes, Meeting held on 23 August 1972.
148 RSA, SABC, BOG Minutes, Meeting held on 23 August 1972.
149 See, for example, among others, P.S. Lekgoathi, 'The African National Congress's Radio Freedom and its Audiences in Apartheid South Africa', *Journal of African Media Studies*, Vol. 2, No. 2 (August 2010), pp. 139–153.
150 RSA, SABC, Board Minutes, Meeting on 29 June 1973.
151 RSA, SABC, 'Summary of the Contents of the Report of the Director-General, J.N. Swanepoel, June–Aug 1974'.
152 RSA, SABC, 'Summary of the Contents of the Report of the Director-General, J.N. Swanepoel, June–Aug 1974.' See also, 'Summary of the Contents of the Report of the Director-General, J.N. Swanepoel, March 1974'.
153 RSA, SABC, 'Summary of the Contents of the Report of the Director-General, J.N. Swanepoel, June–Aug 1974.'
154 RSA, SABC, Minutes of a Board Meeting held on 25 June 1975.
155 See A. Harvey, 'Counter-Coup in Lourenço Marques: September 1974', *International Journal of African Historical Studies*, Vol. 39, No. 3 (2006), p. 487 [hereafter Harvey, 'Counter-Coup in Lourenço Marques'].
156 RSA, SABC, Minutes of a Board Meeting held on 26 April 1974.
157 RSA, SABC, Minutes of a Board Meeting held on 22 May 1974.
158 See, for example, 'White Exodus hits Mozambique', *Sunday Times*, 6 April 1975.
159 See Harvey, 'Counter-Coup in Lourenço Marques', and, more especially, points 3–8 and 22–26 in the memorandum prepared on the insurrection by the British Consul, S.F. St. C. Duncan, and incorporated verbatim in the article. See also

'Radio Station seized … DGS Men Freed', *Sunday Times*, 8 September 1974.
160 RSA, SABC, Minutes of a Board Meeting held on 24 September 1975.
161 See RSA, SABC, Minutes of Board Meetings held on 28 August and 27 November 1974; and 'Matters arising from the Report of the Director-General, D. Fuchs, November 1974'.
162 RSA, SABC, Minutes of a Board Meeting held on 25 March 1975.
163 RSA, SABC, Minutes of a Board Meeting held on 28 March 1975.
164 RSA, SABC, Minutes of a Board Meeting held on 22 October 1975.
165 See Meyer, *Hertzog*, pp. 9–15, for the centrality of the issue.
166 *Financial Times*, 7 November 2020.
167 See H. Giliomee, *The Afrikaners: Biography of a People* (Charlottesville, 2002), p. 442 [hereafter Giliomee, *The Afrikaners*].
168 On Verwoerd and Meyer's history, see Prinsloo, 'Piet Meyer', p. 47. On differences Verwoerd and Meyer at the SABC, see RSA, SABC, Minutes of a Meeting of the Board of Governors, 22 March 1966. On political conflict between Vorster and Meyer, see RSA, SABC, Minutes of a Meeting of the Board of Governors, 26 September 1967, and especially RSA, SABC, Report of the Director of Programmes, August 1969. The remainder of this paragraph draws on a letter to the author from Hermann Giliomee, 8 December 2020, and, on Cillié and Pienaar, also Giliomee, *The Afrikaners*, pp. 535 and 549.
169 Meyer, *Hertzog*, pp. 19 and 20 [all translations those of the author].

INDEX

Note: Entries in *italics* indicate photographs.

5FM 149

A

AB *see* Afrikaner Broederbond
ABC *see* African Broadcasting Corporation
Act No. 28 of 1896 (Sunday Act) 3
advertising 11, 20, 82, 84–87, 90, 99–101, 104–105, 107–109, 112, 117–118, 121, 131–132, 136, 138–141, 145, 147, 153, 179
African Broadcasting Corporation (ABC) 82–84, 86
African National Congress (ANC) 66, 144
African Radio Announcer, The 85, 89, 153, 177
Afrikaners, Afrikaans 4, 8–9, 18, 56, 77, 79, 82, 90, 93–96, 110–111, 115–116, 119, 121, 151–152, 160, 176
Afrikaner Broederbond (AB, 'Unseen Elect') 10, 93–97, 99, 101, 109–113, 115–116, 120, 123, 126, 130, 133, 140, 158
agriculture, farming 2, 78, 88–89, 174
AH & W Reid 42, 172
Albertyn, Gezina 101
alcohol consumption 4, 6, 18, 23, 71, 75, 120, 130
Allegro, Solar 127
ANC *see* African National Congress
Anglo-Boer War (South African War) 18, 25–26, 30, 38, 78, 94, 106, 121, 176
Angola 129–131, 134, 182
apartheid 10–11, 56, 62, 64, 95, 99, 115, 127–128, 134, 136, 141–143, 149, 155–159
    see also segregation
Associated Scientific and Technical Societies (AS&TS) 81, 86, 91

AS&T Broadcasting Company Ltd 81, 86, 91

B

Baker, Herbert 42–44
Banco Nacional Ultramarino (BNU) 41, 45
Bank of Lisbon 135
Barnato, Barney 37
BBC *see* British Broadcasting Corporation
Beatles, The 121–122
Bello's Casino 53–54
Beukes, Charlotte 60–61
black labour 49, 56, 70, 78
Black Peril cases 34
Blackwell, Leslie 60
BNU *see* Banco Nacional Ultramarino
Board of Control, SABC 125–126, 129, 144, 157, 166
Board of Governors, SABC 111–113, 121, 123, 125, 144, 177, 185
Bonnell, Leslie 138
Boschian, Luigi 40–43
Botha, Louis 127
Botha, PW 11, 123, 125, 128, 130, 134–135
Botswana 127, 139
Bradshaw, Brian 123–124, 158, 181
British Broadcasting Corporation (BBC) 9, 81–82, *83*–85, 90, 101, 106, 152, 157
Broadcasting Act 22 of 1936 9, 83, 92, 131–132, 143, 151, 156, 159–161
Brother No. 787 *see* Meyer, Piet
Buncher, SABC regional manager 124

C

Caborra Bassa dam 134–135
Caetano, Marcello 146

INDEX | 187

Calvin, Jean 23, 61, 106
Calvinism 2–10, 12–13, 23, 53, 56, 58–59, 61, 63, 72–74, 81–82, 86–89, 91, 93–96, 103–104, 109–110, 112, 116, 118, 120, 128, 133, 137, 151–154, 156–157, 159
Camacho, Brito 44, 66
Caminhos de Ferro de Lourenço Marques (CFLM) 50, 52–54
Cape Town 7, 42, 47, 50, 58, 65, 100, 159
Cardoso, Augusto 25, 32–33, 39–43
Carnation Revolution 146–147
Carpenter, Edward 17
casino industry 7, 38–39, 45–47, 53–55, 57, 61–69, 73–74, 173–174
Castle Wine & Spirits 40
Catholicism, Roman Catholic Church 2, 5–7, 9, 12–13, 23, 36, 48, 53, 55–56, 72–74, 87, 89, 110, 118, 154, 160
CDT *see* Conselho de Turismo
censorship 12, 122, 130, 137, 143–145, 150
CFLM *see* Caminhos de Ferro de Lourenço Marques
Christianity 89, 120, 123, 125
'Christianity vs Communism' congress 123
Cillié, PJ 159
class-colour separation, exclusion 34–35, 63
Coetzee, Blaar 108–109, 111–112, 119
Cohen, Leāl (Leon) 38–39, 40, 46, 171
colonisation, colonialism 2, 137, 148, 150–151, 155, 160
Commission of Enquiry into the Operations of the SABC 99–100
Commission on Assaults on Women, 1913 34
communism 123, 125, 127, 130, 137, 160, 182
'Communism in Western Culture' paper 123
compound system, mines 34, 78
Conselho de Turismo (CDT) 32, 35, 37–42, 50, 52, 58, 71–72, 171

Consolidated East Coast Engineers 43
Costa's Casino 52, 63
Costa, Leonida 39, 53, 63
crime 4, 16, 18, 29, 31, 43, 61, 155

D

Dagbreek 96
Davenport, John 101, 116, 179
Davenport & Meyer (Pty) Ltd (D&M) 10–11, 101–105, 107, 116–118, 120, 122, 126, 129, 135, 138–139, 145, 155, 166, 179
Davies, Brenda 102
Davies, David 102, 117, 135
DBLS *see* Delagoa Bay Lands Syndicate
de Amorim, PF Massano 40–41, 43
de Bettencourt, Tristão 67–68
Decree No. 16/75, Mozambique 150
Decree No. 1029, Mozambique 32
Defence Amendment Act, 1967 120
Delagoa Bay 14, 23, 29–30, 32, 36–39, 43–44, 46, 53, 56–58, 63, 73, 75, 86, 172–173
Delagoa Bay Engineering Works 43
Delagoa Bay Lands Syndicate (DBLS) 37–41, 44, 46, 48, 65–66, 171
Delagoa Bay Lottery 36
Delagoa Bay Turf Club 52, 173–174
Delbridge, William 42, 43
de Oliviera, JN 66
de Serpa Pinto, Alexandre 25
de Sousa, Romeu 63
de Spínola, António 146–147
DETA (airline) 19
de Toulouse-Lautrec, Henri 22
'Developments in Radio' memorandum 111–112
de Vries, J van Wyk 111
diamonds 2–3, 14, 70
D&M *see* Davenport & Meyer (Pty) Ltd
do Sacramento, José Vicente 36, 73, 86
dos Santos, Paulino 46
Durban 7, 32, 63, 65, 67–68, 71–72
Dutch East India Company 100
Dutch Reformed churches 2, 91

Dutch Reformed Church (NGK) 2, 120, 125

E
Eiffel, Gustave 42
English speakers 3, 5, 7–9, 29, 48, 56, 119, 123, 151–152
Estado Novo 146
Estoril 7, 39, 45–46
Ewan, Alfred 124
External Services, SABC 127–128, 132, 143

F
Fatti, Luigi 40
FBS *see* Forces Broadcasting Service
Federation of Afrikaner Cultural Organisations (FAK) 94–95, 121
Financial Mail 115
FM radio 113, 115, 139, 143, 149
Forces Broadcasting Service (FBS, British Army) 102, 104
Frelimo 11, 122, 126–127, 129, 146, 148–150
Friedman, Max 89
Fuchs, Douglas 124
Fusion government 80, 82–83, 90, 92

G
Galvão, Alexandre Lopes 38–43, 45
gambling, gaming 3–6, 17–18, 23, 36, 38, 53, 65, 68, 75, 89
   see also lotteries, sweepstakes
Gandhi, Mohandas K 89
Gazeta dos Caminhos de Ferro 39
'General JBM Hertzog, Sir John Reith and the Broadcasting Act of 1936' (lecture) 160
genocide 150, 155
German East Africa Line 26
GJ McHarry (Pty) Ltd 100, 108, 117, 118, 126, 130, 136, 138, 140
Godfrey, William 89
'God Save the King' 116
Goebbels, Joseph 94
gold mining 2–3, 14, 16–17, 41, 50, 63, 66, 70, 86
Gordimer, Nadine 8, 13, 15, 22–23, 49, 76
Gordon, David 102
Goudvis, Bertha 25–26
Great Depression 5, 15, 29, 49–50, 55, 59, 65, 74, 82, 85–87, 94, 153, 177
Grundlingh, Albert 176
Guardian, The 33, 63–64, 66

H
Heidegger, Martin 95, 147
Hertz, Joseph 26
Hertzog, Albert 96, 112, 127
Hertzog, JBM 9, 82, 84, 92, 109, 160–161, 177
Hertzog Memorial Lecture 160
Hess, Rudolf 94, 122
hippy music, culture 122
Hitler, Adolf 92, 94, 157–158
Hofmeyr, JH 91
Hofmeyr, N 2
Hollis, Stanley 14, 25–26
Horn, EF 64
horse-racing industry 38, 46
House of Assembly 80, 96, 108, 152
'House with the Bronze Door' 64
Huguenots 2
Hutus 155

I
IBC *see* International Broadcasting Company
Ibrahim, Abdullah 144
immigrants 3, 21, 78
Immorality Act 21 of 1950 63
imperialism 37, 132, 150, 170
Imroth, Gustav 38, 43
industrial revolution 3, 5, 29, 70, 74–76, 78, 81, 151
International Broadcasting Company (IBC) 84, 102
International Broadcasting Union 85
International Criminal Tribunal for Rwanda 155
International Telecommunications

Convention, 1972 132

J
Jansen, EG 13
jazz 9, 85, 87, 89, 119, 121, 153, 157
JB radio station 81, 91
JCI *see* Johannesburg Consolidated Investments (JCI)
Jesus Christ Superstar 125
Joel, Solly 37, 44
Johannesburg 3–7, 9–10, 13–20, 22–24, 26, 28–32, 36, 38–40, 42, 47, 49, 53, 57–58, 63, 65, 68, 71–72, 81, 85, 87–91, 97, 101, 104, 107, 117–118, 133, 148, 166, 172–173, 176
Johannesburg Consolidated Investments (JCI) 28, 37–38, 44, 46, 65

K
'Kaffir Boom' 37
Kerzner, Sol 689
Kimberley 2–3, 14, 89
Kruger, Paul 3, 18, 37

L
Labour Party 50, 81–82
Lansky, Meyer 67
Leggate, WM 46–47
le May, Hugh 43
Lennon, John 121
Lesotho 127, 139, 182
Lewis & Marks 38
liberalism 12, 87, 101, 118–119, 123, 125, 130, 132, 134, 137
licensing, licence fees, broadcasting 81, 88, 90, 132, 136, 141–143, 153
Lisbon 7, 11, 13, 39, 48, 59, 61–62, 67, 99, 122, 126–131, 133–136, 138, 146–148, 183
'LM Hit Parade' 10, 104, 118–119, 153
LMR *see* Lourenço Marques Radio
longue durée 77
Lord's Day Observance Act No. 19 of 1895 (Cape Colony) 3
Lorentz, Carlos 59

lotteries 18, 23, 35–37, 45–46, 53, 73, 86, 171
 see also gambling, gaming, sweepstakes
Lourenço Marques 5–8, 10–11, 13–20, 22–23, 25–27, 28, 29–31, 35–39, 41–44, 45–53, 56–65, 68–69, 71–74, 76–77, 84–87, 89–90, 98–100, 102–103, 105, 107–108, 115, 117, 120, 131, 133, 136, 139–141, 145, 147–149, 153, 166, 176–177, 182
Lourenço Marques Lottery 35
Lourenço Marques Radio (LMR) 8–11, 77, 84, 86–90, 93, 97–98, 100–108, 111, 115–122, 126–139, 141–150, 153–160, 166, 179, 181

M
MacDonnell, Errol 30–31, 170
Machado, DFV 54
Machado, Leonardino 39
Machel, Samora 149
Macmillan, Harold 119
Maia, Adriano 39–41
Makeba, Miriam 144
Malan, DF 96
Mandela, Nelson 120
Market Research Africa 105
McHarry, GJ (Gabby) 9–11, 85–89, 96–105, 107, 116–118, 126, 129–131, 135–136, 138–139, 141–142, 145, 150, 153, 166, 177, 179–182
 see also GJ McHarry (Pty) Ltd
McHarry, Irene *see* Irene Rainsford
McHarry, Michiel Johannes 88
McHarry, Patrick 129–130, 177
McHarry, Trevor 108, 130, 141
Meiring, Gertruida 57, 60
'Memorandum with a View to Discussions between the SABC and Portuguese Quarters' 135, 183
mestiços 22, 62–63, 72
Methodist Church 5
Meyer, Piet (PJ) 10–12, 94–97, 109, 111–116, 121–150, 155–160, 180–182, 184

Meyer, Richard (RL) 101–102, 105, 116, 179
Milner, Alfred 18
Mines and Works Act 12 of 1911 4
mineworkers' strike, 1922 77
mining, miners 2–4, 6–7, 14, 16–20, 22–23, 27–28, 36, 38–43, 56, 63, 65–66, 70–71, 73–74, 77–78, 86, 91, 95
mining capital, capitalists 3, 7, 40, 41, 44, 65, 66
miniskirt ban, SABC 125
Monteiro, J Dias 65–68
morality, Christian moral prescription 3–4, 6–7, 9, 29–31, 34, 56–57, 60–61, 63, 74, 112, 115, 121, 125, 129, 140, 156–157, 174
Mount Nelson Hotel 42–43, 46, 48, 75
Mozambique 5–7, 9–14, 21–22, 29, 31, 34–35, 40, 48–49, 56, 59–60, 62–65, 72, 74–75, 87, 89–90, 98, 100, 105, 107, 118, 122, 125–127, 129–131, 134–135, 146–149, 153, 156, 182
Mozambique Liberation Front *see* Frelimo
Muller, Hilgard 131, 140
Mussolini, Benito 92

N
Nance, FJ 22–23, 27, 58
nationalism 12, 149, 152
    African 12, 77, 79–80, 115, 122, 139–140, 148, 159
    Afrikaner, ultra- 10, 12–13, 55–56, 59, 61, 74, 78–82, 88, 90–97, 99, 101–102, 105–113, 115, 119–120, 122, 124, 157–160
    Portuguese 45–48
National Party 10, 81–82, 95–97, 99, 108, 111, 116, 120, 123, 125, 136, 140–142, 144, 158–159, 184
National Publishers Association, UK 84
nation-states 150–151
Natives (Urban Areas) Act, 1923 34
Naude, WC 60
Naylor, Rupert 'Rufe' 36, 46, 73, 86

Nazism 92, 94, 158
Nederduitse Gereformeerde Kerk (NGK) 89, 120
    see also Dutch Reformed Church

O
Oppenheimer, Ernest 38
Ordinance No. 1 of March 1838 (Cape Colony) 3
Oxford University 94

P
Pact government 50, 80–81, 90
Pan American Radio Company (PAR) 117, 141–142, 145
Park Station, Johannesburg 24, 31, 36
Pellissier, SH 111
Pepper-Tanner Company 117
Philco 84, 89
Pienaar, General 59
Pienaar, Schalk 159
Pinnell, David 117, 138
'Pirate Radio Act' 127, 131, 135
Pirow, Oswald 92
Plugge, Leonard F 84, 101–102
Polana Beach Pavilion 47
Polana Hotel 7, 41, 43–46, 48–50, 52, 65–66, 71–73, 75, 102, 172, 174–175
pop music, culture 12, 118–119, 125–126, 129, 133, 136–137, 140, 145, 157
Portugal, Portuguese 7, 11, 13, 22, 27, 31, 34–35, 39–46, 48–50, 53, 55–62, 64–66, 69, 71–75, 86, 89, 100, 118, 122, 126, 133–134, 136, 138, 145, 147, 153, 158, 176, 182–183
Portugal e o Futuro 147
Portuguese Curator of Natives 39
Pratt, Ambrose 17
predestination doctrine 2
Pretoria 24, 29, 32, 57, 59–60, 62, 64, 72, 123, 129, 134, 139, 146, 148
prostitution, brothels 4, 6–7, 17–18, 25–26, 29–31, 53, 55, 57–58, 61–63, 71, 74–75, 169
Protestantism 2, 4–5, 23, 53, 55, 62,

68, 72–73
'psychedelic music' 125
public broadcasting 81, 87, 151–154, 157, 160

R
racism 34, 53, 62–63, 72, 79, 90, 119, 129, 150, 155, 158
radio 8–10, 11, 12, 17, 20, 27, 36, 47, 80, 81–87, 88, 89, 90, 91–95, 97, 98–110, 111–113, 115, 116, 117–119, 120–121, 122, 125–126, 128–132, 133, 135, 136–145, 147–149, 150–159, 160, 178, 179, 181
  see also British Broadcasting Corporation, Lourenço Marques Radio, Rádio Clube de Moçambique, South African Broadcasting Corporation
Radio Amendment Act ('Piracy Act') 11, 126, 135, 140, 144–145, 149, 155
Rádio Clube de Moçambique (RCM) 11, 85–86, 89–90, 97–100, 105, 107, 117, 126–127, 131–135, 137–139, 141–142, 145–146, 147–149, 156, 177
'Radio Palace', Lourenço Marques 11, 98, 107, 129, 139, 148–149, 166
Rainsford, Irene 89, 108
Rand Afrikaans University 160
RCM see Rádio Clube de Moçambique
Rand Daily Mail 28, 46, 51, 103, 118, 171–172
Reader's Digest 101
Rebelo, Horácio José de Sá Viana 130–131, 135
Reid, Cyril 42, 43, 173
Reid, Walter 42
Reith, John 9, 82–85, 87, 90, 92–93, 99, 103, 106, 109, 118, 124, 151–154, 156–161, 177
religion 2–3, 5, 84, 93–95, 110, 125, 143, 145, 153, 155, 157, 181
  see also Calvinism, Catholicism, Dutch Reformed churches, Protestantism
Rembrandt 96

Rhodesia, Rhodesians 15, 46, 56, 102
Rivonia trial 120
Roos, Gideon 99, 110–113, 119, 180
Roman Catholic Church see Catholicism
'Rufe Naylor Express' 36, 49, *51*
Rupert, Anton 96

S
SABC see South African Broadcasting Corporation
SADF see South African Defence Force
Said, Edward 14
Salazar, António de Oliveira 92, 127, 146
SAR-CFLM 50, 52–54
Saunders, EJ 59
Schlesinger, IW 46, 65–69, 73, 81–83, 86, 97–100, 153
Schoch, AA 99–100
Schreiner, Olive 17
Scully, EC 27
security police 80, 124
  see also South African Police
segregation 13, 15, 34–35, 56, 62, 64–66, 68, 72–73, 115
  see also apartheid
Seme, Pixley ka Isaka 35, 66
Serfontein, JJ 111
Sharpeville massacre 79, 120, 149, 156
Siegel, Bugsy 66
Smuts, Jan 99, 108
South African Academy for Science and Arts 124
South African Broadcasting Corporation (SABC) 10–12, 80, 86–88, 90, 93, 95–96, 99–100, 103, 105–108, 110–115, 118–133, 135–136, 137–139, 140–150, 155–160, 166, 178, 184
South African Defence Force (SADF) 126, 129–130
South African Party 81–82
South African Police (SAP) 30, 36, 60–62, 80
  see also security police

South African Railways (SAR) 31–32, 49–53
South African Republic (ZAR) 3, 18, 37
South African Reserve Bank 141, 184
South African War *see* Anglo-Boer War
sport 3–5, 23, 27, 38, 46, 68, 157
Springbok Radio 10, 99, 103, 105–106, 109–110, 112, 118–122, 138, 150, 155
Stark, Roy 100
Strijdom, JG 112
subsidy by state (radio) 132, 141
Sul do Save 38, 43, 49, 86, 147
Sun City 68
'Sunday Night Wars' 77, 129, 165
    see also Sunday observance laws, rules
Sunday Observance Commission 4
Sunday observance laws, rules 3–5, 8, 10, 23, 29, 77, 84–85, 87, 103–106, 112, 118–120, 129, 133, 153–154, 157, 159, 165, 181
Swan, Catherine 89
Swanepoel, JN 143–145
Swaziland 127, 139, 182
sweepstakes 23, 53
    see also gambling, lotteries

T
'taxi-girls' 57
    see also prostitution
'Top 20' programme 118
tourism 7–8, 13, 16–20, 22, 24, 27–40, 45, 48–50, 52–64, 66–74, 89
tourist zone, Lourenço Marques 64, 66–67, 73
trade unions 5
Transvaler, Die 95
Trans World Radio (TWR) 141
Tsonga radio service 147
Tutsis 155

U
Union-Castle line 50

Unionist Party 60
Union of South Africa 4, 12–13, 18, 20, 29–30, 33–34, 38, 53, 55–56, 59–61, 64, 68, 74, 77–78, 83, 92, 118
United Nations General Assembly 132
United Party 9, 82–83, 108, 151
'Unseen Elect' *see* Afrikaner Broederbond

V
van der Hoven, Colonel 125
van der Spuy, JP 137–138, 140–144
van Riebeeck, Jan 2
van Zyl, Ruby (aka Ruby Steen) 59
Verwoerd, HF 95–96, 112, 126–127, 140, 159, 180, 185
Vicente, José *see* do Sacramento, José Vicente
Viljoen, Marais 142
Vorster, John 121, 127, 140–144, 159, 184–185
Vrije Universiteit, Amsterdam 94

W
Weiss, PDF 124, 128, 182
Wesley, John 5
white slaves 30, 75
white working class 4–6, 18, 20, 23, 27, 29–30, 49–50, 54, 65–66, 70, 154
'Wind of Change' speech 119
Witwatersrand 4–6, 9, 14, 18, 23, 29–30, 34, 36–37, 39–41, 43, 46, 71, 73, 81, 86–88, 90, 93, 100, 107
Witwatersrand Native Labour Association 39
World War I 4, 7, 15, 17–18, 23, 26, 31–32, 34, 36–37, 45, 50, 55–56, 58, 71, 73, 75, 81, 88, 150
World War II 10, 16, 50, 55–56, 59–60, 62–63, 69, 92, 97, 116, 159

Z
Zambia 144–145

www.ingramcontent.com/pod-product-compliance
Lightning Source LLC
Chambersburg PA
CBHW060758110426

42739CB00033BA/3229